The Project Management Coaching Workbook

SIX STEPS TO UNLEASHING YOUR POTENTIAL

The Project Management Coaching Workbook

SIX STEPS TO UNLEASHING YOUR POTENTIAL

SUSANNE MADSEN

ⵊⵊⵊ
MANAGEMENTCONCEPTSPRESS

MANAGEMENTCONCEPTSPRESS

8230 Leesburg Pike, Suite 800
Tysons Corner, VA 22182
(703) 790-9595
Fax: (703) 790-1371
www.managementconceptspress.com

Printed in the United States of America

ISBN 978-1-56726-357-2

10   9   8   7   6   5   4   3   2   1

Praise for *The Project Management Coaching Workbook*

"Clear, practical and valuable. We all need to raise our game in this challenging project management world and Susanne's book will no doubt help you work smarter rather than harder."

—Peter Taylor,
author of *The Lazy Project Manager* and *The Lazy Winner*

"Unlike some coaching guides which stop at assessment, this one actually provides the material and lessons you need to round out your skills and leadership profile. Susanne Madsen is clearly a project management expert with both brains and heart, and a passion for coaching. Take the time to let Susanne coach you step-by-step—you're worth it!"

—Pam Stanton, consultant, coach, speaker, and author of
The Project Whisperer: Understanding the Human Part of the Gantt Chart

"Whether you are building your own project management career development plan or managing the professional development of project managers, this book is a must-have. It provides a unique methodology for developing the task management and team management/leadership skills of the project manager and would be an excellent tool for formal professional development and mentoring programs."

—Martin Chernenkoff, founder of pduOTD.com—PDU of the Day

"I wish I had this book when I first started out as a project manager. This great book provides easy-to-follow steps that anyone can use. The exercises and comprehensive insights will help anyone interested in learning about project management."

—Bernardo Tirado, PMP, Six Sigma Blackbelt,
and founder of The Project Box, *http://theprojectbox.us*

About the Author

Susanne Madsen is a program and project manager, mentor, and coach with over 15 years of experience in managing and rolling out major change programs, using both agile and waterfall methodologies. Susanne is a PRINCE2 and MSP practitioner and holds several qualifications in the area of personal performance and corporate and executive coaching.

The majority of her experience stems from working with investment banks, for which she has successfully managed a number of large, multimillion dollar programs. She has also set up and run several coaching and mentoring programs to improve project management performance. Susanne is dedicated to helping organizations deliver better projects and coaching and mentoring project managers in how to improve their capabilities, performance, and well-being.

The Project Management Coaching Workbook is a direct result of Susanne's project management coaching work over the years. Most of the tools, approaches, and topics presented in the book have grown out of the needs and challenges of the project managers she has coached. She has refined the material based on their feedback and progress over time. In Susanne's experience, attending just a few coaching sessions can give people the tools and support they need to excel and make rapid progress as project managers and leaders.

To find out more about Susanne, please visit her website at *www.susannemadsen.com*. You can also follow Susanne on Twitter: @SusanneMadsen.

To all the magnificent and wonderful people who are ready to unleash their potential and become highly valued and truly successful project management leaders. Believe in yourselves, harness your abilities, and never give up. I hope that the tips, tools, and exercises in this book will assist you and inspire you to reach new heights.

Contents

Foreword

I heard an amusing anecdote a number of years ago, about three frogs that had been relaxing for a while on a lily pad. Suddenly, with great excitement and enthusiasm, one turned to the other two and announced that, after much thought and consideration, he had decided to jump off the pad. His declaration was met with surprise, admiration, congratulations, best wishes for future success, and, if the truth be told, a not-inconsequential amount of envy. When a reasonable amount of time had passed, an observer looked around to determine how many frogs remained on the lily pad. Imagine his surprise when he saw the same three frogs! After a moment's befuddlement, he understood what had happened: The frog had *decided* to jump off but had never actually jumped.

In *The Project Management Coaching Workbook*, Susanne Madsen helps you address the most essential requirement for improving your project management performance— transferring your *knowledge* of the skills, techniques, practices, and behaviors that can help you achieve superior project results into *actions* that you consistently take every day. She does this by sharing with you important guiding principles, such as:

➤ It is your ability to help people embrace your vision, organize and coordinate their efforts, and sustain dynamic and productive interpersonal relationships—more than your use of graphs, charts, and procedures—that will lead you to project success.

➤ To achieve outstanding results, you must encourage people to buy in and commit to achieving project success by meaningfully involving them at all points throughout the project.

She does this by introducing you to many and varied ways to develop, analyze, interpret, and present important project information that can provide improved clarity and understanding of your project's intended results as well as how you propose to go about achieving them. Examples include how to frame the specific criteria that define whether project results meet or exceed project expectations and how to identify, organize, and engage the people who will determine what the project is to accomplish, who will be affected by the project outcomes, and who will perform the work to achieve results.

But most important, Susanne helps you improve your project management performance by guiding you through the following steps to create and implement a personalized plan for molding yourself into the project manager you want to be:

➤ Developing a clear and specific picture of the values you want to live by, how you want to guide and treat the people with whom you work, how you want to approach your assignments, and what you feel will make each of your projects truly successful

➤ Assessing through your own eyes, as well as through those of the people with whom you work, how your behaviors today compare with those to which you aspire in the future

➤ Creating a plan to ensure you both continue to use those best practices you have already embraced and develop and adopt behaviors and actions you have not yet internalized

➤ Continually assessing your progress in acquiring and using the skills, knowledge, and behaviors you seek to develop.

The information, guidance, and suggestions in this book are based on the belief that you must choose for yourself those behaviors on which you will ultimately rely to perform your project management tasks. Throughout the book, Susanne encourages you to clarify your personal vision of the project manager you ultimately want to become. This approach has the effect of gently helping you progress from *understanding* what project management success means to you to *committing* to do whatever it takes to accomplish it. Successfully making this transition is the key to ensuring that you will actually realize your vision.

In sum, *The Project Management Coaching Workbook* offers a unique blend of interpersonal and analytical tools, techniques, and behaviors. As you follow Susanne's tips and guidance, she eases you off the lily pad and launches you on your journey to become the project manager you want to be.

—Stanley E. Portny, PMP,
author of *Project Management For Dummies, Third Edition*

Preface

Most of the tools, approaches, and topics I present to you in this workbook grew out of the needs and challenges of the project managers I have coached. The workbook is a direct result of the many sessions and conversations I had with them and has gradually been refined based on their feedback and progression. Without their engagement and collaboration, it would not have been possible to write this workbook.

I originally started coaching and mentoring project managers because I wanted to make a difference. I wanted to contribute by helping others overcome some of the challenges I had experienced. I had seen the positive effects of coaching in other walks of life and was keen to use it in project management. But although I expected it to have an impact, I did not know that it would be quite as powerful as it proved to be. I did not know that only a few coaching sessions could be enough to give people the tools and support they needed to make rapid progress and excel as project managers and leaders.

Coaching and mentoring project managers gave me great insight into the most common project management challenges, and it enabled me to start identifying ways in which these challenges could be overcome. With the help of my peers, I began to develop some unique tools and approaches, which I tested out during the coaching sessions. The project managers made use of the material and progressed in their personal and professional lives. I grew as a mentor and coach and gradually created the toolbox and foundation for this workbook. In particular, I developed the self-assessment, which plays a vital role in the workbook, in close cooperation with other project managers. Other people's comments and suggestions inspired the use of spider diagrams, free-response text boxes, and the many open and incisive questions.

The workbook is organized into six steps that are designed to increase your confidence and competence as a project manager and leader. Working through the steps will help you understand and articulate what you want to achieve and will subsequently assist you in achieving those goals. You will uncover your strongest and weakest points and be empowered to take action to leverage your strengths and address your weaknesses.

The workbook will also help you overcome some of the most common challenges project managers face: effectively managing a demanding workload, leading and motivating a team, initiating and estimating a project, building effective relationships with senior stakeholders, being confident enough to say no to unreasonable demands, managing risks, issues, and changes to scope, and delegating effectively. It is by strengthening these fundamental competencies that you will be able to generate real results and excel as a project manager.

It is my sincere hope that this book will serve you and your coworkers well and that you will find its tools, approaches, and topics useful. I hope that it will help you fulfill your ambitions and that you will become a more confident and competent project manager as a result.

Please be in touch to share your successes, thoughts, and ideas. Together we can help our colleagues become more confident and competent project managers.

—*Susanne Madsen*
November 2011
www.susannemadsen.com

Acknowledgments

I would like to thank Johan Bleeker and Paul Chapman for their encouragement and for their belief in the philosophy and coaching methods underpinning this workbook. Further, I would like to thank Andrew Doran and Geoff Pope for their detailed reviews and invaluable comments. Finally, I would like to thank Myra Strauss from Management Concepts Press for her kindness, support, and professionalism and for giving me the opportunity to serve others through this workbook.

Introduction

The need for highly competent, confident, and effective project managers is growing, in a world where projects are becoming larger, more complex, and increasingly cross-cultural. It is no longer enough to master the essential tools and techniques involved in managing tasks, costs, and resources. To be an excellent project manager, you must have drive, confidence, and attitude, and you must be able to lead your team to success through your vision and engagement. You must be able to manage your own state of mind, build effective relationships, and have sufficient self-discipline and personal insight to set a great example for others to follow. To be truly successful, you must become a project management champion and a personal leader.

> *It is not your ability to manage tasks and resources that will set you apart. It is your ability to build relationships and lead the team to success through your vision and engagement. As much as knowledge matters, it is your drive, confidence, and attitude that will really help you get your projects over the finishing line.*

This workbook will guide you through a number of practical and insightful questions, tools, assessments, reviews, guiding practices, and exercises that are designed to help you unleash your potential and become a highly valued and truly successful project management leader. The workbook is interactive; to realize the most benefit, it will require you to reflect, make notes, come to conclusions, and take action. Use it if you want to become a better project manager or if you want to coach and mentor others to become one.

I will be your mentor and coach throughout the book, empowering you to leverage your strengths and encouraging you to take action to achieve the things you want. I will stimulate you to take responsibility for your career and professional development and encourage you to look inward as much as outward—inward to manage yourself and be the best you can, outward to manage tasks and the people around you. I will also emphasize the importance of turning obstacles into opportunities and reframing a situation to look at how you can best move forward.

THE SIX-STEP JOURNEY

The workbook is organized into six steps. The steps are based on a coaching model of identifying what your goal is; understanding what your current situation and capabilities are; seeking feedback from others; taking action; learning more; and reviewing your progress and taking more action.

If you work through all six steps and spend the necessary time on the exercises, you will actively learn new behaviors, habits, and techniques that will set you up for a fulfilling career as a project manager.

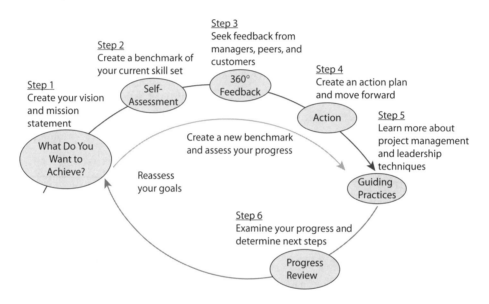

STEP 1: WHAT DO YOU WANT TO ACHIEVE? CREATE YOUR VISION AND MISSION STATEMENT

In Step 1, we will look at what project management is and what kind of project manager and leader you want to become. Who has inspired you in your career, and how can you start inspiring others in a similar way? Having a clear understanding of what you want to achieve is important, as your chances of becoming successful are much greater when you know what you are aiming for. We will look at your strengths, weaknesses, self-image, and aspirations, and I will ask you to write a vision and mission statement to encapsulate the essence of your ambitions and intentions. The vision and mission statement becomes your beacon of inspiration and summarizes what you want to achieve and how you want to carry yourself as a project manager.

STEP 2: SELF-ASSESSMENT: CREATE A BENCHMARK OF YOUR CURRENT SKILL SET

In Step 2, you will be presented with a comprehensive self-assessment to evaluate your project management skills, knowledge, attributes, and capabilities. The aim is to help you reflect upon your current skill set and to generate a personal performance benchmark, which is a summarized view of your strongest and weakest points. Step 2 concludes with a gap analysis, where you will capture the main competencies you need to develop in order to fulfill your goals as a project manager and leader.

STEP 3: 360° FEEDBACK: SEEK FEEDBACK FROM MANAGERS, PEERS, AND CUSTOMERS

To counterbalance the subjective nature of the self-assessment, I will ask you to seek feedback from your managers, peers, and customers in Step 3. Asking others for feedback can be daunting and will require courage, strength, and determination. It may, however, be one of the most determining actions you take and is certain to add further weight to your self-assessment. The 360° review can lead to remarkable results and breakthroughs, as it highlights any discrepancies between how others perceive your capabilities and performance and how you perceive them. Step 3 concludes with a review of your gap analysis.

STEP 4: ACTION: CREATE AN ACTION PLAN AND MOVE FORWARD

In Step 4 you will create a plan of action so that you can start holding yourself accountable, actively moving forward, and becoming a highly valued and truly successful project management leader. When you write down what you *will* do, not only do you create a written record of your intentions, but you are also much more likely to follow through with these intentions. You will start to change undesired behavior and try out new techniques to address a shortcoming or leverage a strength. It is by taking action that real results are created.

STEP 5: GUIDING PRACTICES: LEARN MORE ABOUT PROJECT MANAGEMENT AND LEADERSHIP TECHNIQUES

To accelerate your development, add to your knowledge base, and inspire you, Step 5 offers a number of guiding practices and exercises relating to project management and personal leadership. Focus on the topics and areas you most need to develop. The guiding practices cover topics such as project initiation, risk and issue management, team management, and stakeholder management. Compare these practices with how you manage yourself and your projects today, and decide which new techniques you want to incorporate into the way you work.

STEP 6: PROGRESS REVIEW: EXAMINE YOUR PROGRESS AND DETERMINE NEXT STEPS

In the last step of the workbook, we will review the progress you are making and determine what your next action steps should be. Carry out the review four to eight weeks after finalizing your action plan so that you have had time to implement your initial actions and work on certain behaviors. It is important to regularly review your progress, actions, goals, and capabilities, because huge changes happen when you start to work on yourself and your professional development. You can go through the review several times, until you have established a good routine for setting and achieving your goals.

HOW TO USE THIS WORKBOOK

I recommend that you go through all six steps of the workbook and that you complete the review process in the last step several times, until you have reached your goals and become a highly valued and truly successful project management leader.

The first time you go through the book, you will have a certain view of what your capabilities are, what you want to achieve, and what you want to change. However, after having taken action and worked on your development plans, you may have a different view, and new goals will become more important to you. For this reason it is important to keep reviewing where you are and where you want to go.

Use a different colored pen every time you carry out a review so that you can easily identify what you wrote, and how you scored yourself, at each point in time.

The workbook requires you to reflect, make notes, and take action—and it may take you between three and five months to complete all the steps. Devote time, be patient, and progress through the steps at a steady pace. You will soon start to feel the benefits of the assessments and exercises.

Always remember that the full benefits and the real results come from taking action and continually working with your development plans. Take full responsibility for your current situation and for where you want to go. Relate the examples, exercises, and questions back to your project and to your management and leadership style. Then commit to taking action. Only by applying what you learn will you move forward and become a more confident and competent project manager.

If you are a line manager and would like to use the workbook as a tool for coaching and managing the performance of your project management team, first go through it on your own. Once you understand the true value of all of the steps, you can start to apply them to others. The workbook can easily be used as a complementary tool to existing HR appraisal systems that help employees determine their year-end goals, objectives, and development plans.

Always explain a process you would like to use to the people you manage and get their buy-in before using it. Keep in mind that the focus should be on the aspirations and potential of individual project managers rather than on what the organization would like to achieve. Fully tuning in to the values and goals of individual employees unlocks their true potential. When working with your project management team, use your intuition, listen, be honest, and have integrity.

Today's Date

Please make a note of today's date so that you can use your answers as a reference point and benchmark in the future.

Date: _____

What Do You Want to Achieve? Create Your Vision and Mission Statement

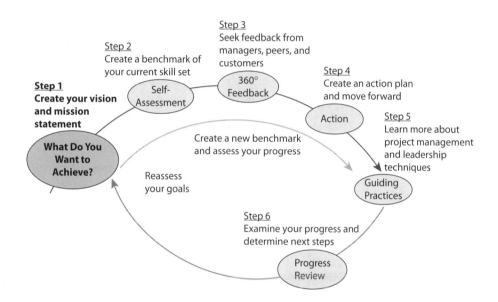

Knowing what you want to achieve is the first step in becoming as successful as possible. Only when you know what you are aiming for can you reach your goals and fulfill your ambitions.

The subconscious mind works to achieve the things that you think about most of the time, whether you want them or not. This is why I encourage you to switch your thinking away from what you do not want to what you *do* want.

The first part of this workbook, Step 1, is designed to make you think about what kind of project manager you want to become. Which qualities would you like to be known for, and what would you like to achieve in your career as a project manager? How do you define success, and what does excellence look like to you? There are many ways of achieving excellence, but you are the only one who can determine what it means to you.

I will guide you through a number of insightful questions that relate to your personal characteristics and to your behavior as a project manager. I will also ask you to write a vision and mission statement that encapsulates who and what you would like to be, do, and have. The vision and mission statement becomes your beacon and measure of success.

After completing Step 1 you will know what your strengths and challenges are as a project manager, what your goals are and what success means to you. A discussion of specific project management tips, tools, and techniques will follow shortly. But first we need to know a bit about who you are and what you want to achieve in your career as a project manager.

WHAT IS PROJECT MANAGEMENT?

Project management is about establishing what is in scope and out of scope of a project and subsequently organizing and managing resources in such a way that specific goals and objectives are achieved within a certain set of criteria.

Project management is the art and science of making a project's vision come alive and getting things done—more so than determining what the vision itself is. Of course, there will be no project without a vision and clear objectives, but determining the "why and what" of a project is more a concern for the customer or change manager than for the project manager.

You could say that change management provides the project's vision and is concerned with the human impact of change, whereas project management is related to how that vision is executed. These two disciplines go hand in hand and are both concerned with the transformation process between a present and a future state. The more experienced you become, the more likely it is that you will take on the role of a change manager in addition to your role as project manager.

Project management involves many different types of activities that all serve the purpose of ensuring that the project's vision is executed and turned into reality within certain time, quality, and budget constraints. These activities relate to planning and coordinating tasks and to directing and supervising people. Scope and deliverables need to be specified, estimated, and executed, and quality must be assured. Risks, issues, and change requests need to be effectively managed, and a significant amount of time needs to be spent liaising with stakeholders and ensuring that the team remains focused and motivated.

In accordance with the philosophy that you manage tasks and lead people, it could be argued that project management contains an equal number of management and leadership activities. On that basis, we could go on to define project management as:

> *The management role that defines, plans, coordinates, and controls a project's scope and operational activities, and the leadership role that inspires and focuses everyone contributing to the successful completion of the project's goals and objectives.*

To become a highly valued and truly successful project management leader, you need to be an excellent manager as well as a good leader. You must be able to access and make use of both skill sets, depending on the immediate need and the situation to which you are responding. In addition, you must be excellent at managing your time and consistently focus on the right activities. Some of the activities you engage in are essential to the dynamics and ongoing progress of the project and must be completed by you. Others are less important and could potentially be delegated to someone else.

Doing something very well that does not need to be done at all is a poor use of time. Before starting any activity, check how important it is to the overall success of the project or to the functioning of the team. Aim to always focus on the highest-value activities and delegate or defer the others. The tasks and activities that matter the most must never be at the mercy of the tasks and activities that matter the least.

Exercise: Project Management Activities

1. Brainstorm all of the tasks and activities that, in your experience, form part of a project manager's job. Consider aspects that relate to the management of tasks as well as people. Write them down on a separate piece of paper.

2. Write each of the project management activities you identified in the leftmost column of the table below.

3. Assign a high, medium, or low rating to each activity depending on how much you believe it benefits your current project.

4. Next, assign each activity a high, medium, or low rating depending on how much you personally enjoy the activity.

5. Indicate how many hours per week you typically spend on each activity.

Project Management Task and Activities	Benefit to Project	Personal Enjoyment	Hours Spent per Week
Example: Liaise with stakeholders	*High*	*Low*	*2 hours*
Example: Update document repository	*Low*	*Medium*	*3 hours*

6. Look at how you rated the activities in terms of how much benefit they add to your current project. Which activities have you identified as adding the most benefit?

7. Which of the high-benefit activities do you need to spend relatively more time on in order to maximize your value to the project, and which lower-value activities can you spend less time on?

8. Examine the items that add a lot of benefit but which you do not particularly enjoy doing. How can you either make them more enjoyable or delegate them to someone else without jeopardizing the success of the project?

9. To add more weight to this exercise, talk it through with your manager. Get her views on what your tasks and responsibilities are and what you need to be spending relatively more or less time on.

_____

_____

_____

_____

_____

MANAGEMENT VS. LEADERSHIP

The concepts of management and leadership are recurring themes throughout this workbook. I have chosen to use the word *management* to describe anything that relates to the control and direction of tasks, events, and processes, and *leadership* for anything that relates to the control and direction of people. On that basis, leadership and management encompass different but overlapping elements. It is possible to be good at one but not the other. It is, however, also possible to be good at both disciplines at the same time.

As a manager, you are typically involved in scheduling work, delegating tasks, coordinating effort and resources, monitoring and guiding progress, building teams, and appealing to rational thinking. As a leader, however, your role is to inspire people, explain goals, share the vision, provide focus, be a role model, monitor morale, create a positive team feeling, and unleash potential.

Field Marshal William Slim elegantly explained the difference between leadership and management in the following way: "Leadership is of the spirit, compounded of personality and vision. Its practice is an art. Management is of the mind, more a matter of accurate calculations, statistics, methods, timetables, and routine. Its practice is a science".

One of the biggest differences between managers and leaders is the way they motivate people who work for them. Managers are in a position of authority, and their subordinates largely do as they are told because they get a reward (or a salary) for doing so. Leaders see their role quite differently and typically offer more creative opportunities when it comes to motivating staff. Leaders focus on inspiring people and on giving credit to others. They focus on the overall vision and end goal and on how they can best engage and serve others so that they in turn feel inspired and motivated to contribute to the vision.

> *Leaders tend to have followers rather than subordinates. They do not tell people what to do; that would not inspire them to follow. People follow because they feel inspired and because they want to contribute, not because they are told to.*

Many associate the word *leader* with a particular role, such as the CEO of a major company. But leadership is not a function of what you do or what your job title is; rather, it is a

Exercise: Management and Leadership Activities

Think about project management and how it overlaps with general management and leadership.

1. Make a list of typical project management activities that fall within the classic discipline of management.

2. Make a similar list of project management activities that predominantly reside within the discipline of leadership.

3. In which situations would you benefit from acting more like a leader than a manager, and vice versa?

_____

_____

_____

_____

_____

function of your personal capabilities. Leaders can be found in many guises and in all walks of life; many parents, for instance, are leaders.

We will be examining the concept of leadership throughout this workbook and will assess what you can do to actively incorporate some of the most important qualities of leadership into the way you interact with your team and project stakeholders.

WHAT IS A GOOD PROJECT MANAGER?

Managing projects requires a great deal of effort, skill, and finesse. As a project manager, you are expected to engage with a big-picture vision and make a certain promise to execute it and turn it into reality within certain time, quality, and budget constraints. This requires thoughtful consideration and a great deal of skill and personal leadership. It requires you to fully understand the vision, scope, and constraints of the project and to continually work to remove blockages. You must consistently spend time on those things that matter the most to the success of the project, and you must focus on people as much as you focus on tasks.

There are as many ways of executing a project as there are people. We all have different ways of doing things, and we experience different degrees of success in what we do. Yet some people stand out from the crowd. They seem to have a different mindset and tend to succeed at most things they venture into. That is not to say that they do not fail, because they do. What matters is that they have the drive, confidence, and attitude to keep going and to turn failure into key learning points which will eventually help them succeed. They have a winning mentality, and they set a great example for others to follow.

When you come across a person who has a winning mentality and whom you admire, it may be because you feel that you lack some of what he has. You admire him for having a particular skill that you would love to have. If you are searching for guidance on what you can do to enhance your own career, a natural first step is to look at people who inspire you.

Exercise: Inspirational People

Take a moment to consider the people who have inspired you in your life and career to date. This could be anyone you have worked with professionally, a family member, a friend, or a person you have admired from a distance.

1. Below, write the names of people who have made a positive impression on you because of their management or leadership skills. List people who stood out for one reason or another. Maybe they were particularly courageous, charismatic, driven, or inspirational.
2. Write down what you admired in each of them.

3. Which of those qualities do you most want to develop?

4. How would you feel if you embodied these qualities? What would you be doing differently from what you are doing today?

_____

_____

_____

_____

ROLE MODELS

Role models can play an important part in your ongoing development. But when you look to people you admire, be careful not to put yourself down or say that you can never be as good as them. Each of us has unique qualities, and each of us is at a different stage in our personal and professional development. Even your role models are in many ways still students who continue to learn and grow.

Use your role models as a compass for the direction in which you want to go. Take a close look at their best qualities and ask yourself how you can incorporate some of them into your own personality and behavior. Visualize the person you would like to be, then act as if you are already that person. When you can imagine it, you can do it!

When I looked at my own role models and what I admired about them, I found that I was particularly inspired by people who remained calm during times of conflict and pressure and who always managed to keep their teams focused on the end goal. When I became aware of this, I examined myself more closely. I found that I was very task-oriented and at times very reactive. I wanted to become more visionary, calm, and measured in my responses to challenging situations.

When I realized this, I began to identify situations where I could proactively make a change. I visualized how I wanted to behave, and I imagined what I would say and do in particular situations. I also asked myself hypothetical questions such as, "What would the head of the department do in this situation? What would my role model advise me to do?" I found that this technique made it easier for me to actually make a change.

Questions

- Who are your role models in the area of project management? You may not be able to think of one person who is excellent in all areas, so identify several people who inspire you in different ways.
- What does each of them do well?
- How would you define a good project manager and his or her role?

_____

_____

_____

_____

_____

IDENTIFY YOUR STRENGTHS

We all have strengths, unique talents, and abilities that set us apart from others. Your strengths are your most powerful skills and attributes and your best tools for accomplishment. They illustrate what you do really well and how you differentiate yourself from others.

When you play to your strengths, you create a positive situation for yourself and for the project, and all parties benefit. The project and people around you benefit from your expertise and positive energy, and you benefit from feeling good, being in control, and being in your flow.

When you do the things you are good at, you have an opportunity to shine, and you are more likely to be of value and a source of inspiration to people around you. Your confidence naturally grows, and you feel successful, calm, and resourceful.

Consider the following questions about the strengths and abilities that you contribute to project management.

Questions

- What are your strengths, talents, and abilities? Think about all your good qualities, things you are proud of, and past successes. These might include your personal characteristics, people skills, knowledge, or ability to handle specific tasks and situations. Write down everything you can think of.

- How can you make better use of your strengths and talents in your current role?
- What is your hidden potential, and what are some ways in which you could make use of it?
- How can you become a role model for others to follow?

_____

_____

_____

_____

My Story

We all have different backgrounds, aspirations, and experiences, and we all have different stories to tell. Let me share my story with you.

A number of years ago I was, like many other project managers, working hard on a project that seemed to be getting increasingly complex, with tighter and tighter deadlines. I was stressed and overworked, and I was not leveraging my capabilities in the best possible way. I spent most of my time planning and tracking tasks and dealing with urgent issues. There was not much time left for being proactive, thinking ahead, or spending quality time with team members or stakeholders. I was under a lot of pressure and did not feel that I had anyone to delegate to. But more importantly, I was not enjoying myself, and I was not always in control of the project.

A number of things made me change.

The defining moment was a coaching session in which I discussed my issues with stress and managing my workload. Within just one hour, I realized that one of my core beliefs was that *project management is inherently stressful (and painful), and there is nothing I can do about it.* At that stage in my career I had been managing projects for well over ten years, and my experiences told me that project management was a very demanding and stressful job. Period.

Recognizing that project management *does not have to be stressful* was a true eureka moment for me. I instantly understood that my belief was subjective, not the objective truth, and that I had the power to challenge it and change it. What a shift that was! Understanding that my belief was not necessarily true allowed me to start working with it and to slowly dissolve it and become more effective and valuable in my job.

When you realize that you have the power to change your beliefs and remove a limiting factor that has been constraining you, you have an "aha!" moment. You feel relieved and empowered.

Today I have the audacity to challenge most people's beliefs, as they are just that: beliefs. They are true only because we believe in them. When we replace them with more empowering thoughts, our worldview can change in a split second.

My eureka moment made me pause, take a step back, and do less. I did this to regain my energy and to free up time to collect my thoughts. And then something magical happened. New ideas started to pop up, and I began to see patterns and connections that I had not noticed before. I looked at the bigger picture and started to understand how I could leverage my strengths and work more effectively. I gave myself the opportunity to be more proactive and to work smarter.

I took a closer look at myself as a project manager and the values that were driving my work. I examined my own worth, and I explored my boundaries. Why was it so important for me to work long hours and to micromanage my team? Was there a better way to get things done? I had to acknowledge that it was not the hours I put in that mattered, but the quality of my work. I realized that in order to produce better-quality work, I would have to change the way I spent my time.

One of the changes I made that had a significant impact was delegating more. I recognized that I could not do everything by myself and that I needed to get better at asking for help and support. I got a project administrator on board to help with lower-level task tracking and administrative work. It was essential work, but it was not essential that *I* did it.

Delegating more freed me up to spend time with the team and key stakeholders, listening to their ideas and concerns and looking at what we could do better. I started focusing more on picturing the end state of the project and proactively reducing the risks associated with the road to getting there.

Today, I put as much emphasis on people as I do on tasks. I listen, I build strong relationships, and I trust others. I manage and lead people in a way that complements their individual needs, as opposed to micromanaging everyone across the board.

I often take a step back, observe the project, and ask the following questions:

- What is the core problem we are here to solve?
- How clear are the project's goal and vision?
- What can I do to make everyone on the team understand it and buy into it?
- What could get in our way of achieving the end goal? What have we not yet thought of?
- How do I know that what we are building is what the users need?
- What can we do to improve the way we test and verify requirements?
- How has the project progressed to date, and what issues have come up (e.g., people, quality, scope, stakeholders, communication)?
- What can we do to improve the way we work?
- How motivated and committed is the team?
- What can I do to inspire people and use everyone's potential better?

- Who are my key stakeholders, and how close am I to them?
- Who do I need to spend more quality time with?
- How effectively am I spending my own time?
- What can I do differently to optimize the way I work?

Previously, I probably spent up to 75 percent of my time focusing on tasks and as little as 25 percent on people. Most of my time was spent firefighting and making up for the fact that we had not analyzed the problem and the end goal properly.

When I started delegating, my focus shifted. I spent more time liaising with the team and the stakeholders and ensuring that high-level and strategic tasks were executed smoothly. I was moving toward taking on the role of change manager in addition to my role as project manager. This shift enabled me to become more effective and to leverage my strengths better.

IDENTIFY YOUR PROJECT MANAGEMENT CHALLENGES

Your beliefs about the world and yourself have a powerful effect on your behavior as a project manager. The way you think determines everything you say, do, believe, and feel. If you want to change the way you *do* things and the way you deal with challenges, you first have to change the way you *think* about things. Any improvement you desire on the outside as a project manager begins with improvements on the inside. When you change your inner world, you will notice that your external world changes too.

One of the differences between ordinary and successful people is that successful people do not give up when presented with an obstacle or a challenge. They pick themselves up, get to the root cause of the issue, and change their approach accordingly. Successful people come across as many roadblocks as everyone else, but instead of giving in and blaming others, they change their approach and do something about the situation. They are proactive and keep trying new ways.

Exercise: Challenges and Root Causes

1. On a separate piece of paper, identify the biggest challenges you are facing right now as a project manager. This could be anything from dealing with specific tasks to managing and directing people or handling stress. List anything that concerns you and that you seem to spend a lot of time and energy worrying about.

2. Select the five topics that concern you the most and list them in the leftmost column of the table below.

3. For each of the five entries, carefully examine what the root cause could be. What is the bottom line? What does the challenge ultimately come down to? To help you identify the

root cause, keep asking "why" until you have found the ultimate reason for your concern. It is by identifying and addressing the root causes of your concerns and challenges that you are able to overcome them.

For example, imagine that a project manager is finding it difficult to manage her workload. She feels that there is too much work and that she never gets to do any of her tasks properly. On the face of it, the reason may seem to be the workload itself, or that her managers are giving her too much to do. But when she asks *why*, she may find that the root cause relates to her own desire to please and to her reluctance to ask for help and support from others.

4. Which actions could you take to address the root causes of your concerns and challenges? Record your findings in the column to the right.

	Concern/Challenge	Root Cause	Possible Actions
A			
B			
C			
D			
E			

IDENTIFY YOUR LIMITING FACTOR

In almost everything you do, a single factor sets the speed at which you achieve your goals or complete a job. This factor is a constraint that determines how effectively you manage yourself and others and how successful you are at achieving a specific outcome.

To put it another way, we could say that your performance is determined by your potential, less interference. This interference could be a limiting thought, an unhelpful behavior, or any external influences or distractions that have a negative impact on your focus and ability to perform an activity.

Many people are limited by a negative self-image and hold themselves back unnecessarily because they do not believe in their own abilities. If this rings true for you, you need to come to an understanding of what you have learned to think and believe about yourself so that you can unwind any negative thought patterns and start thinking and behaving in new ways.

To improve your performance and unleash your potential, you must identify and remove your limiting factor and limiting beliefs. Focus on what it is that interferes with your abilities and prevents you from performing at your best. When you take action at that level, you address the root cause of some of your biggest challenges.

Identifying your limiting factor and reducing interference could be the one of the most important actions you take on your road to success.

Exercise: Your Limiting Factor

Take a moment to think about what your limiting factor might be.

1. On a separate piece of paper, identify and write down all the situations you can think of in which you tend to hold yourself back or not perform at your best. Examples might include giving presentations, facing off with senior stakeholders, challenging team members, or any other project-related activity.

2. Look at each of the situations you have identified and examine which underlying beliefs and habits might be interfering with your performance. Do you, for instance, believe that you are not good enough at certain things? Do you deliberately put yourself down? Perhaps you avoid certain situations or tasks because you do not enjoy them. Write down anything that comes to mind.

3. Go back to the previous exercise and examine the root causes you identified. Could any of these root causes be your limiting factor?

4. Which beliefs and habits do you need to change in order to address your limiting factor?

_____

_____

_____

WRITE YOUR VISION AND MISSION STATEMENT

Formulating a personal vision and mission statement for your project management practice is an important step in becoming more successful at what you do because it articulates your aspirations and ambitions. A vision and mission statement expresses, in just one paragraph, who you want to be and what you want to do and have as a project manager. It also functions as a measure of your success in reaching those goals. If you have a vision and mission statement, it is much easier for you to direct your development plan and understand which capabilities you must strive to enhance and which behaviors you need to change.

A vision and mission statement encapsulates the essence of what you want to achieve and how you want to present yourself. It states your intentions, summarizes your values, and demonstrates your commitment to living up to these values.

A vision and mission statement should reflect your values, vision, goals, and purpose. It is really important that you feel excited and inspired by it. When you read it aloud, it should make you feel good and compelled to live by it.

Exercise: Composing Your Vision and Mission Statement

1. Answer the following questions as honestly and with as much passion and commitment as you can. The answers will help you compose a vision and mission statement of your own.
   - What personal qualities do you most want to emphasize?
   - How can you use and display these qualities in a working environment?
   - What are the most important values you want to express at work?

   _____

   _____

   _____

2. Visualize yourself five years from now. Imagine that you are managing and leading the project of your dreams. Envision that everything is exactly the way you want it to be: the type of project you are running, the industry it is in, its size and complexity, the people involved, and your own capabilities and confidence as a project manager. Imagine that you are every bit as successful as you want to be. Feel it and see it.

   Use the space below to draw a picture of yourself and your surroundings five years from now. Draw the things you see, feel, and hear. Use as many colors as you want.

3. Keep imagining yourself in the future, and be as specific as possible in your observations. Where exactly are you? What are you doing? Who are you talking to? What does the project look like? How big is it? How complex is it? How are you feeling? Why do you

want to be exactly where you are? Add more detail and descriptive words to the illustration.

4. How would you sum up your vision and mission as a project manager? What are the things you ultimately want to achieve? Who do you want to be? What do you want to do?

5. What will need to happen in order for you to feel proud of your progress as a project manager in five years' time?

EXAMPLES OF VISION AND MISSION STATEMENTS

"My vision is to live each day to the fullest and to treat others with the same respect I deserve myself. I look for strengths in others and the good in every situation. I grow stronger with each accomplishment, and even stronger with each setback. My mission and ultimate goal is to pass on these values to my family and to everyone I work with."

"The project manager I choose to be is someone who lives life honestly and compassionately, and who inspires and motivates others to deliver remarkable projects with the philosophy that everything is possible."

"My vision is to be honest and empathetic towards others and to build my reputation based on performance. I am committed to growing as a leader by learning from those with more experience than myself and to champion others to grow personally and professionally. My mission is to create and lead a dream team where everyone is playing to their strengths in order to deliver value-added projects that provide the end users with a superior experience."

"I am calm and resourceful in everything that I do. I listen, I observe, and I make effective decisions. I build strong and trusting relationships and I put pride in being open, honest, and proactive. I choose to filter out negative and pessimistic views and strive to show strength during adversity. I find support and balance inside myself. My pleasure comes from seeing my team thrive and succeed in the delivery of great projects to a satisfied customer."

Compose Your Vision and Mission Statement

Write your own vision and mission statement. Remember that above all, you must feel excited and inspired by it. For the remainder of the workbook we will be referring back to this statement as your measure of success. It illustrates what you want to achieve as a project manager and how you want to carry yourself.

_____

_____

_____

_____

_____

_____

_____

_____

_____

Feel free to also make a drawing that complements your words.

Self-Assessment: Create a Benchmark of Your Current Skill Set

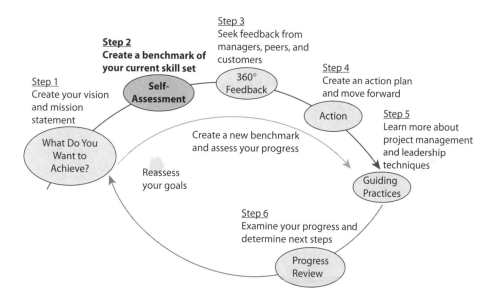

The purpose of the self-assessment in Step 2 is to establish a benchmark of your current skill set so that you have a baseline from which you can progress. You will be asked to score your proficiency on a scale from 1 to 10 in a number of project management disciplines and competencies.

By assessing yourself, you become more aware of the areas where you are strong and the areas where you might need to improve. You then will be able to leverage your strengths, develop your project management capabilities, and focus on removing your limiting factor.

Use a colored pen when filling in the self-assessment. Later, you will go back and reassess yourself using a different color. You can then overlay your scores to easily determine your progress.

At the end of Step 2, you will have a realistic picture of your current capabilities as a project manager. I will ask you to reflect on your scores and look at them in the context of the vision and mission statement you wrote earlier. This will set up a comparison between your capabilities and those of the project manager you really want to become; the direction in which you should direct your efforts will become more obvious.

Date of 1st assessment (and color used): _____

Date of 2nd assessment (and color used): _____

Date of 3rd assessment (and color used): _____

YOUR SELF-ASSESSMENT

To assess your capabilities and establish a benchmark, we first need to determine the project management themes against which you will be assessed. There are many different ways of doing this; your way could be as good as mine.

I have chosen ten overarching project management themes as evaluation categories for the self-assessment. Each theme relates to either the management of tasks or the management and leadership of people.

Task Management

1. Skills and knowledge
2. Project initiation and planning
3. Managing product quality
4. Tracking cost and schedule
5. Risk, issue, and scope management

People Management and Leadership

6. Managing and motivating the team
7. Stakeholder relationships and communication
8. Self-management
9. Leadership behavior
10. Project stability and identity

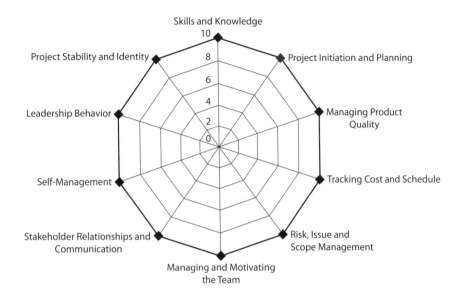

The equal weighting of task and people management is essential to the self-assessment. Many project managers are well-versed in managing tasks and spend most of their time planning and tracking work. Others are great at dealing with people but spend little time attending to the detailed tasks of the project.

To become a highly valued and truly successful project management leader, you need to master both sides of the job. You need to build strong and honest relationships with the team and stakeholders, but you also need to spend sufficient time keeping track of completed work, scope changes, and budgets—otherwise, you will not be fully in control of a project. Most important of all, you need to have a good relationship with yourself, enjoy what you do, and want to be the best you can.

Each of the ten project management themes contains eight subcategories—characteristics or tasks associated with that theme—and there is a spider diagram listing these subcategories for each theme. You will record your scores for the characteristics or tasks for each theme on the diagrams.

Case Study: Tim's Self-Assessment

Tim is a project manager who has been managing technology projects for nearly four years. He previously worked as a developer and team leader but fell into project management when his employer urgently needed someone to run a small integration project. At the time, he received no formal project management training; he had to learn on the job. He felt he had flair for managing projects, so he continued down this career path.

Tim has received mostly positive feedback from his managers and peers about his performance over the last four years, but a complex project that he recently managed did not go quite as expected. During user acceptance testing, a significant amount of the product's functionality did not match the user's expectations, and further issues were identified after go live. The senior stakeholders openly voiced their discontent. They felt that they had not been consulted enough during the project.

In Tim's latest appraisal, his manager picked up on these issues, and they jointly agreed that Tim would spend extra time learning about project management best practices to improve his performance. They also agreed that Tim would be formally mentored by Andy, a highly respected senior project manager within the organization.

Tim and Andy quickly arranged to meet, and they spent quite a bit of time during their first mentoring session exploring Tim's work experience, performance, and aspirations. Andy suggested that Tim carry out a self-assessment to get an overview of his strengths as well as the areas in which he needs to improve. The outcome of Tim's evaluation is illustrated in the web below. Each node in the web shows Tim's aggregated score for each of the ten categories of the self-assessment.

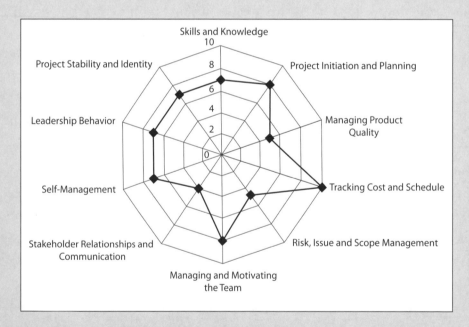

Overall, Tim scored himself highly in the areas of Tracking Cost and Schedule, Project Initiation and Planning, and Managing and Motivating the Team. He scored himself lowest in Managing Product Quality, Stakeholder Relationships and Communication, and Risk, Issue, and Scope Management.

After completing the self-assessment, Tim went through the scores with his manager to get a second opinion. He did not adjust his scores as a result, but he found it useful to discuss his capabilities and thoughts with someone who knew him well.

The manager agreed that the capabilities Tim had identified as areas for development were not his strongest skills, and he added further nuances to the picture, which helped Tim get a better understanding of where and how he needed to focus his efforts. Tim and his manager had a detailed discussion about particular project management situations and capabilities to make sure that they were talking about the same thing and understood each other's point of view. They agreed that Tim needed to improve his capabilities in the following areas:

- **Managing product quality.** Because he has a background as a developer, Tim is very focused on running detailed technical tests and ensuring that source code and configuration management are under control. He also feels that he spends a fair amount of time attending to functional testing but admits that the quality of the test cases is generally poor, as the team finds it difficult to engage the users to verify the requirements. Most of the time, the team has to start developing functionality without knowing exactly what the sign-off criteria are, and this uncertainty filters through into the testing phase. The team is not effective enough at eliciting requirements and test criteria, and the feedback loop between the development team and user representatives is slow and ineffective.

- **Risk, issue, and scope management.** Although Tim reliably logs risks and issues, he rarely carries out a thorough impact analysis or assigns an owner to the entries other than himself. He feels that as the project manager, he is responsible for the issues and tends to deal with them himself. Because he does not assign and escalate risks and issues frequently enough, they often spiral out of control. Senior stakeholders cannot provide much-needed support if they are not aware of the risks and issues. A similar problem is occurring with change requests: Tim does not always get around to logging them or raising them to the steering committee for approval.

- **Stakeholder relationships and communication.** Tim focuses a lot of his energy on the project team, creating a great environment where everyone feels involved and motivated, but he rarely spends any length of time with the major stakeholders, other than at the monthly steering committee meeting or when a pressing issue comes up. He thinks the sponsor and user representatives are busy people, and he does not want to take up any of their time unnecessarily. He feels somewhat uncomfortable asking for advice and support and therefore rarely interacts with them to get general feedback or discuss how the team might be able to mitigate certain risks or work more effectively. In other words, he has a reactive rather than a proactive relationship with them.

After filling in the self-assessment and talking it through with his manager and mentor, it became easier for Tim to determine which particular areas he needed to focus on in order to improve his performance and the success rate of his projects. Tim decided to immediately take action and make some improvements in each of the three identified areas. With the help of his mentor, Andy, he settled on three things he could do right away:

1. To address the concerns around product quality, Tim decided to set up a number of workshops with the key team members and end users to address the team's uncertainties about requirements, test cases, and sign-off criteria. He believed that the best approach for the workshops was to ask team members to illustrate and write out their understanding of the requirements and acceptance criteria received to date on a whiteboard. The users could then correct the team where necessary and fill in the gaps. Tim thought that this was a powerful first step in ensuring that everyone understood the requirements, which in turn would help define the detailed test cases and improve overall quality. Andy volunteered to speak to the most senior user representative to explain the importance of the end users attending the workshops.

2. Tim also decided to set aside one hour twice a week to carefully review the project's risks, issues, and scope changes, either on his own or with the team. After careful consideration, Tim decided that once a week he would involve four of the team members in a review process, and once a week he would spend time on his own to reflect on risks and issues and chase any outstanding actions. He set up a weekly recurring meeting where the team could brainstorm and analyze new risks and issues, discuss the resolution and ownership of existing items, and talk through any new scope changes that needed to be analyzed and presented to the steering committee for approval.

3. The last action Tim took was to set aside time on a daily basis to start liaising more with the senior stakeholders of the project. To identify which stakeholders were the most important to spend time with, he analyzed each of them to determine who had the most power and influence over the project. Based on this analysis, he settled on three people with whom to start building stronger relationships. He decided to schedule one-on-one meetings with each of them to get a better understanding of their interests, knowledge, and concerns, how they could best support the project, and how he could best support them.

However, Tim and his mentor did not just focus on Tim's shortcomings in their discussions. They also spent a considerable amount of time examining Tim's strengths and unique contributions, particularly with regard to managing and motivating the team, and how he could leverage these strengths in other areas of the project. In particular, they talked about his outstanding ability to build strong and lasting relationships with his coworkers (team members) and about how he could start to use the same skills and techniques for building better relationships with the project's senior stakeholders.

Tim always felt very focused and energized after his mentoring sessions with Andy. These sessions continued for a period of six months, during which time Tim significantly improved his performance and image across the organization.

SKILLS AND KNOWLEDGE

One of the prerequisites for operating effectively as a project manager is having some understanding of the business domain and subject matter you are dealing with.

You need to understand what fundamental problems the project is there to resolve, what benefits the customer and end users want to obtain, and how the project can help deliver these benefits. When you understand the details of what the customer wants to achieve and which systems and business processes are already in place (if any), you are in a much better position to help identify a solution that meets or exceeds the customer's needs. The more knowledge you have about the relevant sector, industry, products, and services, the easier this will be. When you have that knowledge, you are able to understand the business implications of the project and establish what needs to happen in order for it to ultimately be a success.

In addition to understanding the business domain, you also need to understand the solution domain of the project. By *solution domain*, I mean the specific technologies, materials, methods, tools, and techniques your team will make use of in creating the end product. The better your grasp of the solution domain, the easier it will be for you to effectively challenge the design of the solution and manage the end-to-end process for the project.

It is possible to run a project and do a good job without having much subject matter knowledge. However, in order to really apply yourself and become as effective as possible, you must have a certain understanding of the project's domain.

As a project manager, you furthermore need a good understanding of project management best practices and how to effectively manage each stage of a project. This knowledge will help you assess which project management methodologies to use (unless the methodology is preselected by the organization) and which quality assurance (QA) processes are most suited for the project.

It is unlikely that you will need to be an expert in every area of your project; your team will probably be comprised of specialists. However, you need *enough* knowledge to get the right kind of people involved, challenge proposed solutions, technologies, and tools, and effectively manage risks, issues, and changes to scope. In other words, you need to have sufficient knowledge about project management, the business domain, and the solution domain to effectively manage and control the project.

Remember, though, that knowledge is, of course, not the only factor that matters in your overall level of success. You also need the right amount of attitude, drive, and confidence, and you must know *how* to effectively apply your knowledge.

Questions

- How good are you at applying the knowledge you have to the projects you manage?
- In what ways do you use your knowledge of technologies, methods, tools, materials, client industry, and business domain to produce the best possible and most cost-effective solution for the client?
- In what ways do you use your knowledge of project management best practices and processes to optimize the way your projects are run and executed?

Project Management Methodologies

There are lots of standards, methodologies, and approaches that relate to project management. A select few deserve to be mentioned very briefly at this stage.

The PMBOK® Guide (*A Guide to the Project Management Body of Knowledge*) is a process-based framework that contains standards, guidelines, and characteristics of, project management. It is sponsored and published by the Project Management Institute (PMI®) and is the most widely used methodology for managing projects in the United States and around the world. The fourth edition of the *PMBOK® Guide* is based on five process groups: initiating, planning, executing, monitoring/controlling, and closing. It is further supported by nine knowledge areas: integration management, scope management, time management, cost management, quality management, human resource management, communications management, risk management, and procurement management. PMI® offers two main levels of project management certification: CAPM® and PMP®.

The APM Body of Knowledge is a well-established collection of knowledge and common guides within project management. It is developed by the Association for Project Management (APM) and is widely used in Europe and throughout the world. The fifth edition of the *APM Body of Knowledge* covers 52 topics divided into seven sections: project management in context, planning the strategy, executing the strategy, techniques, business and commercial, organization and governance, and people and profession. APM offers several certifications, such as the APM Introductory Certificate, APMP and APM Practitioner Qualification (PQ), and Certified Project Manager (CPM).

PRINCE2® (*PRojects IN Controlled Environments*) is a product- and process-based framework that contains a set of best practices and guidelines for managing the various elements and stages of a project. It is administered by the Association for Project Management Group (APMG) on behalf of the Office of Government Commerce (OGC). PRINCE2 is a de facto standard and is used extensively by the private and public sector in the UK and Europe. Not only does it cover the management, control, and organization of a project, it also defines a number of templates and processes for managing a project. There are two sets of PRINCE2 qualifications: PRINCE2 Foundation and PRINCE2 Practitioner. Both require the candidate to study the PRINCE2 manual and sit for an exam.

Six Sigma is a business performance and management methodology originally developed by Motorola. It seeks to help businesses improve the capability of their processes and outputs by identifying and removing the causes of defects. It does so by combining a number of quality-management methods to evaluate and improve an organization's operational performance and design and manufacturing practices. The goal of Six Sigma is to achieve near-perfect quality.

Each Six Sigma project follows a defined sequence of steps and has quantified financial targets. Organizations using the methodology establish a special infrastructure of people within the organization (e.g., "Black Belts" and "Green Belts") who are experts in each of the quality management methods.

Capability Maturity Model Integration® (*CMMI®*) is a framework for improving organizational performance and business processes. It is used across many different industries and areas and can be applied to a project, a division, or an entire organization. It defines a set of practices that can be used to support process improvements in areas such as eliciting and managing requirements, decision-making, measuring performance, planning work, and handling risks. CMMI® is a registered trademark of Carnegie Mellon Software Engineering Institute (SEI).

Waterfall is a term used to describe a traditional way of delivering a software development project. It refers to a sequential process in which one stage of the project life cycle is completed before the next begins. These life cycle stages typically include analysis, design, execution (construction), verification (test), implementation (release), and maintenance (support). On a traditional waterfall project, testing will not begin until all components of the system have been built, and the execution phase will not begin until all requirements have been analyzed and designed. A waterfall project typically has one long test phase and a big-bang implementation.

Agile is an iterative and incremental approach to software development. It is different from the traditional waterfall approach in that the development team typically touches upon all life cycle activities at any one time during the project. Instead of the end product being developed sequentially, it emerges gradually because one function is being designed, built, tested, and released before the next function is embarked upon. In the agile approach, there is a constant feedback loop between the development team and the end user, as functionality is continually being designed, tested, and delivered. This approach is thus highly collaborative and user-centric.

Exercise: Knowledge Assessment

Use the spider diagram to assess your level of knowledge. Use a scale of 1 to 10 to score yourself. A score of 10 out of 10 represents the ideal state. It is what you are aiming for in each knowledge area.

1. For each of the eight knowledge areas in the diagram below, imagine what a score of 10 out of 10 would look like. For example, what would you be doing and feeling, or what would you have, if you had sufficient knowledge of the client's industry and sector to effectively manage the project?

2. For each knowledge area, indicate on the diagram where on the 1 to 10 scale you are today by making a dot on the line that represents your score. If, for example, you would give yourself an 8 for Knowledge of Client Industry/Sector, place a dot on the line labeled 8 in front of Knowledge of Client Industry/Sector. Be as realistic as possible, and give yourself credit for all of the things you already know.

3. After you have scored yourself, draw a line between the dots to see the outline of your web. Remember to use a colored pen so that you can later go back and reassess yourself using a different color and compare your scores.

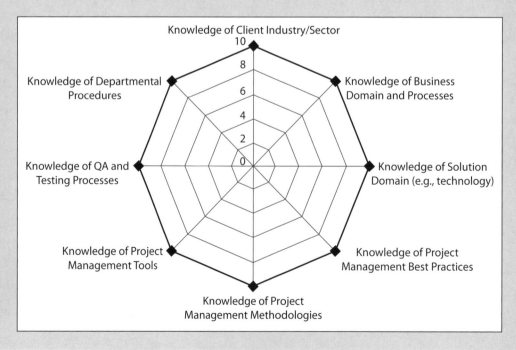

Examine your scores . . .

1. Look at your scores. Which areas stand out as needing attention?
2. What could you do to raise your rating just one point in each of these areas?

_____

_____

_____

_____

_____

_____

This self-assessment should be an honest representation of how you perceive your skills and capabilities as a person and project manager. To add more weight to the self-assessment, run through it with someone you trust and respect after you have completed it. Use this person as a sounding board, and discuss aspects of the assessment about which you were in doubt.

I suggest that you do not change your scores as a result of your discussions. Your initial scores are your benchmark, and you will need them for later comparison. Write down the comments you get on a separate piece of paper, and take them into consideration when you begin to take action or next time you go through the assessment.

Talking your self-assessment through with someone you trust and whose opinion you respect gives you an opportunity to "sanity-check" your scores. (In Step 3, 360° Feedback, you will take this concept one step further by asking your managers and peers to directly assess your capabilities. This will draw out any blind spots of which you are not aware. It will also highlight your hidden potential and reveal the ways in which others believe you can better leverage your strengths.)

In addition to sanity-checking your self-assessment, I recommend that you form a group of project managers who can function as your sounding board for day-to-day project management issues. The project manager role can be very lonely and at times demanding, so form a group of peers who can support and mentor one another.

PROJECT INITIATION AND PLANNING

The project initiation phase is the first major phase of a project, in which the project's aims, objectives, and approach are established. This is where you define the ground rules and lay the foundation for everything that is to come later.

This phase may have a different name, depending on the methodology you use. I have used the term *initiation* phase to cover any project activity intended to formally define and plan the project before it enters into the execution, construction, or build phase.

Note that for the purpose of this self-assessment, we will assume that senior managers have already engaged in some project activity before you get involved. Usually, this activity consists of establishing the business drivers and the business case behind the project and endorsing its initiation. The business case is the document that captures the reasons and rationale for the project—why it is important to undertake and what the expected benefits are. It also highlights specific project constraints and assumptions related to cost and time.

So, at the point where you get involved in a project, we assume that someone has already explored the expected benefits, explained why the project is important, and determined the overall cost and time constraints to which the project may be subject. However, even if someone else has already explored these business-related aspects of the project, you as the project manager still must fully understand them and query them if they are too vague or if they do not make sense.

The value of your role and the success of your project are heavily dependent on how well you plan and initiate the project. In the words of time management expert Alan Lakein, "Failing to plan is planning to fail." If you start to execute a project without planning what is to be done, you may actively contribute to its failure. The same holds true if you do not adjust or change the project's plans if they are no longer accurate or do not work.

The purpose of planning is not to create a map that is set in stone but to think through the project's critical elements and steps before you make irreversible commitments and take irrevocable actions. When you take the time to establish the project's scope and analyze the requirements, problem domain, and solution up front, you are much more likely to understand the project's core challenges and recognize what it takes to address them and deliver a quality product to the client.

Up-front planning is required for all types of projects. However, the extent to which you plan a project in detail during the initiation phase depends on the specific domain and nature of your project as well as the chosen methodology. Some projects are large, complex, and volatile, while others are smaller and much simpler to define, plan, and deliver. For this self-assessment, we will assume that your project is somewhere in between: a medium-sized project of medium complexity, with a project methodology that is neither rigid nor extremely flexible. As a result, you will plan the project at a high level during the initiation phase and subsequently refine and adjust the plan as you move through the execution of the project.

Among the reasons why planning is required up front is that the organization and customer need you to estimate the project's size, cost, and completion date before they fully commit to undertaking it. Likewise, as the project manager, you need to understand the exact scope of what your team is expected to deliver and how you plan to deliver it. These questions need to be answered during the first phase of the project before it is fully committed to and kicked off in earnest.

The best way to begin the initiation of a project is to start with the end in mind. The end represents the purpose and the end deliverables of your project. Knowing the purpose provides direction, focus, and motivation and is a frame of reference against which to make decisions. If you do not know what the aims, objectives, and end products are, you will not be able to direct the team and the project in a manner that will bring it to a successful completion.

> *Visualize the end state of your project once all changes have taken place and all benefits have been realized. What does that look like, and how does it differ from the current state? Really feel the end product and its purpose. Imagine the benefits and how they will affect the users.*

In many cases, you will be able to find out what the project's aims and objectives are by consulting the customer or reading the project's business case. If the business case has not been written by the time you get involved, it may be up to you as the project manager to extract the information and put together this document.

Many activities take place during the initiation phase in addition to understanding the project's scope, objectives, high-level constraints, and business case. One of them is to identify who the main stakeholders are. You can do that by asking and finding out *who* will be affected by the project and who has an interest in the project's completion. To learn about your stakeholders, identify what each of them will have gained in the end and what would make each of them say that the project was a success.

We will cover the subject of stakeholders and project success criteria in more depth later on.

Once you understand why the project is important and what it is supposed to deliver and for whom, you can start to work backwards with your team to identify what the detailed requirements are and how you can best deliver them. It is important, however, that the project's vision, business benefits, scope, and constraints are uncovered before you start exploring *how* the project can be delivered.

At a minimum, the following questions should be explored and answered in the initiation phase:

➤ What is the project intending to achieve?

➤ What are the motives for completing it?

➤ What business benefits will it lead to?

➤ Who will the beneficiaries be?

➤ What are the project's success criteria?

➤ What are the project's time, cost, and quality constraints?

➤ Who are the main stakeholders?

➤ What is in scope and out of scope?

➤ What are the requirements?

➤ What is the proposed solution?

➤ Who and what is required in order to deliver the project?

➤ What risks, issues, and dependencies surround the project?

➤ What is the project team likely to look like in terms of size, types of roles, and skill sets?

➤ Who will be responsible for each aspect of the project?

➤ What is the likely duration of the project?

➤ How much is it likely to cost?

➤ What high-level phases is the project likely to go through?

➤ How will the project be executed and controlled?

➤ How will the products and outcomes be quality checked?

➤ How will the project be closed down and handed over to the users and maintenance teams?

➤ How will the product be supported and maintained after handover?

➤ How will the project be governed?

Tip for Getting a Project Back on Track

If a project goes off track, or if you get involved in a project that is already in its execution stage, go back and revisit these key questions. Taking a step back and checking whether the foundations of the project are still solid can prove very worthwhile.

When analyzing the project's goals and objectives, it is not enough to consider the functions or products the project will deliver. You also need to understand the business benefits these products will ultimately bring about for the customer. It is in the tracking and delivery of business benefits that you will be able to add ultimate value. A project, therefore, does not end when you have delivered a new feature or function. It ends when that feature has been fully transitioned and integrated into the client's environment and when the resulting benefits have been realized.

Note that the initiation phase may be broken up into a subset of smaller, and somewhat informal, phases. When you first get involved, there may be a lot of uncertainty about whether the project is going ahead or not, and the organization may not want you to spend a lot of time and effort doing the initial investigations. However, as time passes and the organization or customer starts to commit to a more serious examination of scope, solution, and preliminary budgets, you will be able to move into a more established part of the initiation phase, where you can draw on more resources to help plan and scope the work.

The initiation phase is all about exploring and understanding what the scope of the project is and how to best go about delivering what the users want and need within the given constraints. The initiation phase is also an ideal time to be building relationships and securing buy-in for the project. You need to engage the customer, users, and senior executives as well as the team members.

The team members you need to involve from day one of the initiation phase are people who can effectively help you answer the questions listed above and explore what needs to be delivered. These people might include a domain or solution expert, a business analyst, a user representative, and maybe a more hands-on person who can help prototype the proposed solution. Anything you can show, illustrate, or demonstrate to the client at this stage provides a big advantage, as doing so will help ensure that what you plan to build matches what the customer needs and wants.

Exercise: Project Initiation Self-Assessment

Use the spider diagram to assess your ability to effectively initiate a project. Use a scale of 1 to 10 to score yourself.

1. For each activity in the diagram below, imagine what a score of 10 out of 10 would look like. For example, what does effectively capturing the project's aims, objectives, business case, and benefits entail?

2. For each activity, indicate on the diagram where on the 1 to 10 scale you are today by making a dot on the line that represents your score. After you have scored yourself, draw a line between the dots to see the outline of your web.

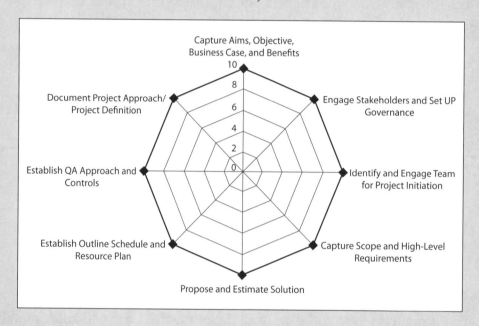

Examine your scores . . .

3. Look at your scores. Which areas stand out as needing attention?

4. What could you do to raise your rating just one point in each of these areas?

_____

_____

_____

_____

_____

PROJECT GOVERNANCE

When you start to engage the stakeholders, you must formalize their roles and responsibilities and set up the project's governance, or management structure. This is important because it ensures that effective decisionmaking can take place.

The first step in establishing the project's governance structure is to identify who the project sponsor (or executive sponsor) is. This person will be a senior stakeholder who is or who represents the customer. He or she is not involved in the day-to-day running of the project, but he or she remains the project's ultimate decisionmaker and the person who is ultimately responsible for ensuring that the business benefits are delivered and realized. The project sponsor provides project funding, defines the overall aims and objectives, resolves major issues, endorses key deliverables, approves major changes to scope, and provides high-level direction. In most cases, it is the project sponsor who owns and formulates the project's business case.

The second step is to set up and formalize the project's steering committee, that is, the group of people who, together with the project sponsor, form the project's decisionmaking body. The steering committee (sometimes referred to as the project board) will typically consist of senior executives who are able to support the project sponsor in making decisions, setting the project's direction, and allocating resources. The project sponsor is the head of the steering committee.

It is your role as the project manager to ensure that the steering committee is established as early as possible during the initiation phase and that the project sponsor and steering committee members acknowledge their responsibilities. It is important that the steering committee only consists of decisionmakers who have real influence over the project. It should not turn into a forum of stakeholders who are just looking for a project update.

Keep the size of the committee to between three and five people if you can. Make sure that all roles and aspects of the project are represented—for example, a steering committee might consist of the sponsor (responsible for the business case), the supplier (responsible for supplying resources to produce the end product[s]), and various user groups (responsible for providing the requirements). It may not be practical to have any external suppliers or vendors represented on the steering committee. Use your sense of judgment and consider splitting steering committee meetings in two if you need input from any external partners.

A steering committee will normally meet on a monthly basis to provide direction and make decisions on risks, issues, and scope changes presented to it. As the project progresses and intensifies, you may need to increase the frequency of steering committee meetings.

Under normal circumstances, a steering committee is not involved in the day-to-day administration of a project, so consider setting up a working group that meets on a more frequent basis and that can make lower-level decisions. Involve all relevant stakeholder groups, but let each be represented by a less senior manager than the representative on the steering committee.

Finally, remember that there is no point in having a perfect governance structure if no one knows about it or buys into it. Let everyone know what your intentions are, and reach agreement with each participant about their specific roles and responsibilities.

GETTING BUY-IN

One of the biggest challenges when starting up a new project can be to engage the stakeholders. This may be especially true when working on in-house mandatory projects that do not seem to benefit anyone directly. You may have a team ready to capture the requirements and estimate the solution, but if the users, domain experts, and stakeholders are not coming to the table, you will not get very far. You will have to engage them by appealing to their interest in the project and by focusing on the benefits they will receive directly or indirectly as a result of it.

If you continually struggle to get your stakeholders to devote time to a project, you will need to escalate this problem as an issue that is preventing you from making progress. Resist the temptation, and withstand pressure, to start executing the project without having defined it first. Delaying execution may not suit everyone, but explain that only when the stakeholders are engaged and the project team knows what it is working toward and understands the desired outcome will you be able to deliver that outcome. This may be common sense, but it is not necessarily commonplace. Far too many project managers kick off projects without knowing what the end game is.

DOCUMENTING THE PROJECT'S APPROACH

The project management plan, project initiation or project definition document are artifacts that describe what the project's goals and objectives are and how the project will go about achieving them. Each lays out the project's purpose, sponsorship, funding, scope, and proposed solution, and it highlights the project's exclusions and out-of-scope items. The document furthermore describes the main stakeholders and their roles and responsibilities. It also defines the high-level schedule and expected costs and how the project will be controlled. In other words, it answers the questions *what, why, who, how, where, how much,* and *when.*

You could say that the project definition is a "contract" between the project manager and the steering committee stating what will be delivered, when, and for how much. It is unlikely that you will have a detailed plan to show at this stage, as the requirements will not have been analyzed in depth. Plan for what you can and outline the main phases, activities, and target milestones.

The project's business case may either be included in the project definition document or be represented in a standalone document. The specific contents of the project definition document are discussed in more detail in Step 5, in Initiating and Planning a Project.

The signed off project definition document is one of the most important outcomes of the initiation phase, along with a description of the requirements and a functional prototype or proof of concept of the proposed solution.

An effective project definition document must be *closed*, meaning that it can only be interpreted in one way. If it is open, it can be interpreted in a variety of ways, which can cause misunderstandings and failed deliveries later in the project. You will need to work with the team and stakeholders to make the approach as specific as possible and close it, for instance by clearly stating what is *not* in scope of the project.

Although I refer to the project definition as a document, the real work is not in the writing process but in the days or weeks of combined team effort to analyze, discuss, and agree how to best deliver the project's scope and objectives.

The project is ready to move into its execution stage when all major aspects of the project initiation phase have been analyzed and agreed on and when the business case and project definition document have been signed off by the steering committee. In addition, you will need the necessary resources, such as funding, people, space, and materials, to be made available before you can move on.

Test Yourself

How well can you explain your current project's objectives, solution, and plan?

1. Take five to ten minutes to prepare an imaginary project presentation. Visualize yourself speaking to a new stakeholder who has not been involved in the project before. You will talk about the project's major milestones, dates, budget figures, and end deliverables and will explain the requirements, business benefits, and the vision.

2. Stand up now and deliver the presentation you have prepared. Speak uninterrupted for five minutes, and imagine that the senior stakeholder is listening.

3. How well did you do?

PROVIDING THE INITIAL ESTIMATE

Understanding what the users want, and how much it will cost to produce what they want, is essential to successful delivery. Many projects start off on the wrong foot because they have been insufficiently analyzed or underestimated. It is human nature to want to deliver something well and quickly, but underestimating the complexities of a project can lead to problems such as lack of budget to complete the project, missed deadlines, or both.

One of the tasks you and your team need to complete before you can effectively estimate the effort required is to spend a sufficient amount of time analyzing and understanding the user's requirements as well as the proposed solution. *Sufficient* means that you have uncovered all of the risky areas and that a robust solution is emerging. Do this by engaging the key users (or user representatives) and eliciting, documenting, and prioritizing all their key requirements. Use a structured approach, and engage a strong business analyst or domain expert. We will explore the subject of eliciting requirements in more detail in the next theme: Managing Product Quality.

There is no golden rule regarding the number of requirements to analyze in the initiation phase. For one project, 40 percent may be appropriate, while it may be 70 percent for another. This will depend on the nature of your project and the culture of your organization. Remember that the initiation phase is all about laying down the foundation and mitigating project risk by understanding what needs to be delivered and how it will be delivered. Start off by analyzing the most important and most risky parts of the project first, and leave the less important aspects to be analyzed and refined during later stages of the project.

Tips for Estimating Project Effort

There are many different tools and methods for estimating project effort. Below are a few tips and guidelines that can help you improve your estimates:

✔ **Gradually refine estimates.** Bear in mind that estimation is an ongoing activity that should take place regularly throughout a project, for instance at the beginning of each new phase. In the initial phase, a high-level estimate may be required in order to determine the feasibility of the project, whereas later, a more thorough analysis and estimate will be needed. Resist the temptation to provide an estimate without having any detailed requirements or analysis to back it up. If senior management needs a quick indication of potential costs in connection with an initiative, provide them with a best guess, and make sure they do not take it as an official estimate.

✔ **Understand the requirements.** Analyze all key requirements to a reasonable level and break the effort down into manageable pieces. The more granularity, the easier it will be for you to estimate. Hold workshops to illustrate and talk the requirements and proposed solution through in detail with the team and customer. Make sure you are all in agreement about what needs to be delivered and thus estimated. If time allows, you may want to demonstrate or prototype key aspects of the product in order to further validate the user's requirements and proposed solution.

✔ **Involve the right people.** Involve experienced people in the analysis and estimation process and brainstorm with the people who are actually going to do the work—the more the better. Have different groups of people estimate the same thing, then compare the outcomes. A big disparity between numbers points to uncertainties in the proposed solution. Add extra contingency to compensate, or spend more time analyzing the uncertain elements.

✔ **Use estimation tools.** Research and experiment with different estimation tools and techniques. Ask around in the organization to find out which tools other teams have used. Understanding how estimation tools work will generally improve your ability to estimate a project even if you end up not making use of them directly. These tools will help you consider all the different aspects of the project and make you aware that you need to compensate with more contingency if your team is relatively inexperienced or if the solution is particularly complex.

✔ **Use factors and complexities.** If your project consists of many common factors or products (for instance, rooms or floors in a building), estimate how much effort one would take to build and then multiply by the number you need to deliver. Refine this method by operating with different types of complexities, for instance high-, medium-, or low-complexity rooms. Note that this method will not be applicable to highly complex projects that have very few common factors and products.

✔ **Quantify the unknowns.** All estimates carry an inherent degree of uncertainty (or risk), especially in the early stages of the project, when there are more unknowns. It is crucial that you quantify the percentage of unknowns in your estimate and compensate with an equivalent level of contingency. Remember that relatively speaking, you will be much better off overestimating the effort, as this will give you a chance to come in under budget and thereby over-deliver.

✔ **Be pragmatic.** Be careful to not just estimate the "sunny path" scenario for a project. Unexpected things always come up, and requirements are often more complex to implement than originally thought. Remind everyone to be pragmatic and realistic when providing estimates, and ask people for best-case and worst-case numbers.

✔ **Factor in all phases.** Make sure you factor in all phases and activities of the project, including initiation, analysis, design, build, testing, rework, delivery, handover, post-project support, training, documentation, and project closedown. Also include specific time for management and support activities such as project management, project support, team management, technical management, and test management if these are not already accounted for.

✔ **Estimate effort in points.** Estimate the effort in points or labor-hours as opposed to calendar time to account for the fact that no team is ever 100 percent effective. You can then apply a separate conversion factor to translate your estimated effort into calendar time. The translation of effort into calendar time is based on how many effective hours a team member can spend on project tasks per day. For example, if your team spends 30 percent of an average day attending meetings, answering queries, checking emails, and doing other activities that are not part of the project's estimated effort, you will need to add a conversion factor of 1.3. Estimating your project in points will make it easier to track the accuracy of your estimates as you move through the project. It also will enable you to measure the effectiveness of your team.

✔ **Add contingency.** Add a downright contingency factor to your estimate to account for events you cannot foresee, such as unexpected problems with the proposed solution or vendor or unexpectedly having to onboard new or more expensive project resources. Also bear in mind that labor rates and exchange rates may change as the project progresses. These are risks which you must account for with contingency.

✔ **Have a change budget.** If you foresee that the requirements will change as you move through the project, consider setting money aside specifically for scope changes. If you do not have a change budget, any major scope changes will eat into your contingency, or you will have to go back to your sponsor and ask for more money. Neither situation is ideal.

✔ **Record estimates.** Formally record your estimates and document how you arrived at them. Make the estimated scope and assumptions clear, and also highlight what is out of scope. Not only will this put you in a better position to defend and adjust your numbers, but it will also help you review and improve your estimation process going forward.

CREATING AN OUTLINE PLAN

There are many different ways of creating a plan. One of them is a product-based planning technique. With product-based planning, your focus is first and foremost on the products that need to be delivered as opposed to the activities the project needs to undertake. It means that you plan the project from the client's and user's perspective, because you put the focus on tangible deliverables and outcomes.

Note that the plans you produce during the initiation phase will mostly be high level, unless you operate within a domain where your plans for some reason *must* be fixed and contain a minimum amount of uncertainty. Under most circumstances, though, I would recommend that you only plan in detail for as far ahead as is sensible. Keep your plans realistic yet simple. It is better to be broadly right than precisely wrong.

Do not attempt to plan your project in isolation, but seek assistance from your team members. You need them to help you break down high-level products into subproducts, tasks, and activities with durations and dependencies.

Use the below tips and techniques to help you create a high-level product-based plan. Note that you will only be able to produce the plan once you have a reasonable understanding of what the requirements are and once you have estimated these requirements. Planning is an iterative process, so do not worry if you do not have all of the detailed information up front. Create a high-level plan and refine it as you go along.

1. **Create a product breakdown structure.** The first step in creating a product-based plan is to create a product breakdown structure in hierarchical format, similar to one you would use to build an organizational chart. It should contain all of the major products (i.e., components and deliverables) you plan to produce and deliver.

   › At the top of the hierarchy, you depict the final product—the finished system, building, or deliverable.

   › In the level below, you document its constituent parts. This could consist of two, ten, or more subproducts depending on your project.

   › On the third level of the hierarchy, you break down the subproducts even further.

   Continue breaking down your products and deliverables to a level that makes sense for the project. The product breakdown structure does not contain any dependencies or activities but is a pure representation of what the users need and how their needs break down into sub-subdeliverables.

2. **Create a product flow diagram.** The next step is to turn the product breakdown structure into a product flow diagram, which is a view of the *sequence* in which the different products are likely to be delivered. Use the products and subproducts from the product breakdown structure, and rearrange them according to their priorities and dependencies. Make the diagram flow from left to right, ending up with the final product on the far right side. Use your knowledge of interdependencies between the subproducts and their relative business priority to create the diagram.

3. **Produce a high-level plan.** Use the product flow diagram as the guide for creating a road map and a straw-model scenario that you can use to jump start more in-depth planning conversations and activities. In the early stages of the planning process, you may have to make many assumptions and use approximate durations and timings. Determine the sequence in which you aim to deliver the products, then arrange them into phases with clearly defined milestones. Aim to deliver the core and most critical part of the solution first.

Once you know what the distinct phases are, focus on the first phase and break down its subdeliverables into as much detail as you can, preferably until you have individual tasks and activities that would take days, rather than weeks, for a team member to execute. Continue breaking down the subsequent phases of the project, but use a broader brush for the later phases, where you might not yet have full understanding of the detailed activities that need to be carried out.

4. **Assign resources.** Start assigning resources to your plan, and tighten up the estimated duration of individual tasks. In order to do that, you must understand which resources are available and also plan for the possibility of their being unavailable. Play around with different resource levels to get a good feel for when the project might complete.

When doing so, identify and pay special attention to the project's critical path. The critical path is the longest sequence of dependent activities in your schedule that must be completed by the due date in order for the project to be on time. It is the critical path that will determine the actual duration of the project, as all other activities can be scheduled in parallel. More than anything, it is the critical path that you must pay close attention to throughout the execution of the project to make sure that the overall project time line does not slip.

5. **Present the plan.** Before you provide your sponsor and steering committee with the outline plan, review it one last time with members of the team, and make sure you have added sufficient contingency to the critical path. Remember that it is better to under-promise and over-deliver than the other way around.

Once stakeholders see a schedule, they have a tendency to think it is set in stone. Plan for worst-case scenarios, and provide a range of dates within which you expect to deliver the project, as opposed to just one fixed date. Explain to your stakeholders what your planning assumptions, risks, and issues are, and make it very clear that events are not set in stone. Explain that you will update and refine the plan frequently as you move through the project and that you will keep them informed of any changes.

MANAGING PRODUCT QUALITY

Understanding the detailed scope of a project, and managing the quality of that scope, are critical to a successful outcome because scope defines the products and benefits the customer and users will receive. A project that does not deliver the required functionality, at the level of quality the users need, may be of no use and is likely to end in failure.

Acceptance criteria play an important role in defining and measuring quality. They can be defined as the conditions that must be met in order for a particular feature or product to be considered accepted by the customer. The key to successful quality management is to first and foremost define these acceptance criteria and to continually check that the products being produced match them. To effectively ensure quality, you must have clearly defined acceptance criteria for each product and subproduct you plan to deliver. Each product should also have a test case associated with it. Test cases explain how the product will be tested to ensure that the acceptance criteria are met.

Remember that acceptance criteria must be measurable in order to be useful. It is all well and good that the customer wants you to produce a blue chair, but what exact qualities and dimensions must it have, and how will the customer decide if the shade of blue is the correct one?

When capturing the detailed requirements, acceptance criteria, and test cases, liaise closely with the customer, end users, and other key stakeholders, and engage the entire team to make sure that everyone understands the scope and feels responsible for its quality. It is not enough for the business analyst or domain expert to understand the detailed scope and its quality measures. All team members must understand it, feel it, and know what each of their specific roles and responsibilities are so that they can contribute to it. When the entire team internalizes the scope and quality measures, testing and checking that the products meet the acceptance criteria may become a trivial exercise.

The activity of capturing the requirements and acceptance criteria is an art as well as a science–especially when it comes to capturing needs that are not easily verbalized. It takes great listening, questioning, and analysis skills to dissect what is being said and to ask about that which is unsaid.

> *Many users and stakeholders are not trained in conveying what they need and may only relay part of the picture. The more you probe them about what they want, the more likely you are to create a solution that meets their real needs.*

Put on your detective's hat when eliciting requirements, and get your team and business analysts to do the same. Ask, probe, question, and illustrate. Put yourself in the users' shoes, and see the end product with their eyes. What is it that they need, and how can you best ensure that they get what they need?

| How the customer explained it | How the team designed it | What the customer really needed |

You may already have seen this cartoon.[1] Although it is old, the principle still holds true.

The challenge for the project team is to truly understand and deliver what the customer needs rather than blindly designing to the requirements that are initially expressed.

Interacting as much as you can with the customer and making use of workshops, storyboarding, demonstrations, and prototyping helps ensure that everyone understands and agrees to what needs to be delivered. But as with anything, the devil is in the details, so you will need to continuously confirm that what is being produced corresponds to the users' needs and requirements.

To help you keep track of the detailed requirements and their associated acceptance criteria and test cases, consider creating a *requirements traceability matrix.* The matrix is a simple tool, often in spreadsheet form, that helps you effectively manage a project's requirements from conception through testing and delivery. Specifically, you can use it to track the progress of each individual requirement, its priority, and its test status.

Construct the matrix so that it shows the relationship between business objectives, requirements, and their associated test cases. List all of the project's requirements (or products) in the left-hand column of a spreadsheet. Assign each requirement or product a unique reference number. Place the identifiers for the other documents or activities you want to track, such as test cases, across the top row. Figure 2-1 is a simple example of what your matrix might look like.

Different types of projects use different terminology for their artifacts. Use the best-suited terminology for your project. Similarly, track the activities that add the most benefit to what you want to achieve. You may, for instance, want to track the status of design documents, test cases, and user acceptance testing against each of your requirements. You may also want to add several levels of requirements, such as business requirements which map

Reference number	Requirement	Priority	Test case	User Acceptance Validation	Comments
Business Objective 1					
1					
2					
Business Objective 2					
3					

FIGURE 2-1.   Requirements Traceability Matrix

to more granular system requirements. Remember to account for both functional and non-functional requirements. To add more weight to the matrix, work with your team to assign clear responsibilities for each of the listed activities.

Using a requirements traceability matrix helps you ensure that no requirements are forgotten, that there is a business objective behind each requirement, and that nothing gets delivered without having been tested and signed off. It also serves as a firm baseline against which you can track changes to your requirements.

There are various ways to test the project's requirements, depending on the nature and domain of your project. On some projects, it makes sense to carry out automated tests, while this is not applicable on others. However, on most projects you will be able to perform some form of functional testing and user acceptance testing to verify the quality and suitability of the products you plan to deliver. These types of tests tend to be most effective if they are performed against predefined test cases and if the end users are direct participants. Another QA method that can be adopted on most projects is peer reviews. Peer reviewing can be done at various stages, for instance to review requirements specifications, design documents, and test cases.

Although frequent interaction with the end users is a main factor in ensuring quality, always get your team to thoroughly test a product before it is presented to the users for final acceptance. Asking the users for feedback throughout the project is vital, but when it comes to final delivery of the products, you want the users to verify and sign off on deliverables rather than having to thoroughly test them.

A good way to measure quality throughout a project is to look at the defect count. Determine an effective way to record and track all defects, and monitor the total number. If the number is too high or if it all of a sudden changes dramatically, investigate the reason and find a way to address it. It is likely that your QA and testing processes are not good enough, or that they are not being correctly followed.

Exercise: Product Quality Management Self-Assessment

Use the spider diagram to assess your ability to effectively manage product quality. Use a scale of 1 to 10 to score yourself.

1. For each of the activities listed in the diagram, imagine what a score of 10 out of 10 would look like. For example, what does effectively capturing the project's scope and acceptance criteria entail?

   Note that although you may not necessarily be carrying out all of the product quality activities yourself, you remain firmly responsible for managing and monitoring them as a project manager. This responsibility encompasses business analysis, development activities, and test management. A score of 10 out of 10 in this exercise therefore means that you are fully in control of the individual activity as a project manager.

2. For each activity, indicate on the diagram where on the 1 to 10 scale you are today by making a dot on the line that represents your score.

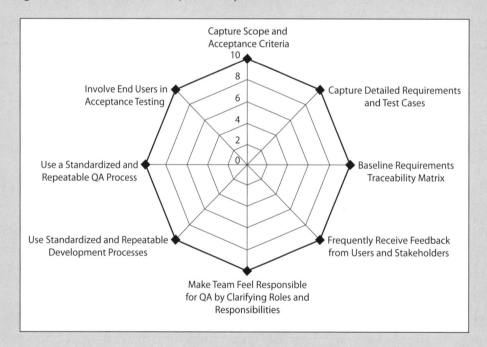

Examine your scores . . .

3. Look at your scores. Which areas stand out as needing attention?
4. What could you do to raise your rating just one point in each of these areas?

_____

_____

_____

USER INVOLVEMENT

End-user involvement[2] is imperative to producing a high-quality project outcome, both because the users (or their representatives) play an imperative role in specifying what needs to be built and because they are normally the ones who sign off on the deliverable to indicate that it matches the requirements. Make sure you involve all of the main user groups, including those who will actually be maintaining and supporting the product after it has been produced and handed over to the customer.

To benefit the most from the users' knowledge and experience, it may make sense for the project team to be seated next to the users (or their representatives) for the duration of the project. Ask the users to document acceptance criteria and test cases before the team starts developing a feature, and have them verify emerging functionality throughout the project. Be careful, though, not to push all of the testing onto the users. They are there to verify functionality, not to thoroughly test it. The advantage of checking back with the users as often as possible is not only to sanity-check the functionality but to give the users a great opportunity to refine their requirements so that they will get what they truly need.

Holding workshops can be an excellent way to engage the users. Ask them to illustrate their requirements and to walk through key scenarios that show how they intend to use the solution. Let the project team ask questions about anything that is not clear. After the users have explained their requirements, team members can write up their understanding of the requirements on a whiteboard. This will very quickly highlight any gaps or misunderstandings.

Another way to minimize the risk of developing something your users do not need is to have a senior user representative peer-review and sign off on requirements, acceptance criteria, and test cases before you start development. Again, use prototyping whenever you can. It is an excellent way to obtain feedback and to verify that what you are about to develop matches the requirements.

Come to agreement with the project sponsor and stakeholders up front about how much time and attention you can get from the users and how you intend to work together, so that it is clear to everyone exactly what is expected of them. If despite this agreement, you do not get enough attention from the users, escalate the problem as soon as you can to someone who can help change the situation. Lack of user involvement is one of the most common reasons for project failure.

Caution

When it comes to product quality, it is very important not to make assumptions. Do not assume that you know what the customer and end users want, and do not assume that what you are developing matches their requirements. Be skeptical, and check everything you do not have evidence for.

- How can you confirm that all requirements for a particular feature or product have been captured correctly?

- How can you confirm that what you are developing (or planning to develop) matches the users' needs and requirements?

- How can you ensure that the requirements are well understood by all team members?

- What can you do to involve the users more on your project?

Tips for Gathering Requirements

You may be in a situation in which the customer delivers the requirements to you in a neat and structured way, ready for your team to estimate and deliver a solution. More often, however, it is up to the project team to work with the customer and users to extract, analyze, and document the requirements. If that is the case, try the following:

- ✔ **Agree on the approach to managing requirements.** First of all, come to agreement with your team, customer, and end users on a process for gathering, documenting, and controlling requirements, and determine who will be responsible for each part of the process. Formally capture the steps, tools, and roles and responsibilities in a requirements management plan, and get it signed off by the stakeholders.

- ✔ **Engage the right people.** Make sure you talk to the end users and senior stakeholders who have the actual authority to sign off on requirements and who will ultimately be using the end product. They can tell you what they want and what they expect from the product you are building.

- ✔ **Be proactive.** Do not sit back and wait for the customer to deliver a detailed, concise, well-structured requirements document. Usually, you will need to be proactive and work with the stakeholders and end users to help them structure and articulate their needs.

- ✔ **Organize a workshop.** Workshops are a very powerful way to gather requirements. Set up an initial workshop to uncover the vision and high-level requirements. This workshop may last several days, if necessary. Involve all major stakeholders.

- ✔ **Describe the product vision.** Take a top-down view and capture the essence of the envisaged product to be developed. Determine the objectives, needs, wants, limitations, and constraints. Document the vision, and get the customer to sign off on your interpretation.

✔ **Identify the users.** Identify all of the users who in one way or another will be using and interacting with the end product. Each user group is likely to have unique requirements.

✔ **Specify what is out of scope.** Specifically focus on and write down items that are out of scope. Make this document as explicit as possible; clearly draw boundaries between what you will and what you will not deliver.

✔ **Analyze the problem.** Come to agreement with the senior stakeholders on the overall problem that your product is being developed to resolve. Drill down: identify the problems behind the problem. Prioritize these problems and document them.

✔ **Break the requirements down.** Break the high-level requirements and products down into their constituent parts. Set up workshops that focus on specific parts or components of the product, and invite the necessary stakeholders.

✔ **Ask open questions.** Engage all user groups, interview them, and ask open questions about what they want from a specific component, product, or subproduct. Ask them what the product will enable them to do and how they will be interacting with it. Focus on their needs and problems and how they will determine if the product works according to their specifications.

✔ **Be creative.** Use a variety of techniques in addition to workshops, such as interviewing, storyboarding, brainstorming, role-playing, and prototyping.

✔ **Verify the requirements.** Play back your understanding of the requirements to the stakeholders to ensure your team understands them and has correctly captured them. This can be done in any way you choose. The important thing is to ensure mutual understanding of the requirements and obtain formal sign-off.

✔ **Capture nonfunctional requirements.** Users may not have thought of nonfunctional requirements, which include requirements around maintainability, scalability, security, and performance. Seek to understand what will happen after the project completes and which nonfunctional requirements pertain to the long-term usability of the solution.

✔ **Organize the requirements.** Depending on the size of the project, you may not be able to define all of the requirements in a single document or model. In that case, maintain multiple sets of requirements—one set for each of the products and subproducts you have identified.

✔ **Incorporate acceptance criteria and test cases.** As you gather and document the requirements, simultaneously document how each product or requirement will be tested and what its acceptance criteria are.

✔ **Use a requirements traceability matrix.** Keep track of all requirements and their associated test cases in a requirements traceability matrix. This document helps you carry out completeness checks and track the progression of each requirement. It serves as a baseline scope document against which you can track and control changes. Be sure your requirements traceability matrix is signed off by the steering committee.

AGILE DEVELOPMENT

If you are running a software project, you probably know that it is becoming more and more commonplace to use agile approaches for delivering projects. Agile development is iterative and user-centric in nature. This approach implicitly promotes quality because functionality is specified, built, tested, integrated, and delivered gradually.

The agile philosophy is based on the fact that requirements change and that they must be easily incorporated into the project. The team will continuously check what the highest-priority and most risky requirements are and focus on analyzing, developing, and implementing those. They will iterate through the deliverables in close cooperation with the end users until an acceptable level of satisfaction is achieved.

In agile, the emphasis is on face-to-face communication and on building the right product. Fixed parameters such as cost, time, and scope are less important than efficiency, feedback, and quality. When used correctly, the agile approach leaves less room for misunderstandings because of the constant feedback loop between team and user.

One of the biggest advantages of agile is that features and benefits are delivered early and incrementally throughout the project, as opposed to one big-bang delivery. The users receive working software on a regular basis, which minimizes the risk of producing an incorrect deliverable.

Depending on the nature and type of project you are running, you may be able to implement and benefit from some agile principles, even if you are running a non-software project. The earlier you are able to show your customer and users what you are building, and the earlier you can test and integrate the work into their environment, the better placed you are likely to be to build a quality product.

Questions

- How agile is your project?

- In what ways could you implement some of the agile practices to help improve quality on your current project?

TRACKING COST AND SCHEDULE

Once the project has been defined and approved, it enters into the build, construction, or execution stage, where the majority of the development and actual work take place. From that point on, a major part of your role is to manage and track the schedule of work and costs incurred. The way you go about this will depend on the nature of your project and the chosen methodology. On projects that are executed using a traditional methodology, you will primarily track to an agreed-upon plan defined during the initiation phase. If you are running a project that is more iterative in nature, you will define much of the detailed plan as you move through the project.

For the purpose of the self-assessment on cost and schedule management, assume that your project is somewhere in between: an outline plan was created during the initiation phase that must be refined and adjusted as you move through the execution of the project.

Tell your stakeholders that the plan will be refined and adjusted as the project progresses, and get them to agree to this early on. If you do not make this clear, there is a risk that they will expect the schedule to be fixed. They may forget that projects are dynamic and that the schedule will change every time there is a change to requirements, priorities, dependencies, estimates, or availability of resources.

> *Effective project managers know that things change and are flexible enough to account for this by recalibrating their plans when change happens. At the same time, they have enough foresight to manage stakeholders' expectations so that they never receive unexpected bad news.*

One way you can manage your stakeholders' expectations is by proactively identifying and discussing risks before they turn into issues. Give senior stakeholders a heads up when you discover a significant risk, and do what you can to avoid it or mitigate it. (We will talk more about how you can effectively manage project stakeholders in Step 5.)

Two of the key elements of ongoing planning and tracking are adaptability and accuracy. Adaptability is needed in the planning process to accommodate changing circumstances, and accuracy is essential to tracking and reporting on progress made and costs incurred. Without these two elements, your project plan may not be a true reflection of what is actually going on, and you are unlikely to be aware of the exact status of the project.

There are three parameters you must regularly and rigorously track during the execution of a project: scope, cost, and time.

➤ **Scope** relates to the products and outcomes being produced by your team and how much work (or effort) is still outstanding to complete the project. Scope may also refer to the quality of the products, but here we will primarily use scope to refer to progress on project work.

➤ **Cost** relates to how much money the project is spending compared to the amount that has been estimated and budgeted. You need to know if the estimates still stack up and whether you have enough money to complete the project.

➤ **Time** relates to the speed at which products are being produced and whether the project is on track to meet its outlined delivery dates and anticipated end date.

To effectively track cost and schedule, you need to be able to answer the following questions at any given time:

➤ What actual progress has been made on the project (i.e., how much work has been completed, and which milestones have been met)?

➤ What is the actual vs. planned progress (i.e., how much work has been completed compared to plan)?

➤ How much time has passed?

➤ How much money has been spent?

➤ What is the anticipated end date of the project? (Provide a range of dates that indicates when the final products are expected to be delivered, as well as one that indicates when all business benefits will have been realized.)

➤ How much additional money do you expect to spend?

Exercise: Cost and Schedule Management Self-Assessment

Use the spider diagram to assess your ability to track and manage a project's costs and schedule on an ongoing basis. Use a scale of 1 to 10 to score yourself.

1. For each activity shown in the diagram, imagine what a score of 10 out of 10 would look like. For example, what must be done to effectively track actual costs vs. planned costs?

2. For each activity, indicate on the diagram where on the 1 to 10 scale you are today by making a dot on the line that represents your score.

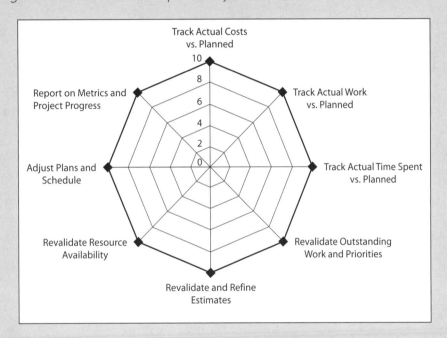

Examine your scores . . .

3. Look at your scores. Which areas stand out as needing attention?

4. What could you do to raise your rating just one point in each of these areas?

_____

_____

_____

_____

_____

METRICS

Metrics are numerical data used to quantify results. When used correctly, they become valuable measurements that help you report on a project's status with confidence and reliability. Metrics can tell you whether your team is making progress at the expected rate and if your project is within budget. You can find these out by measuring how much the project is earning (i.e., producing) compared to how much it is burning (in terms of time and money). In other words, you want to measure what you have produced against the amount of time that has passed and how much money has been spent.

A prerequisite for calculating metrics effectively is having something against which you can measure progress. You must have a baseline scope, a baseline budget, and a baseline time frame. You also have to use valid units as measures. Time and cost are relatively easy to measure, but when it comes to scope, there are various ways of determining and measuring progress. The measure I recommend you use for calculating progress is *points* (or any other unit that is independent from time). You must convert all of the products in scope into points to get a measure of the project's total effort. For example, a task you estimate to take three person-days of effort might represent three points. As you move through the project, you can calculate how many points you are earning (or producing) compared to how much money and time you are burning.

Some of the metrics you (and your stakeholders) might find useful to track are listed below. In project management–speak, these metrics are sometimes called earned value methods.

Scope (What are you earning?)

1. Actual products completed in real terms. (What has the team delivered and achieved to date? Report actual deliverables as well as the number of points earned.)

2. Actual products completed, or effort earned, in percentage terms. (What percentage of scope has been completed? How many points have you earned compared to the total number of project points?)

3. Actual vs. planned products completed. (How much scope has been completed compared to how much you planned to have completed?)

Tip for Tracking Progress

Only count work as complete if a task or a piece of functionality has been validated by the users. This provides a true picture of progress and prevents you from inflating numbers and believing that something has been done while in reality it is still incomplete.

Cost (What are you burning?)

1. Actual costs incurred in real terms. (How much money has been spent, or burned, in actual dollar terms?)

2. Actual cost incurred, or burned, in percentage terms. (What percentage of the total budget has been spent?)

3. Actual vs. planned cost. (How much money has been spent compared to how much you planned to have spent?)

Time (What are you burning?)

1. Actual amount of time spent. (How much time has passed since the project started in terms of days, weeks, iterations, or months?)

2. Actual amount of time spent (or burned) in percentage terms. (What percentage of the allotted time has passed?)

3. Actual vs. planned time. (How much of the allotted time has passed compared to how much you planned to have passed at this point?)

TRACKING AND MEASURING PROGRESS

Example 1: Tracking and Measuring Progress

Figures 2-2 and 2-3 show examples of how you can track and measure your project's progress over time.

First, read through the text so that you understand what the graphs show. Then create your own spreadsheet and try out the tracking techniques for yourself. Insert real budget, time, and effort numbers and play around until you get some meaningful metrics. In the end, you should have some powerful yet simple graphs that you can start to include in your project reports.

Remember that a prerequisite for doing this exercise on your own is that you have estimates of your project's total scope or effort and its cost. Without these, you will not be able to produce any meaningful metrics.

In this example, the project's baseline scope is 110 points, the time frame is 17 weeks, and the budget is $340,000.

Example 1, Step 1: Establish a Baseline

Figure 2-2 is an example of a burn-up chart, which shows how scope or effort can be measured over time.

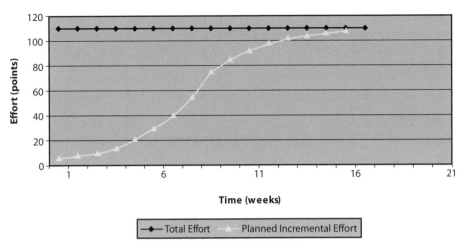

FIGURE 2-2. Planned Project Progress over Time

The vertical axis measures the project's work or effort in terms of points and includes all of the collective features and products in the project's scope. The straight line across the top shows the total effort of the project: 110 points.

The horizontal axis is a measure of time in weeks. The curved line represents how much effort (or how many points) the project manager expects the team to deliver over time. The point at which the two lines intersect signifies the date when the entire project is expected to complete, in this case 17 weeks after it started.

Example 1, Step 2: Track and Monitor Actual Progress

As time passes, you can start to track whether you are making progress in line with your plan.

Figure 2-3 is an example of how your project's progress might look after eight weeks.

The short, curved line with squares shows the actual effort your team has completed. In this example, your team is making significantly less progress than planned.

The straight line across the top, which represents total effort (or scope), has moved upward. This has happened in response to approved change requests that increased the project's scope. The total effort your team has to work through has gone from 110 points to 115 points to 120 points.

Because the team has completed less work than planned *and* because the scope has increased, the project is unlikely to meet its original delivery date unless the scope is reduced or the size or efficiency of the team is improved. The corrective action you need to take as a project manager to resolve this problem depends on the root cause of the issue.

To get a view of what the revised delivery date is likely to be if no corrective action is taken, extrapolate the short line with the squares to see the point at which it meets the straight line

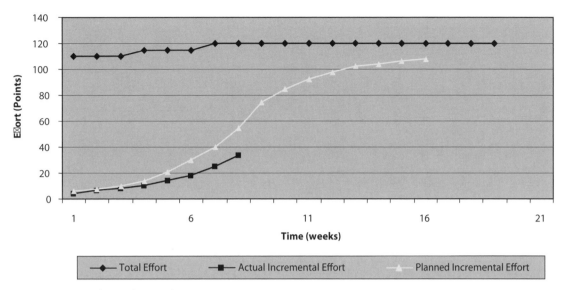

FIGURE 2-3.   Actual vs. Planned Project Progress over Time

along the top. It is by observing the effort (or number of points) your team delivers over time that you can best predict when your project will be delivered.

TRACKING AND MEASURING COST

> **Example 2: Tracking and Measuring Cost**
>
> Figure 2-4 illustrates how you can track and measure your project's cost over time.
>
> The first step is to establish the baseline against which you are tracking cost. To do this, you have to know what the project's total budget is and how much money you expect to burn each week (or month).

In Figure 2-4, the baseline budget is $340,000 (as shown by the straight line), which is expected to be burned within 17 weeks, as illustrated by the curved line with the triangles. The curved, short line with the squares illustrates how much money has actually been spent eight weeks into the project.

When your project is spending more money than expected, you must identify the root cause and take corrective action as soon as you can. You also must raise the issue to the steering committee and discuss its severity and impact as well as the identified action plan.

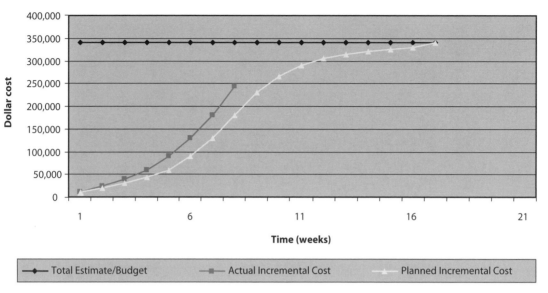

FIGURE 2-4. Actual vs. Planned Project Cost over Time

COMPARING EFFORT, COST AND TIME METRICS

Example 3: Comparing Effort, Cost, and Time Metrics

Figure 2-5 illustrates how you can show and compare how much effort your project is earning with how much money and time it is burning.

This graph is a snapshot of progress eight weeks into the project.

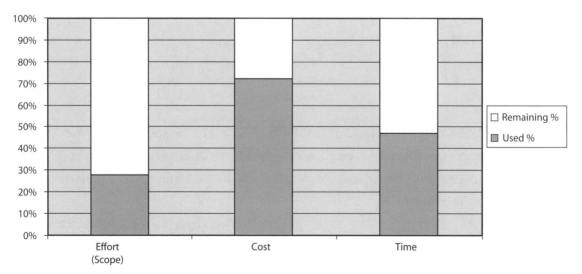

FIGURE 2-5. Project Effort Earned vs. Cost and Time Burned

As Figure 2-5 shows, the project has earned 28 percent of effort, or 33 of 120 points, after eight weeks.

At the same time, the project has burned 72 percent of budget; you have spent $245,000 out of $340,000.

The project has also burned 47 percent of time, as you are eight weeks into a 17-week project.

Take Action

1. Take time out to create a set of cost and effort metrics for your project, following the process outlined above. Remember to first establish a sound baseline from which to track spending and progress. If you have not collected metrics from your project up until now, go back and do so retroactively.

2. Update your metrics on a weekly or monthly basis, and use bar charts and diagrams to convey the information to your stakeholders in weekly project reports and monthly steering committee meetings.

MANAGING PROJECT COSTS

We have already discussed the importance of managing project costs and the metrics you need to collect in order to track and report on them. The tips below can help you better manage and control costs.

Tips for Managing Project Costs

✔ **Produce an estimate.** Compile a realistic estimate with the help of your team. Make sure it covers all of the project's phases and activities and that it contains sufficient contingency. Account for all people costs as well as the cost of materials, services, hardware, and software.

✔ **Establish a baseline budget.** Get the estimate signed off by the sponsor and steering committee and ensure that the funds are actually released and allocated to the project. This will give you a baseline budget to work from.

✔ **Establish a monthly budget.** Determine what you expect the project's monthly running costs to be based on your knowledge of the project's resource plan and schedule. Document the expected expenditure for each month for the duration of the project in a spreadsheet.

✔ **Establish cost controls.** Set up clear cost controls and sign-off responsibilities for the different types of expenditures. Consider who will be approving and signing off on time sheets, materials, hardware, software, and vendor invoices. Cost controls are crucial, as they (not surprisingly) are how you control the actual costs that will be booked to your project.

✔ **Record actual costs.** Check the actual dollar amount accounted to your project at the end of each month. The finance department will normally provide this figure to you. Record the amount in your spreadsheet so that you can compare it to your budget.

✔ **Calculate metrics.** Calculate and update your cost metrics at the end of each reporting period. Measure how much money the project has actually spent compared to how much money you had expected it to spend by this point in time. Include your cost metrics in your project reports and steering committee presentations.

✔ **Update forecasts.** Adjust your budget forecasts on a monthly basis to account for any changes that have taken place. Changes could be caused by actual running costs being higher (or lower) than forecast or estimates being higher (or lower) than forecast.

✔ **Communicate.** Be open with senior management about the project's costs by including your cost metrics and key numbers in your project reports and steering committee presentations. If your costs are not on track, treat this as an issue to be analyzed, resolved, and discussed with the steering committee.

PROJECT REPORTING

Regular and honest project reporting to all involved parties is essential for a number of reasons. It increases your awareness of the true state of the project by forcing you to collate project metrics and review outstanding risks and issues. It also shows the whole team what is going on and provides senior stakeholders and executives with opportunities to step in and offer their support and guidance when required.

Written reports should never replace face-to-face contact with stakeholders, but they work well as supporting material for regular steering committee meetings or working group meetings. Keep your reports simple, brief, and focused, and deliver them in a format that is acceptable to the recipients.

Again, project reports must be an honest reflection of what is going on; otherwise, they serve little purpose. There should be no need to give a false impression that the project is doing well if it is not. Spell out the risks and issues—this is your chance to get the more influential stakeholders to help you resolve them. And make sure to mention all of the project's successes and achievements in the report. You are closest to the project, so you are the one who should promote it the most.

Your organization may well have guidelines for how often you are required to publish a project report. If not, you may want to compile a report weekly or biweekly and send it out to all main stakeholders.

When you report on metrics, illustrate them with burn-up charts or bar charts similar to the ones presented in Figures 2-2–2-5. This is a great way to illustrate your progress.

What to Include in a Project Report

At a minimum, the following should be included in your project report:

- Basic information, including project name, reporting period, and the name of the project manager and project sponsor.

- A visual time line that clearly indicates which milestones have been met and which are still outstanding.

- A brief description of what has been achieved since the last report.

- A description of top-ten risks and issues, including their impact, agreed-upon actions, and assigned owner.

- Key metrics, such as actual progress vs. plan and actual cost vs. plan.

- Visual elements that support the message your words convey.

If your organization uses RED/AMBER/GREEN (RAG) statuses, then include them in your reports, but make sure everyone understands the definition of each status. Does GREEN mean that the project is on track for scope, budget, and time, or does it mean that you have no current issues, or both? Likewise, does RED mean that the project is slipping behind the original schedule, or does it mean that you cannot currently progress due to a pressing issue?

Caution

Never report a major issue in a project report without telling senior stakeholders about it beforehand. No one likes to receive bad news, so make sure contentious risks and issues are communicated face-to-face or over the phone. That will put you in a much better position to talk people through the impact and explain what you are doing to address the issue. In this way, the project report functions as a formal record of what is already known and therefore does not contain any negative surprises.

RISK, ISSUE, AND SCOPE MANAGEMENT

A significant part of a project manager's job revolves around problem-solving and removing real or potential blockages to enable the team to work unhindered on assigned tasks. Risks and issues need to be managed so that they do not get out of hand, and changes to scope need to be controlled so that quality, time, and cost parameters are not unintentionally affected.

Risks, issues, and scope changes are different, and to handle them effectively, you need to understand the differences between them.

A *risk* is an event that has not yet occurred but would have a noteworthy impact on the execution of your project if it were to occur. To manage risks effectively, you first need an efficient way to identify them. This could be by brainstorming different risk categories with team members and stakeholders, or simply by taking a step back and imagining all of the things that could cause your project plan to change – be it in a positive or negative direction.

Once you have identified all likely risks, analyze each of them and determine whether each risk has a high, medium, or low likelihood of occurring and if the impact on the project would be high, medium, or low. Assign an owner to each risk, and determine what action should be taken to lower the likelihood and potential impact of the risk. Where risks are positive, and hence represent an opportunity rather than a threat for the project, you will need to identify actions that can increase rather than decrease the likelihood of the risk occurring. Monitor risks over time and follow up with their owners to make sure preventive action is being taken as agreed. Always pay the most attention to those risks that have the highest likelihood of occurring and the highest potential impact on the project.

An *issue* is a problem that is affecting the progress of your project right now. Issues can pertain to people, resources, requirements, technology, funding, estimation, quality, processes, a vendor, or anything else. In short, anything that is slowing you down or preventing you from moving forward in a productive manner is an issue.

Issues need to be handled effectively as soon as they emerge. Carefully analyze the root cause of the issue and determine how it affects your project's cost, scope, quality, and schedule. Meet with your team to brainstorm ideas and possible resolutions. Assign an owner to the issue, and agree on exactly what he or she will do to help resolve it.

If you do not have the authority or resources to deal effectively with an issue, escalate it to a senior stakeholder or to the steering committee. Provide as much detail as you can, and await their guidance. Make sure the stakeholders understand the root cause and impact of the issue.

Get into the habit of identifying and reviewing risks and issues on a weekly, if not daily, basis. Managing Risks and Issues in Step 5 provides more detail on this subject.

A *scope change* is an event that modifies the requirements and the products you have agreed to deliver. That is, it changes the project's baseline scope. As the project progresses, new information comes to light, and changes invariably happen. The idea is not to avoid changes to scope but to manage them effectively when they occur.

There are many reasons a project's scope may change. Scope changes may or may not represent an underlying issue. If changes happen frequently and have a profound impact on the project, they may be the result of insufficient consideration of the requirements or solution at the beginning of the project. But it is almost impossible to get the requirements 100 percent right up front. It can be very difficult for users to predict the real outcome and usability of the solution they have specified until they get to see it, feel it, and test it. Users' understanding of what they need improves as the project progresses, and you must take the change requests that arise as a result into account. If you do not, you run the risk of delivering an end product that does not suite the purpose for which it was intended.

Scope can also change as a result of external factors, such as new regulations or delays in expected deliveries from a vendor.

The challenge is not so much in dealing with formal changes to scope as it is in recognizing when informal changes happen. If scope changes are allowed to go undetected, they can end up significantly affecting the cost, schedule, or quality of the entire project.

To control changes to scope, you must first and foremost know what your baseline scope is. Capture the collective scope in a requirements traceability matrix and get it signed off by the steering committee. Then you must make sure that the impact of every change is properly analyzed and that each change is approved by the steering committee (or change control board) before you incorporate it into the schedule.

A large change with a significant impact on budget and schedule may require that the sponsor releases extra funds or resources. It is your job to make sure that happens—and it must, or you will struggle to deliver everything on time and within budget.

If scope changes are not controlled, you will end up with extra work that is not accounted or planned for. That is what we call scope creep.

Managing Changes to Scope in Step 5 goes into more detail on this topic.

Exercise: Risk, Issue, and Change Management Self-Assessment

Use the spider diagram to assess your ability to effectively manage risks, issues, and changes to scope. Use a scale of 1 to 10 to score yourself.

1. For each of the activities in the diagram below, imagine what a score of 10 out of 10 would look like. For example, what would you do to proactively work to remove project blockages?

2. For each activity, indicate on the diagram where on the 1 to 10 scale you are today by making a dot on the line that represents your score. After you have scored yourself, draw a line between the dots to see the outline of your web.

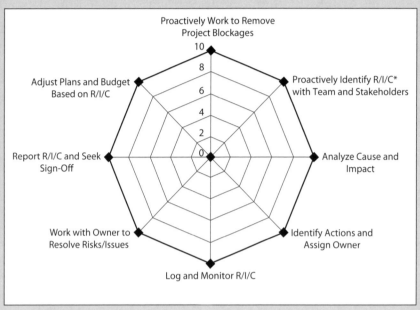

*Risks/issues/changes

Examine your scores . . .

3. Look at your scores. Which areas stand out as needing attention?

4. What could you do to raise your rating just one point in each of these areas?

_____

_____

_____

_____

_____

_____

RISK IDENTIFICATION

The best way to identify risks is to talk to people. Spend time with each team member and stakeholder, and ask them what is worrying them or what could potentially get in their way. Go through all of the factors that are essential to completing the project, and brainstorm things that could go wrong with each and jeopardize the success of the project. These eventualities are all possible risks.

Brainstorming is an excellent technique for identifying risks with the help of your team. In addition to this, spend time on your own, away from the project, asking yourself what could go wrong. Ask yourself what you would worry about if you were the customer or user or development lead. What has the team not yet thought about?

> *It is easy to get so absorbed into the details of a project that we forget to take a step back and look at the stage from afar. Take a high-level view of the project. Play out different scenarios in your head, and try to see the project from different points of view.*

Once you have identified the risks, assess and prioritize them so that your team can focus their efforts on the most important ones. Talk the risks through with the team so that everyone understands their possible root causes, potential impacts, and what you can do to avoid them or mitigate them.

One tool that can be helpful is an impact/probability matrix, as shown in Figure 2-6. Plot your risks on the matrix according to their potential impact and probability, and make sure

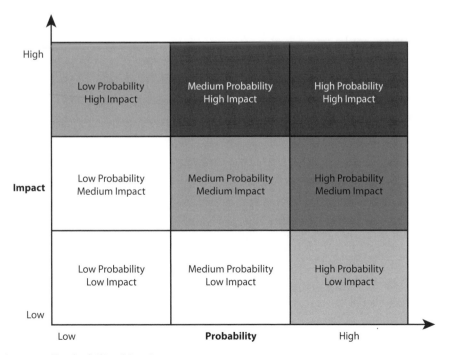

FIGURE 2-6. Impact/Probability Matrix

your team's focus is on those risks with the highest probability of occurring and the highest potential impact on the project.

Note that a risk with high impact and low probability is more serious than a risk with high probability and low impact. A low chance of a catastrophe warrants more attention than a high chance of a hiccup.

When you identify risks, also factor in opportunities; i.e. events that in some ways could affect your project in a positive manner. What would the impact be, for instance, if the uptake of your product was bigger than expected, or if it was delivered ahead of schedule? What could you do to explore this opportunity and plan for it? Likewise, what would you do if new and more effective technology became available half way through the execution of your project? What could you do to take advantage of this opportunity?

Take Action

1. Brainstorm and write down anything that could go wrong on your project—your threats or negative risks.

2. Identify events that could have a positive impact on your project—your opportunities or positive risks.

3. Schedule time with your team and stakeholders to elaborate on the risks you have recorded and identify new ones. As a group, brainstorm anything that could go wrong, and consider lessons learned from similar projects.

4. Plot the risks on the impact/probability matrix.

5. Focus on the risks with the highest potential impact and highest probability of occurring. Identify what you can do to lower the probability of each negative risk happening and to mitigate its impact if it does occur.

6. Look at the opportunities you have identified and decide if any action needs to be taken to exploit them and plan for them.

To effectively manage a project's risks, you need to do more than identify and analyze them. It is in taking action to mitigate or avoid the identified risks that you get the real benefit. The multipart Risk Management exercise in Step 5 guides you through the entire risk management process from beginning to end.

RISK AND ISSUE OWNERSHIP

Many project managers feel as if they are singlehandedly responsible for owning and resolving all of their projects' risks and issues. Not so. If you carry the entire burden yourself, you will quickly feel weighed down and can end up exhausted. What is more, you are usually not the best person to resolve a risk or an issue. Do not try to hide risks. Make them as visible as possible, and get the right people involved to help resolve them.

Your primary responsibility is to instill a robust process to identify, assess, and monitor risks and issues. You may own *some* of these items yourself, but you need to assign owners to the remainder and expect these owners to develop solutions. Do not hesitate to chase risk and issue owners as needed. Chasing outstanding actions is part of your job, and people expect you to do it.

Questions

- What risks and issues are you currently taking ownership of but should not?
- Who would be better placed to take ownership of these particular items?

MANAGING AND MOTIVATING THE TEAM

To become a highly valued and truly successful project management leader, you must be able to relate to others on a deep level and have excellent people-management and leadership skills. It is not enough to be good at managing plans, tasks, and budgets, although these skills are certainly required. To succeed, you must be as good with people as you are with tasks. You must embrace the fact that to get real results and to build a high-performing team, you have to liaise with people and help others succeed. Do not make the mistake of handing over the management of your project team to someone else. Even if you are not your team members' actual line manager, you need to take on the responsibility for providing leadership and direction on behalf of the project.

> *To set yourself apart, you need to build effective relationships and understand how to motivate each person within your team. Fine-tune your listening skills, spend time with people, and create a team in which everyone buys into the project's goals and objectives.*

To build a great team, you have to focus on enabling your team members to *thrive*. Look after them, value their contributions, and make sure that communications and relationships are good. Allow for people's individuality, and play to their strengths. Investigate how you can best enable them to shine and help them do their jobs even better. You can do this by spending more quality time with your team members, listening to their views, and finding out what matters most to them in their work. Seek to understand what their aspirations and career goals are and how you can create synergy between personal and professional goals. When you uncover the factors that truly motivate people, you can tap into a powerful source of energy and help them become high performers on your project.

Building relationships and gaining the trust of team members require you to be patient, open, and trustworthy. But more important, you need to set sufficient time aside in your schedule for impromptu conversations as well as regular one-on-one sessions with people. Make your team members a high priority; show them that their welfare is important to you. If that is not the case, they will not trust you or give you their best.

Exercise: If Team Members Were Volunteers

To improve the way you work with and relate to your team, play with the idea that all of your team members are volunteers who are giving up their personal time to work on the project. Imagine that even though they receive no income for the work they do, they *choose* to be there for other reasons: they want to contribute and achieve certain personal goals.

- In what ways would you treat your team members differently if everyone were a volunteer?
- What would you start doing that you are not doing today?

Remember, if people do not feel that their contributions are making a difference, or if they are not deriving a sense of personal satisfaction, meaning, and purpose from their work, they will choose to go elsewhere.

People perform best in high-trust environments where they feel safe, secure, and respected by you and other people around them. The worst thing you can do is to ignore your team or distrust or criticize its members. Doing so will create hostility, discourage people, and lead to underperformance. If your team has these issues, identify the root cause and talk about it. What are the reasons for the mistrust or underperformance? Do you need to change your leadership style, appreciate your team more, or improve the way you manage performance by agreeing to clearer personal objectives? Do you need to put more emphasis on making people feel responsible for the results they produce? Only by listening, asking for feedback, and spending time with people will you find out.

The success of your project will to a large extent depend on the quality of your team and how driven it is. Make an effort to select good people with the right skills and attitudes, then help them grow and develop. Agree on objectives and responsibilities that play to their strengths but also stretch them, and look after their well-being by ensuring that long hours do not lead to negative stress and burnout. Remember to reward and celebrate project successes. Your team is your biggest asset, so value it, appreciate it, and nurture it.

In addition to valuing and appreciating your team, you also have to challenge people and make them feel personally responsible for the results they produce. Be as clear as you can about what you expect to be done, when it should be done, and to what standards. Knowing what is expected can be a major performance motivator.

Below are some of the characteristics of productive, motivated, happy—and high-performing—teams. The more each trait rings true, the greater the chances that your team is performing well.

➤ Being united around a common goal

➤ Having the motivation to achieve the common goal

➤ Feeling appreciated, recognized, and rewarded

➤ Having a sense of purpose and satisfaction

➤ Being empowered to contribute ideas and implement decisions

➤ Having clear roles that maximize the strengths of each team member

➤ Having a complementary range of skills and styles

➤ Having a culture of shared ownership, participation, and trust

➤ Having a culture of open communication, learning, and development

➤ Having the necessary tools, processes, and knowledge to do the job.

Unfortunately, a team does not become great or high-performing overnight. It first has to go through a number of distinct stages in which roles, responsibilities, and team purposes are clarified and relationships and working styles are established. For more information on the different stages a team goes through, read up on Bruce Tuckman's Forming, Storming, Norming and Performing team development model. As a project manager, you need to be aware of the stage your team is in. Your team will need different types and levels of guidance and support from you as it moves through the different stages.

Initially, a team requires a lot of direction from you. It also needs your support in defining processes and in helping smooth out conflict. As the team becomes more established, you can start to take a step back, delegate, and let the team take responsibility. Stepping back and delegating too soon may cause confusion and underperformance, as the team may not be ready to handle the autonomy.

Exercise: Team Performance and Motivation Analysis

1. Make a list of everything that is working well on your team and everything that could be improved. What issues stand out as needing attention? Write them down.

2. Look at your own role and how you interact with each team member. Answer the following questions. Where you answer yes, write down examples that support your answer.

- Do you spend enough time with everyone on the team?
- Do you praise people when they do a good job?
- Are you aware of everyone's strengths?
- Do you use people's strengths effectively?
- Do you give people the level of support they need to succeed?
- Do you delegate tasks completely when people are capable of working autonomously?
- Are you working to improve each person's confidence and motivation?
- Do you know how each team member would like to be recognized and rewarded?
- Do you empower people to implement new ideas?
- Do you set clear performance expectations?
- Do you involve team members in the decision-making process?
- Do you discuss the project's vision, road map, and priorities with as much passion and insight as you possibly can?

3. How many of the above questions could you convincingly answer yes to?
4. What can you do to improve your team's performance?

Try out different ideas and approaches. Change your leadership style and behavior to more actively help increase motivation and optimize your team members' strengths. Make each person's role as appealing and rewarding as possible. Review your approaches and actions and ask your team members for feedback. Eventually you will find the right formula.

The guiding practices in Step 5 for Team Motivation go into more depth about the factors behind motivation and what you can do to take best advantage of them.

Exercise: Team Management Self-Assessment

Use the spider diagram to assess your ability to effectively manage your team. Use a scale of 1 to 10 to score yourself.

1. For each of the responsibilities shown in the diagram below, imagine what a score of 10 out of 10 would look like. For example, what would you do to inspire and motivate the team? How would you feel if you were fully able to do so?

2. For each responsibility, indicate on the diagram where on the 1 to 10 scale you are today by making a dot on the line that represents your score. After you have scored yourself, draw a line between the dots to see the outline of your web.

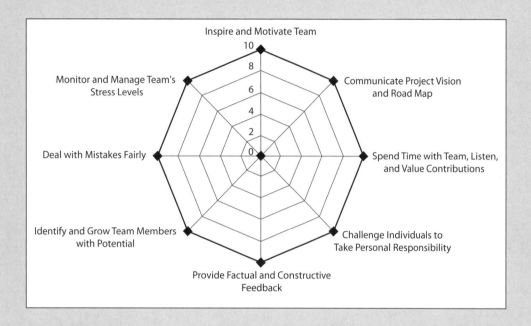

Examine your scores . . .

3. Look at your scores. Which areas stand out as needing attention?

4. What could you do to raise your rating just one point in each of these areas?

_____

_____

_____

_____

_____

_____

_____

SPEND TIME WITH THE TEAM

One of the keys to managing and motivating your team is to spend quality time with its members on a regular basis. If you do not spend time with people, how can you convey project goals and objectives, set direction, manage performance, provide guidance and support, help resolve issues, improve team morale, and understand how to best develop and motivate each person?

Regularly set time aside for one-on-one catch-ups, even if each meeting is only 20 minutes long. These catch-ups will build relationships with team members in a way that big team meetings cannot—not everyone is comfortable speaking up in meetings.

When you catch up with an individual, listen to his ideas and concerns. Try to see the project through his eyes. Listen without interrupting, and give him your undivided attention. This will strengthen your relationship and give you insight into how to best motivate and support him. (If your conversation does not reveal how you can do so, just ask!) You will also glean useful ideas and a view of project risks and issues of which you might not be aware.

In addition to one-on-one catch-ups, hold regular team meetings to share steering committee decisions that affect the project's direction, goals, and vision. These meetings are a great opportunity to motivate and inspire the team, so make sure you speak with passion and confidence when leading one.

Equally important are regular meetings to review progress and make sure that everyone is able to move forward with their tasks. Invite each person to talk about what they have been doing since the last meeting, what is holding them back, and what could help them progress faster. Your main job at these meetings is not to talk, but to listen. When you listen, you will learn what blockages you need to help remove and how you can help improve the team's performance.

If you are working with a geographically dispersed team, you can use a host of tools and communication forms to bring the team together, including conference calls, videoconferencing, instant messaging, and other collaboration tools. Aim to communicate with the virtual team at least once a day, and do what you can to make everyone feel part of the project. Try to see remote team members in person on a regular basis, if possible.

Questions

- Who on your team do you need to spend more time with?
- How much do you know about how to best support and motivate each team member? Give examples.
- How well are each team member's strengths used on the project?

GET THE RIGHT TEAM MEMBERS INVOLVED

As a project manager, you sometimes get to work with pre-established teams who already know their roles and responsibilities well. At other times, you have to engage and attract new team members to a project or even build a team from scratch. When building a team, it is crucial that you hire and select the right people for the right roles. The importance of this cannot be overemphasized.

Your ability to secure and keep the right people is an immensely important factor in the ultimate success of your project. Many of the issues and frustrations you will encounter in project management are likely to be the result of having the wrong person in the wrong position. If you become impatient when building or adding to a team and do not take the necessary time to get the right people involved, you are likely to end up with an underperforming team and will have to deal with the consequences of your choices. A bad hiring decision is often worse than no hiring decision at all, so take the time and effort to find the right people.

Aim to engage people who want to be on the project, who have the necessary skills, and who have the time available to focus on the job. Try to choose individuals who have a few specializations and a range of generic skills that overlap, rather than employing pure specialists. Choose people who will get along with each other and will work together as a team. If you are in doubt about how to craft a good team, draw in help from someone who knows how.

In many cases, you will not have direct line management responsibility for your project team, so you will not always be able to pick and choose who you want on your project. However, you will always be able to influence, to a certain extent, the decisions regarding who will do what. This is especially true the more familiar you are with the organization and the better relationships you have with senior stakeholders and hiring managers.

Whether you are directly or indirectly involved in the selection process, make sure that you, and the other hiring managers, know exactly what you are looking for and what outputs and results you expect from a new person. Think through what you want the candidate to accomplish and what her exact responsibilities will be. Determine the skills and experiences you would like her to have, and identify the ideal personal attributes or qualities, such as honesty, positive mental attitude, confidence, drive, or focus. Finally, consider the team as a whole and the people the candidate will be working with. What type of person would fit in best with the existing team?

Once you have listed all of the qualifications you can think of, prioritize them into "must haves" and "nice to haves," and circulate this job description for review before finalizing it.

Taking time to think through and plan hiring decisions up front is one of the most important things you can do as a project manager. Investing just 10 percent of the time thinking and planning for a new hire could save you up to 90 percent of the time and effort required to find the right person.

Exercise: Writing a Job Description for a New Team Member

This exercise will enable you to craft a thorough job description and person specification that will help you find the right individual for a particular role.

To carry out the exercise, think about a person or project role your team lacks and needs: an analyst, architect, developer, project administrator, tester, or another position.

- **Step 1: Determine job purpose**

  First, be clear about the purpose of the job and what you want to achieve by recruiting someone to fill it. Write a couple of paragraphs about the background a candidate should have and the goals and objectives for the role.

- **Step 2: Determine key responsibilities**

  Clarify what you need the person to do and the role you expect her to play. Liaise with existing team members and senior managers to ensure you capture all aspects of the job. Get everyone together in a room to brainstorm all of the activities and responsibilities the new person will be given.

- **Step 3: Write a draft job description**

  Prioritize the list of activities and responsibilities you have identified, and write a draft job description based on the ten most important responsibilities. Focus on what you expect the person to be doing in an average day and the outputs and results you expect her to produce.

- **Step 4: Formulate a draft person specification**

  Brainstorm the specific skills, knowledge, experience, and qualifications you require from the ideal candidate in order to fulfill the responsibilities of the role. Prioritize your wish list into absolutely required and desirable qualifications. Add the person specification to the job description as a separate section.

- **Step 5: Visualize the ideal candidate**

  Imagine the ideal candidate working on your project and performing her daily tasks. How does she behave toward and communicate with fellow team members, senior managers, and the customer? How does she deal with issues and with interpersonal conflict? Write down what you see and feel.

- **Step 6: Determine interpersonal skills**

  Determine the interpersonal skills and capabilities you require from the ideal candidate. What should her personal makeup be? What values should she embrace?

How important are factors such as drive, initiative, and attention to detail for this role? Add your conclusions and requirements to the person specification.

- **Step 7: Interview and select the best person**
  You now have a firm job and person description and a clear view of what you need and who you need. Use this as the foundation for interviewing and selecting the best person for the role.

PROVIDE FACTUAL AND CONSTRUCTIVE FEEDBACK

A lack of feedback can cause significant difficulties on a project. If people are to do their best, they need to know what they are doing well and what they could do better. Everyone needs feedback, but team members who are relatively inexperienced or new to the project or organization are likely to need more feedback than others.

As the project manager, it is your job to provide feedback to team members. If feedback is to be effective, it must be given in an objective and constructive way; otherwise, it may be ignored or misinterpreted. Take the emotion out and keep it as factual and objective as possible. This is especially important when delivering so-called negative feedback.

Think carefully about how you communicate your message, as everyone reacts differently. If you want the person to have positive feelings about making a change, make sure that your message has that effect. Be mindful of your body language, tone of voice, and facial expressions. Think about what you want to communicate first, and make sure your body language supports that message.

Remember that providing feedback is a two-way process. Who is to say that the team member you are talking to actually did a bad job? Could it be that your instructions and support were lacking? Keep an open mind and allow for the possibility that you could be wrong. Listen carefully to the team member's comments and views without interrupting.

If a team member has made a genuine mistake or truly needs to improve in some way, be as specific about the situation as you can and give concrete examples of the behaviors that concern you. The more specific you are, the more accurate and helpful your feedback may be.

Do not, however, focus on failures and mistakes—a negative focus can make people lose confidence or become discouraged. Always assume that people mean well and that they are doing the very best with what they have. Coach your team members to identify ways in which they can improve. Focus on the way forward, and encourage them to take steps in that direction.

Tips for Providing Feedback

✔ Make your feedback factual and constructive.

✔ Be as specific as you can, and give examples.

✔ Do not criticize; focus on the way forward.

✔ Be mindful of your body language and make sure it supports your message.

✔ Encourage an open dialogue by asking for comments.

✔ Listen without interrupting.

✔ Allow for the possibility that you could be wrong.

✔ Be honest.

✔ Let people know when they have done a good job.

It is important to give feedback when a team member does something well, too. After all, everyone likes to feel important, valued, and appreciated. Often projects get so busy that you may forget about the little things that can make a big difference and boost morale. Make it a habit to give sincere praise on a regular basis. Let your team members know when they have done a good job. If you do not tell them that they are doing well, they may never know that you have noticed and appreciate their performance. They may eventually start doubting themselves. People love the feelings of success, contribution, and knowing that they make a difference.

STAKEHOLDER RELATIONSHIPS AND COMMUNICATION

A stakeholder is an individual or group that has a vested interest in your project and is directly or indirectly affected by it. Examples of stakeholders include the project sponsor, customers, end users, external suppliers, your manager, senior executives, resource managers, team members, shareholders, government bodies, the compliance department, and the public.

For the purpose of assessing your stakeholder management skills, we will leave your team members out for now and focus on the more senior stakeholders. These are the senior managers who have the authority to direct the project and allocate time, people, money, and materials and who can set priorities on behalf of their department or organization. They are the people who can make or break a project and who decide what is in scope or out of scope.

The stakeholders hold the key to your project. Among them are people who own the vision and the business case and who will be the ultimate recipients of the business benefits. Some stakeholders control project finances and need to approve changes that impact cost or time in a material way. Others are responsible for assigning resources such as people or materials to the project. Still others represent the users and are ultimately responsible for the requirements. They need to approve any changes that significantly impact scope or quality.

Building strong relationships with your stakeholders and keeping them involved and informed at all times is critical to success. Their buy-in and contributions are a crucial factor for the continued existence of the project. You need to understand your stakeholders' interests and position and address their concerns before they turn into issues. Investigate what they are worried about and what they are looking for in terms of concrete outcomes. Find out what valuable knowledge they have and how they can best contribute to the project.

> *The way to build strong relationships with your stakeholders is to spend time with them. Actively engage them, and make an effort to understand their roles. Find out what they are looking for and what will make each of them say that the project was a success.*

Building relationships is a time-consuming but essential activity. Analyze each stakeholder in terms of his or her power and influence over the project and how supportive the individual is of the project. Most of your time should be spent with those stakeholders who have the most power and influence.

The matrix in Figure 2-7 illustrates how you can group your stakeholders according to how much power and influence they each have over the project and how supportive they each are.

Those stakeholders who are supportive as well as powerful are your best allies. They can promote the project and help persuade others to accept new ideas and solutions. If you need to ask for help, ask this group first.

Stakeholders who are not supportive but are very powerful have the potential to negatively influence others. Make an effort to understand why they are skeptical so that you can work to win them over and influence them to view the project more positively.

It may or may not be important to build strong relationships with stakeholders who are not powerful. It will depend on the information they have and the role they play on the

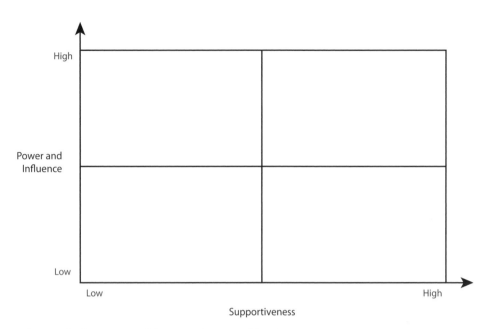

FIGURE 2-7. Power/Influence and Supportiveness Matrix

project. Under normal circumstances, you should never prioritize a stakeholder with less power and influence over someone who is more influential.

The multipart Stakeholder Management exercise in Step 5 goes more into detail on this subject. It helps you analyze and group your stakeholders by their level of power and influence and support for the project, and in turn determine who you should spend your time with. It also shows you how you can get to know your stakeholders better and what you can do to communicate more effectively with each of them.

Exercise: Stakeholder Power, Influence, and Relationships

1. Identify the three most important stakeholders on your project in terms of how much power and influence they have. Write down their names.

2. Rate the relationship you have with each of them according to the following descriptions:

   - **Very good:** You meet with this stakeholder regularly. He or she knows the details of the project and is always happy to help out. You look after each other's interests.

   - **Good:** You have a good and stable relationship with this stakeholder. You respect each other and regularly discuss risks and issues that need attention.

   - **Average:** You do not tend to spend much time with this stakeholder. No bad words have been exchanged between you, but you are just not particularly close.

   - **Poor:** There is some animosity between the two of you. You try to avoid each other.

3. Your relationships with the top three stakeholders of your project should ideally be very good. If you would not describe them as very good, identify what the first step could be to improve them.

4. Spend 30 minutes of quality time with each of the three main stakeholders next week. Ask them how they think the project is progressing and if they have any concerns or recommendations they would like to share with you. If you have not asked them about this before, you will probably be amazed at how much they open up to you.

Exercise: Stakeholder Management and Communication Self-Assessment

Use the spider diagram to assess your ability to effectively manage and communicate with your project's stakeholders. Use a scale of 1 to 10 to score yourself.

1. For each of the competencies listed in the diagram, imagine what a score of 10 out of 10 would look like. For example, what would you be doing or feeling, or what would you have, if you were fully able to build strong relationships with stakeholders?

2. For each competency, indicate on the diagram where on the 1 to 10 scale you are today by making a dot on the line that represents your score.

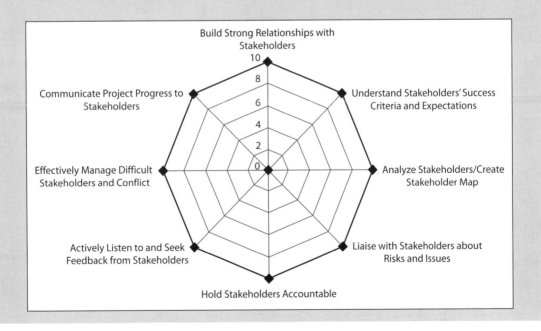

Examine your scores . . .

3. Look at your scores. Which areas stand out as needing attention?

4. What could you do to raise your rating just one point in each of these areas?

_____

_____

_____

_____

_____

COMMUNICATE PROJECT PROGRESS

You must keep the main stakeholders inside and outside of your project informed at all times. This is one of your most important responsibilities as a project manager. Give your stakeholders honest and complete information; that is the only way they will be able to gauge what is going on, provide the correct level of support and guidance, and make decisions.

Project progress can be communicated formally or informally, in writing or verbally. Make use of all types of communication, but vary your methods depending on the situation, purpose, and person you are communicating with.

	Formal	Informal
Written	Status reports Minutes from key meetings Written presentations/newsletters	Ad hoc email updates Instant messaging Informal online communities
Verbal	Decisionmaking forums Steering committee meetings Formal presentations/gatherings	Phone calls Ad hoc meetings Informal face-to-face catch-ups

Formal, written communication encompasses weekly or bimonthly status reports, minutes from key decisionmaking forums, PowerPoint presentations outlining major achievements, and project newsletters. This type of communication is relevant for almost all of your stakeholders. It is one of the most traditional ways of ensuring that everyone is kept updated about the project's status and its main risks and issues.

Formal, verbal communication encompasses decisionmaking forums such as steering committee meetings or other formal gatherings. These forums are a chance to communicate with senior stakeholders who have authority to set the project's direction and allocate resources. Start off with monthly steering committee meetings and increase the frequency if needed.

Insight

Preparing for and attending steering committee meetings is one of your most important roles and responsibilities. This is your opportunity to promote your team and the progress you have made and to escalate any matters (risks, issues, or scope changes) on which you need executive direction and input. This is your chance to shine and to show that you are in control of the project.

Always prepare thoroughly for these meetings, and produce a flawless presentation. People know immediately when you are well prepared for a meeting and when you are not. When you are prepared, your credibility goes up; when you are not prepared, your credibility goes down. The presentation should be short and succinct and cover topics such as key achievements, the project road map, upcoming milestones, top-ten risks and issues, change requests for approval, and a financial overview. Insert graphs and charts to make the presentation more appealing and readable.

To help you prepare and deliver the presentation in the most effective manner, consider the emotional journey you want to take the listeners through. What emotional state is your sponsor and key stakeholders likely to have at the beginning of the meeting and what emotional state would you like them to have at the end of the meeting?

You may or may not chair this meeting. If you are the chair, make sure that all key decisions and actions are summarized at the end of the meeting. Write up key decisions and actions and circulate these written minutes within 24 hours of the meeting.

Informal, written communication mainly encompasses email updates and instant messaging. To optimize the way you communicate progress, tailor this form of communication to each stakeholder's needs. Ask each person what information they would like, how often, and in what format—and respect their requests. Some people may really value project details and want to be updated on a very frequent basis, but do not overload someone with email updates if he or she is not interested. Most executives are busy people and generally only want to know whether the project is on track or not. Give them an update when there is good news, and escalate issues you cannot resolve on your own. Also consider that many executives read their email on a smartphone. Tailor your emails specifically for this medium by making them short, punchy, and to the point.

Informal, verbal communication includes phone calls, ad hoc meetings, and catch-ups. Many project managers communicate too much in writing and not enough verbally. They hide behind their desks instead of picking up the phone or seeing people in person. If this rings true for you, think of email as a tool for delivering documents rather than a way to communicate. See your stakeholders in person on a regular basis, as this is one of the best ways of building trusting, lasting relationships. If you cannot meet face-to-face, make sure you talk to people on the phone on a regular basis.

When a major issue arises, always seek to inform your stakeholders face-to-face, as that will give you more control over the situation. Never convey negative information in writing without having informed the senior executives first. When you do raise an issue, clearly explain what the root cause is, what the impact is, and what you are doing to address it.

Exercise: Communicating with Stakeholders

1. On a separate piece of paper or spreadsheet, make a list of all of the different ways in which you communicate with your stakeholders. To do this, first partition your list into two sections. The top section is for formal, written communication and the bottom section is for formal, verbal communication.

2. Underneath the top heading, specify the reports and artifacts you use; under the bottom heading, list any formal meetings you have to communicate progress to your stakeholders.

3. You now have a list of all of the different means of formal communication you use on your project. For every entry on your list, determine how often you want to use that form of communication, what it entails, and who the recipients or participants should be. For instance, how often will you send out the project status report, what will its contents be, and who will the recipients be? Make sure that all of your stakeholders are listed somewhere. Everyone should receive some type of formal update from you on a regular basis.

4. Create a third section on your sheet for informal communication, and list all of your stakeholders again.

5. For each stakeholder on the list, determine what the individual's needs are. For example, what informal methods of communication does the project sponsor prefer, and how often does he or she want to be updated? If you do not have enough information to complete this section, take it as an opportunity to talk to your stakeholders and find out.

DEALING WITH CONFLICT

Conflict arises when people have contrasting feelings, needs, perceptions, and interests. It often occurs when people feel they are losing something they value or believe that something intangible—their ideals, standards, aspirations, reputation, status, or self-esteem—is being threatened.

As a project manager, you are more than likely to encounter difficulty and conflict. The more complex and high-profile your project is, the higher the likelihood. Disagreements may arise between a group of stakeholders and yourself, or perhaps you will have to function as a mediator in a conflict between several stakeholders.

Conflict is common during the project initiation phase, when stakeholders are supposed to agree on the foundations of the project but may have differing opinions on the project's goals, objectives, success criteria, scope, requirements, solution, or approach. Later in a project, conflict can arise when constraints and agreements such as budget, time, or quality are breached. Unexpected changes in general are likely to give rise to disagreements.

Remember, however, that conflict is not necessarily bad. Sometimes a problem can only really be resolved by getting all opposing emotions, opinions, and views out into the open. Be resourceful and calm, and diplomatically deal with the situation before it escalates out of control.

Tips for Handling Conflict

✔ Do not prejudge the situation. Become aware of your own emotions and interests, and open your mind to the possibility that you could be the one who is wrong.

✔ Where possible, negotiate with people one-on-one instead of letting a conflict flare up at a meeting. No one likes to come across poorly in front of others, so give people a chance to resolve the conflict before the meeting.

✔ Take on the role of a mediator even if you are an active part of the conflict. Listen, speak, and carry yourself the way a respected mediator would.

✔ Do not attack, blame, or defend anyone. See both sides of the situation. As the mediator, your role is to calm the situation down and promote rational thinking.

✔ Make a *big* effort to listen and understand the other parties. Assess their underlying fears, motives, and aims.

✔ Speak up about your own views and thoughts only once you fully understand the other parties' positions. This will help you identify mutual ground and garner respect.

✔ Use phrasing such as "I understand" and repeat the exact words and phrases each party is using. Summarize everyone's position as accurately as you can.

✔ Identify the root cause of the disagreement, and get all parties to agree on what the underlying problem is.

✔ Make people feel good and look good by taking their interests into account.

✔ Focus all discussions and conversations on the way forward.

✔ Maintain an open and positive mind throughout and aim to find a resolution that works for everyone: not a compromised agreement, but an expansive win-win solution that is better than anything either party had thought of when the conflict started.

SELF-MANAGEMENT

To be a highly valued and truly successful project management leader, you must be able to manage yourself and control your own state of mind. The better you know and understand yourself, the better decisions you will make and actions you will take—and the better results you will get.

As a project manager, you are the hub of all daily activities and the one others turn to for day-to-day decisionmaking and issue resolution. It is important that you set a good example and seek to be the best you can in all that you do. When you are proactive, positive, and resourceful, others are likely to copy your example and work more effectively.

There are many ways you can set a good example and show self-mastery. One of them is by applauding your team when things go well and by taking blame and responsibility when things go wrong. Give your team credit for the project's achievements and successes. When something fails, look inward before you look outward. Seek to understand how your actions (or lack of) contributed to the failure. Then assess what you can do about the situation to positively influence it. Resolve the issue as effectively as you can without blaming others or finding excuses.

Great project managers take responsibility for the current situation without blaming external circumstances or other people. They know that what is happening in the external world is a reflection of their own thoughts, actions, and choices. They seek to change the situation by changing their own behavior and by taking action.

The worst thing you can do when a project does not go according to plan is to ignore the situation or focus on who to blame. Instead, keep calm, be proactive, and maintain a positive attitude. When the immediate issue has been resolved, look at what you can do to prevent it from happening again.

Bear in mind that it is much easier to be positive and proactive when things are going well and according to plan. The real test of self-mastery is how well you perform during adversity and in challenging times. That is when we really need to show our strength and courage. As Rudyard Kipling said, "If you can keep your wits about you while all others are losing theirs, and blaming you…. The world will be yours and everything in it, what's more, you'll be a man, my son."

The calmer you remain in a crisis, the better you think, analyze, and decide. One of the keys to calmness and mental clarity is to refuse to spend time worrying about something that you cannot change, such as past events. Focus your energies on what can be done to deal with the situation and solve the problem at hand.

Tip: Say "And," Not "But"

To change the way you think and act in different situations, eliminate the word *but* from your vocabulary. Instead, substitute *and*. When you use *and* instead of *but*, you open up opportunities instead of closing them down. You adopt a more positive attitude, which can help you respond in more creative and resourceful ways.

Try it for a week. Notice how many times you say (or think) the word *but*. Turn it into a game—see what happens when you use *and* instead.

Self-management is all about character and attitude. It is about who you choose to be, how you choose to portray yourself, and what you choose to believe in. It is about being conscious of your thought processes and actions and making sure that they support you and your project in the best possible way. It is also about looking inside yourself for solutions, reassurance, and guidance, as opposed to looking to others for answers and resolution.

Among the characteristics of a highly valued and truly successful project management leader are mental strength and confidence. In order to stand up for your project and lead your team to successful delivery, you need to be strong and comfortable with your own abilities. You must be able to say no and push back when required. This part is really about your self-esteem and confidence. The more of it you have, the stronger you will be and appear.

Note that this is not about being arrogant or headstrong. It is essential to balance confidence and humility. Self-esteem and confidence are simply about valuing your own contributions and believing in yourself. If you are able to do so, it will be easier to respond in calm, proactive, and resourceful ways.

To illustrate this point, imagine a situation in which a senior stakeholder asks you to deliver a product significantly earlier than planned. You know that your team will not be able to achieve this deadline without making drastic changes to scope and quality. You also know that the reason for this request is not business-critical and that incorporating such a drastic change at this point in time will end up costing the client more money and will cause the project to take longer overall.

In this situation, many project managers would feel insecure and would bow to the stakeholder's request without openly questioning it. They may *want* to question it, but they do not have enough self-confidence and belief in themselves to do it.

If this sounds familiar, you might need to work on increasing your self-worth and assertiveness. One way to do that is by noticing and recognizing your strengths and unique talents. It may also be beneficial for you to work with an assertive, self-confident mentor or coach.

Exercise: Self-Management Self-Assessment

Use the spider diagram to assess your ability to effectively manage yourself. Use a scale of 1 to 10 to score yourself.

1. For each of the capabilities listed in the diagram, imagine what a score of 10 out of 10 would look like. For example, what would you be doing or feeling, or what would you have, if you were able to stay calm in stressful situations?

2. For each capability, indicate on the diagram where on the 1 to 10 scale you are today by making a dot on the line that represents your score.

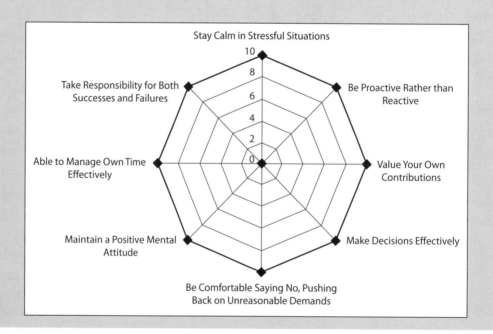

Examine your scores . . .

    3. Look at your scores. Which areas stand out as needing attention?

    4. What could you do to raise your rating just one point in each of these areas?

_____

_____

_____

_____

_____

BE PROACTIVE

Proactive project managers focus their efforts and attention on the long term as opposed to being reactive in the present moment. They believe that their actions matter and that they can positively influence a situation by doing something about it.

One of the best ways you can be proactive as a project manager is to work with your team and stakeholders to actively identify, analyze, and mitigate project risks before they turn into issues.

You can also make a concerted effort to build strong and lasting relationships with your stakeholders so that you are able to draw on their knowledge and support when you need it. When you keep your stakeholders abreast of developments and have an excellent rapport with them, they are very unlikely to turn against you. They respect you, and they know that you are actively working to improve all aspects of the project on their behalf.

Another way to be proactive is to carry out project reviews and to liaise with your team members one-on-one. Ask for feedback: is there anything you can do to optimize the way the team works?

Finally, investigate whether your QA activities are as good as they can be: poor product quality is one of the biggest reasons for project failure.

Reactive is the opposite of _proactive_. Reactive people often believe that they have no control over a situation, whether it is the behavior of an unreasonable stakeholder or issues that arise during a project. They surrender and wait until a potential problem has become a burning issue before they take action.

One of the reasons some project managers become reactive is that their workload is so big that they feel they have no option but to firefight in the present moment. But in reality, you always have another option, even if it is not an easy one. If you feel overloaded and overworked, you might want to look at delegating more, getting better at saying no to new requests and assignments, and optimizing the way you manage your time. The guiding practices for time management in Step 5 go into more depth on this subject.

Activity: How Proactive Are You?

- Think of ten examples from last week of your being proactive on your project. Write them down.

- How often do you attempt to identify new project risks or lead the way by brainstorming resolutions to potential or actual issues? Give examples.

- When did you last initiate a project review or ask your team members and stakeholders for feedback on how the team could be working more effectively?

Tips for Becoming More Proactive

✔ Spend time on your own and with team members identifying anything that could go wrong on the project. Thoroughly analyze the risks, and identify an owner and mitigating actions for each risk. Do this as often as possible.

✔ Ask team members as often as you can what is preventing them from moving forward or what could help them work more effectively.

✔ Build strong relationships with all key players on the project. See things from their point of view, understand their interests, and address their issues and concerns.

✔ Carry out project reviews and encourage a culture of learning and contribution. Discuss how past issues can be avoided, and take action to make improvements.

✔ Demonstrate and prototype the solution to the customer and end users as often as possible. Ask for feedback and verify that what you are building matches their requirements and expectations.

✔ Identify and review your project controls on a regular basis. Assess whether they are working as expected and keeping cost, quality, and time under control.

✔ Actively manage your stakeholders' expectations through face-to-face meetings and regular project reporting. Make sure they appreciate the risks, issues, and constraints you are facing, and ensure there are no negative surprises.

✔ Organize knowledge-sharing and fun team-building activities to improve morale and motivation.

✔ Assess your own working practices and determine how you can optimize the way you spend your time. Could you, for instance, start delegating more?

STRIVE FOR PERSONAL EFFECTIVENESS

To become a highly valued and truly successful project management leader, you must learn to be effective. That is, you must consistently focus on those activities that will bring about the results you are seeking. Effective project managers are highly active, and they do more of what works and less of what does not work. They spend their time well; they focus on the tasks and activities that matter the most to the overall success of a project.

Pareto's Principle is an interesting rule of thumb that can be applied to many different aspects of life. It says that 80 percent of the effects come from 20 percent of the causes. For instance, 80 percent of revenue comes from 20 percent of the customers, or 80 percent of defects stem from 20 percent of the requirements.

When we apply this principle to personal time management, we might say that 80 percent of your results stem from 20 percent of your actions. This 20 percent makes the difference in your effectiveness and is the 20 percent that you need to focus on to really excel. If you are struggling with time and something has to give, make sure that what you give up is not part of the 20 percent of activities that matter the most to your success.

Exercise: Pareto's Principle and Time Management

Take a moment to identify the 20 percent of tasks and activities you do during your day or working week that produce 80 percent of your results.

1. What are the activities that you do very well and that make all the difference in your performance and increase the likelihood of project success? Write them down.
2. Identify what you can do to focus relatively more time on the 20 percent of tasks that matter. Which activities do you need to stop doing?

BUILD SELF-ESTEEM

Self-esteem is a state of mind that is self-created. It is the way you think and feel about yourself and is related to how confident you are in your ability to cope with challenges. Self-esteem is a mirror of your thoughts. If you want to change how you feel about yourself, you first have to change your thoughts.

To be a strong and resourceful project manager who is respected by team members and stakeholders, you have to have enough self-esteem to naturally stand up for yourself, your team, and your project. You have to have enough faith in yourself and in your abilities to comfortably make decisions and lead your team in the right direction.

Building self-esteem is the first step in becoming more assertive as a person and project manager. It is about knowing your boundaries and challenging others when these boundaries are breached. Accept that you cannot please everyone and that your needs, rights, and feelings are as important as everyone else's.

If you struggle with self-esteem, be careful not to be overly critical of yourself, and resist the temptation to focus on what you feel is missing. Make an effort to see the positive in every situation and what you have to bring to the table. Take credit for the tasks and activities you do well and leverage your strengths. If there are skills you feel you are lacking, take a course, read a book, or work with a mentor. Do not ignore these feelings. Empower yourself by being proactive and doing something about them.

One good way to build self-esteem is to practice appreciation—of yourself. Each day, notice what you do well as a person and as a project manager. Write these strengths down in a notebook, and find new areas and capabilities to appreciate every day. See yourself as the confident project manager and leader you want to be.

It can take time to build self-esteem, but with the right support and willingness, you can change the way you feel about yourself more quickly than you think.

Exercise: Confidence

1. Think of a point in time when you felt really confident. Close your eyes and imagine it now. Where were you? What did you do? Who were you with?

2. Focus on the feeling you had in your body at that time. Where in your body did you feel a confident sensation? Be specific. Recall that feeling now.

3. Focus on this feeling in your body every day when you get out of bed and when you get to work. Try this exercise for a week and assess its impact.

4. Make it a habit to feel good and to appreciate your strengths and contributions.

Another action you can take to build self-esteem is to write out your vision and mission statement on a piece of paper and stick it in a place where you can see it. Make sure it is positive and appealing and that it puts emphasis on feeling good and being confident. For example:

> *I feel confident and calm in everything I do as a project manager. I love and respect myself, and I value my uniqueness and my capabilities. My mission is to focus on my strengths and to have the confidence to withstand pressure from demanding stakeholders.*

Read your vision and mission statement as many times as you can during the day. Close your eyes and imagine being strong and confident. Really feel it in your body. This will help you create a new pattern where you feel and think differently about yourself.

Tips for Building Self-Esteem

- ✔ Read uplifting and motivational books.
- ✔ Spend time with confident people.
- ✔ Notice and recognize your strengths, achievements, and uniqueness.
- ✔ Ask others what they think your unique talent is.
- ✔ Imagine being strong, positive, and confident.
- ✔ Identify a self-confident role model and learn from him or her.
- ✔ Set reachable goals, and break difficult tasks into smaller steps.
- ✔ Write an empowering vision and mission statement and live by it.
- ✔ Be objective and fair when assessing your capabilities.
- ✔ Work with a confident mentor or coach.

WORK WITH A MENTOR

It can be difficult to look at ourselves objectively and understand which thought patterns and behaviors we need to change in order to get a different result and become more effective and successful.

Finding and working with a mentor can help. Establishing a mentoring relationship will stretch and challenge you to think deeper. Your mentor will also serve as a sounding board when you are uncertain or need to make difficult decisions.

A mentoring relationship can be formal or informal, depending on whether it is supported by your employer or one in which you and your mentor came together informally, in another setting. If you would like to choose your own mentor, pick someone you trust and admire—and who has made a few mistakes, so that you can learn from them.

Think carefully about what you want to get out of the mentoring relationship and how you can make the most of this learning opportunity. Tell your mentor what you would like to work on, and schedule one-hour sessions every couple of months. The meetings do not have to follow a specific pattern as long as they have a clear focus and a clear outcome.

Prepare thoroughly for each session, recognizing that your mentor's time and energy are precious. Keep a log of positive things that happen at work, as well as frustrating incidents, and review it before each meeting. Provide your mentor with a short agenda a few days before your session so that she can prepare.

Listen to your mentor's views, and be prepared to explore issues and to be challenged. But do not take everything your mentor says for granted. Make up your own mind about what you need to do.

LEADERSHIP BEHAVIOR

Many people think of a leader as the directing chief at the top of a hierarchy. But focusing on a single role paints an incomplete picture of what leadership is. Leadership is more a function of *how you act* than *what you do* or what your job title is. Good leadership requires emotional strength, mental and spiritual reserves, and certain behavioral characteristics. Skill and position alone do not make a leader; attitude and behavior do. Leadership is about behavior first and skill second.

As we touched upon in Step 1, leadership and management are two different talents, but they are not mutually exclusive. A good way to think about these concepts is that you *manage tasks* and *lead people*. Leadership primarily focuses on the achievement of a goal through the involvement of people, whereas management is more concerned with achieving the goal through tasks, events, and processes.

People tend to follow good leaders because they admire and respect *them*, not the skills they possess or the authority they have. Leaders do not need authority to get people to do something. They tap into people's resources by inspiring them to follow on a personal level. They pull rather than push. They paint an appealing picture of the organization's or project's aims, objectives, and vision and make sure people understand what they need to contribute at an individual level in order for that vision to become reality.

There are many views and definitions of what good leadership is, perhaps because a true leader possesses a vast number of traits and capabilities. Some say that the essence lies in being able to get in touch with people, having a vision, and being positive. But traits such as honesty, integrity, and courage are equally important, as is the ability to be assertive without being arrogant.

A good leader is almost always a people person who values others' contributions and who gives credit to others. He is someone who helps others succeed. After all, who would want to follow someone if his or her personal input and hard work were not appreciated?

To become a highly valued and truly successful project management leader, you need to be as good at leading people as you are at managing tasks. You must care about others, listen to their ideas, and lead them to success through your vision and engagement. You must earn respect through your actions, rather than demand it; keep your promises; and treat others the way you want to be treated yourself. This type of behavior creates followers. People will want to work on your team because you are engaging and inspiring and because there is an appealing goal to reach. They will feel appreciated and listened to, but moreover, they will want to work with you because they want some of the appeal that you have.

> *Hold onto the big vision. Be the best you can in all that you do, and others will notice your example. They will be inclined to follow because they want some of whatever you have.*

The opposite of good leadership is failure to recognize your team's efforts or, more generally, failure to acknowledge the hard work of others. If you only speak to people when they have made a mistake, and if you are known for offering negative feedback and criticism, you almost certainly qualify as a poor leader.

As a project management leader, you need to eliminate criticism from your vocabulary. If you are not satisfied with a person's performance, do not criticize her. Look at the underlying causes and provide constructive feedback. Allow for honest mistakes. Build and reinforce people's self-esteem whenever possible. Tell people how good they are. Take time to express compassion, concern, and caring for each person.

Natural leadership abilities are not something we are all born with, but they are skills we can all improve through a process of observation, self-study, and coaching. Remember that practice makes perfect!

Exercise: Leadership Capabilities Self-Assessment

Use the spider diagram to assess your leadership capabilities. Use a scale of 1 to 10 to score yourself.

1. For each of the responsibilities listed in the diagram, imagine what a score of 10 out of 10 would look like. For example, what does sharing the project's vision, plans, and roles entail?

2. For each responsibility, indicate on the diagram where on the 1 to 10 scale you are today by making a dot on the line that represents your score.

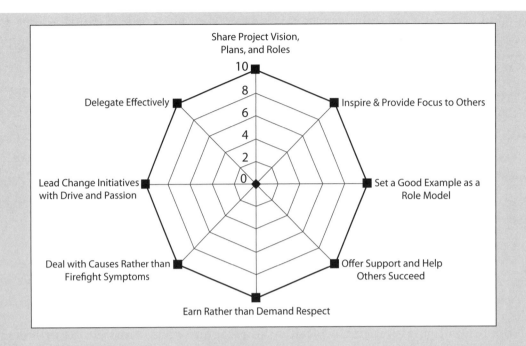

Examine your scores . . .

3. Look at your scores. Which areas stand out as needing attention?

4. What could you do to raise your rating just one point in each of these areas?

_____

_____

_____

_____

_____

BE A PROJECT CHAMPION

To become an outstanding project manager, you must be able to take your team on a journey by sharing an appealing project vision and a road map for achieving that vision. The greater clarity you have regarding the future you wish to create, the easier it will be for you to inspire the team and make the day-to-day decisions necessary to reach that future. Make the vision relevant to your people. Draw them into it by illustrating how they fit in and how their roles matter to its overall execution.

A good way of engaging people in a project vision is to think of yourself as the project champion—someone who fully embraces the goals, objectives, and plans of the project. When you understand and take ownership of the strategy for obtaining a successful outcome, you are able to provide focus and direction to the team.

Visualize the end state of the project once the changes have been fully implemented and the objectives achieved. See it the way the end users and beneficiaries see it. Feel it, taste it, and smell it. Keep the vision vivid, and it will be easier to inspire and motivate others.

As a project champion, you are more than a manager of people and resources. You become an inspiration to the team and the embodiment of the project. You become an agent of change who measures and monitors the ultimate business benefits. You become the person who makes sure that the customer adopts and implements the necessary business processes and procedures to support the end product so that the change initiative is ultimately successful.

Questions

- How well do you understand your project's vision and objectives? Give yourself a score between 1 and 10.
- What would need to happen in order for you to rate your knowledge of the vision and objectives 10 out of 10?
- What can you do to inspire your team to achieve that vision?
- What can you do to become an agent of change?

A Sticky Situation: Not Believing in Your Project

What if you find yourself in a situation where you do not fully believe in the project you are running?

In that case, take time out to examine this feeling as soon as you possibly can. Get to the bottom of your doubts by continuously asking *why* until you identify the root cause. Maybe the mandate to initiate the project is not clear, maybe the stakeholders' buy-in is not strong enough, or maybe the risks and issues are too great.

Whatever the reasons, get to the root cause and address it at that level. When you fully understand the source of your doubts, you are much better placed to take action—and take action you must. If you ignore your uncertainties, you will not be a convincing leader of the project. You may even cause it to fail.

Spend extra time with the customer or project sponsor. Voice your concerns, mitigate the risks, and do what you can to understand and embrace the benefits of the project.

BE PASSIONATE

To be a great leader, you must have a lot of drive, confidence, and love for your work. Do what you can to identify and tap into your passions, inside and outside of work. Take time out to pursue the activities you enjoy, and be good to yourself. Do this to recharge your batteries and sustain your enthusiasm for work and for life. When you make time for fun, you become more positive and passionate in other areas of your life. This will fuel the passion of those you lead and manage.

> *To be a truly successful project manager, you must love what you do and lead by example. When you are passionate, positive, and proactive, others will notice your example and want to follow.*

ADMIT WHEN YOU ARE WRONG

One of the most valuable qualities you can develop as a project manager is openness to the possibility that you could be wrong and that you could have made a mistake. Develop a habit of asking yourself if there are any situations on your project that, knowing what you know now, you would not get into again if you had the opportunity to redo it. If the answer is yes, your next question should be, "How can I get out of this situation, and how fast?"

This way of thinking is especially useful when you experience stress or ongoing irritation about something, such as a bad hire or a bad design decision. These feelings could be a sign that you have made a mistake and need to change course to get yourself and your project out of an undesirable situation. It can take great courage to admit that you were wrong, but doing so shows great strength and builds up other people's trust in you as a project management leader.

Many project managers leave a bad situation as is simply because of ego. They cannot admit that they have made a mistake and are afraid to tell others that they changed their mind. Mistakes need to be resolved and put in the past as quickly as possible. If they are not corrected, they become failures. When they are corrected, they become experiences from which you learn and develop.

Exercise: Leadership Styles

Although you might not see yourself as a leader yet, we are all leaders to someone. Leadership is not about having authority and being assigned a certain role. It is about your attitudes and behavior and how you relate to people and situations.

For each of the below statements, rate yourself with a score between 1 and 10 based on how frequently you exhibit each behavior.

Leading by exception

- I intervene only when there is a problem.
- I change things only when they go wrong.
- I let others know when goals are achieved.

Leading by objectives

- I give others a clear and lucid picture of objectives.
- I allow others to decide how they will reach their goals.
- I offer quantified feedback on goal achievements.

Leading by inspiration

- I inspire with a focus on team values and beliefs.
- I act as the prime motivator of my group or team.
- I offer opportunities for others to do their best.

Leading by charisma

- I enthusiastically and clearly define the benefits of success.
- I see myself as someone who others would wish to follow.
- I believe that I have earned the respect and trust of others.

Leading by reward

- I offer incentives for successful outcomes.
- I reward before, during, or after the outcome.
- I offer promotion or privileges as rewards.

Leading by challenge

- I challenge others' ideas so that they will refine them.
- I invite others to develop creative "what if" solutions.
- I encourage creative problem-solving.

Leading by coaching

- I encourage others to build on their strengths.
- I encourage others to expand their comfort zones.
- I act as a mentor, friend, and guide.

Take action and blend your leadership styles . . .

Most of us have a preferred way of managing and leading others that we consciously or unconsciously use most of the time. A good leader will adapt and blend different approaches and use whichever is most relevant at any one time.

To increase your effectiveness, start to pay more attention to the styles you use in different situations and with different people. Then experiment and draw in new styles and ways of relating to others.

1. Choose two different situations in which you would most like to make a change. For example, perhaps you would like to change how you interact with a specific person about a particular topic. Write each situation down.

2. Ask yourself what you would like to achieve and how you would like to come across in each situation. What is the impact you would like to have, and how would you like the individual(s) you are leading to respond?

3. Identify which of the above leadership styles you use most often in each of these two situations.

4. Assess whether the leadership style(s) you are currently using is the best suited for getting the outcome you want. If not, which other styles could you start using?

5. Take action by trying new ways of interacting with the people around you. Do not judge yourself when you try this out. Treat it as an experiment to find out what works best. Simply observe yourself and adjust your approach as needed. Remember that practice makes perfect!

DELEGATE EFFECTIVELY AND THOUGHTFULLY

You are unlikely to be able to manage a project all by yourself. Delegating some of your tasks and responsibilities is an important part of making sure that you spend your time effectively. You must remain focused on the areas that make the most difference to the success of your project. People used to say, "If you want the job done right, you have to do it yourself." That is old-school thinking. The new-school approach is to say, "If you want the job done right, you have to delegate it properly."[3]

On small projects, the amount of delegation you can do may be limited. However, as you become more experienced and take on bigger projects, delegation becomes an essential way to make the best use of your strengths. When you delegate effectively, you leverage yourself and multiply your value to the project. In short, delegation frees you up to focus on other activities that make better use of your time.

By delegating, you also help grow and develop other people. When you ask a team member to take on a certain task, it may be the one thing that helps motivate and stretch that person. If done correctly, delegation will contribute to your team members' professional development needs, confidence, and competence. It will also help you build relationships characterized by trust and openness with others.

Many project managers do not delegate enough because they believe that they either have no one to delegate to or they do not want to lose control of a certain task. You need to think more broadly, creatively, and strategically. Often team members are perfectly able to perform a task—for instance, one related to planning and estimation—if they are given the opportunity and the right amount of support.

You can either delegate to existing team members or, if their skill sets and aspirations are too different from what you need, get a dedicated project support person on board. Some organizations have a centralized project management office (PMO) facility that might be able to offer additional help and support.

Deciding which tasks to delegate goes back to Pareto's Principle and the 80/20 rule. Never delegate the 20 percent of tasks that contribute to 80 percent of your results. Choose tasks you are not particularly attached to and that someone else could potentially perform better than you can. The easiest tasks for you to delegate may relate to tracking and administering the project. Consider delegating tasks such time sheet approval, financial tracking, taking minutes, documenting procedures and solutions, detailed planning, reporting, creating newsletters, and keeping the document repository up-to-date.

Depending on the size of your project, you can also delegate specific roles such as test management, implementation management, and detailed planning of particular products, work streams, or work packages. On a small project, you might double up and take on these roles yourself, but on a large project, it is essential that you delegate them.

When you have made a decision to delegate a task, take time to think through the job. Decide exactly what is to be done and what results you want. Determine the performance standards you are going to measure the job against, as well as a schedule and a deadline. Explain what is to be done and the reason for doing the task in the first place. Remember to make the outcome as measurable as possible.

When you delegate a piece of work, make sure you hand over the entire task to the person you are delegating to. Check in with him regularly to see how he is getting on and give him the support, direction, and information required to succeed. Gradually step back when you see that he is mastering the task. Be patient, and do not look for mistakes. We were all trainees once and had to learn from someone more experienced. It is your support and direction, more than anything else, that determines how successful you are at delegating.

You may not always have a lot of choice in deciding who to delegate to. Do, however, try to take the following factors into consideration:

1. **Competence.** How competent is the person to whom you want to delegate? What are his expertise and skills in areas such as planning, communication, and time management? The person's competence will determine how much direction he needs from you.

2. **Commitment.** How committed is the person to whom you want to delegate? How motivated, confident, and driven is he? His commitment will determine how much moral support he needs from you. When people are both competent and committed you can manage them by exception and tell them to get back to you if they have a problem.

3. **Availability.** How available is the person to whom you want to delegate? How much time would be required to complete the task, and how could the person be freed up to work for you? How would taking on the task you are delegating affect his other work priorities?

4. **Career development.** How much will the particular task challenge, stretch, and motivate the person to whom you plan to delegate? What is in it for him? In what ways will this assignment contribute to his success and help him develop his skills and capabilities?

PROJECT STABILITY AND IDENTITY

As the project manager, you are ideally positioned to take a step back and observe how the project operates as an entity and how it interacts with the organization and the external world. With that knowledge, you can fine-tune the project to function more optimally on its own and in a wider context. You can do this by, for example, creating a sense of belonging and identity within the team and by protecting the project from external noise and interruptions.

Project stability and identity are more than looking at how the team functions on its own. They involve looking at how the team is interacting with the environment in which it operates. If, for instance, you find that there is too much overall distraction and interruption stemming from sources external to the project, you will have to strengthen the boundaries and shield the team from that external noise. (Think of noise as anything that interferes with your team's performance.)

For example, imagine that your organization is implementing new processes and procedures that affect the people on, and working practices of, your project. Such a change could be very disruptive and time-consuming, especially if the new processes are awkward or overly bureaucratic or if the rollout is badly timed. In that situation, you would need to protect your team and your project's interests by negotiating a solution that works for all parties. Suggest that the rollout be delayed or scaled back so that the impact on your team is limited. It is your job to act as a buffer between the project and the organization and to smooth out any conflict and interference between the two.

You are the external face of the project and the link between the team, stakeholders, and wider organization. Take this opportunity to promote the project and stand up for it. Be the project's ambassador. Never criticize your own players; take responsibility and shield them from the outside. Think of yourself as a protector who is looking for ways to remove obstacles from the project. Take the blame if your team is criticized, protect its reputation, and shield it from internal politics.

> *Creating project stability and identity is about "oiling the machine" so that it performs better. It is about making team members feel at home and giving them optimal conditions for getting on with their work without unnecessary worry or interruptions. It is about protecting the project and being its ambassador to the outside world.*

One way you can "oil the machine" and optimize the project is to look at the team's working practices and the tools it uses. Investigate whether there are more appropriate ways in which the team could be working. Do you, for instance, have the right software and hardware and a good physical space to enable the team to produce its best work? Are you allowing people to work in whatever ways are most conducive to their productivity, and are you giving them the tools and facilities they need? Liaise with people and ask them what could make them work more effectively. Be a facilitator: help remove blockages so that team members can succeed.

Come to an agreement with the team about how you want the project to operate, and provide the necessary support to achieve this vision. When everyone has the same level of understanding, the project is more likely to build up its own rhythm and be more effective.

When new team members join, make sure that they are able to work effectively as quickly as possible. Not only do they need the right tools and information to do so, they also need the right amount of support and encouragement and an understanding of who is who and who does what.

One of the ways in which you can make people feel at home is by creating a strong spirit and identity around the project. People like to feel that they are part of something bigger than themselves, something that gives their work meaning and purpose. Ask yourself what it is that makes your project special and why people would want to work on it. What is the unique identity and culture of the project, or if it is lacking, how can you help create it? To find the answer, encourage teamwork, knowledge-sharing, and fun team-building activities. It is often the small things that matter and that help define a project's unique identity.

Exercise: Project Stability and Identity Self-Assessment

Use the spider diagram to assess your ability to "oil the machine" and foster stability and identity on your project. Use a scale of 1 to 10 to score yourself.

1. For each of the responsibilities listed in the diagram, imagine what a score of 10 out of 10 would look like. For example, what must be done to promote project stability and order?

2. For each responsibility, indicate on the diagram where on the 1 to 10 scale you are today by making a dot on the line that represents your score.

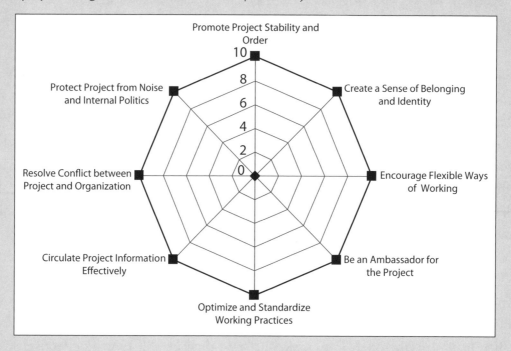

Examine your scores . . .

3. Look at your scores. Which areas stand out as needing attention?

4. What could you do to raise your rating just one point in each of these areas?

_____

_____

_____

_____

_____

CIRCULATE PROJECT INFORMATION EFFECTIVELY

An important part of creating project stability and identity is ensuring that project information is effectively circulated to all relevant parties. The purpose of this is to create transparency around project plans, progress, and decisions so that people can work more effectively and continue to feel positive and motivated about the project. There is nothing worse than being involved in a project and not knowing what is going on or having a feeling that certain information is being withheld.

If you want to optimize the way your project functions, you need to involve and inform people inside (and outside) the project. Show your team members that they matter by disseminating information and project news as soon as you can. If appropriate, copy them on steering committee presentations, and right after the meetings, talk them through what was discussed and decided. Depending on the size and nature of your project, many team members may not have the opportunity to interface directly with the project sponsor and senior stakeholders. They rely on you to provide them with timely and accurate updates about the direction of the project.

In addition to keeping team members informed, you have to keep all major stakeholders and the organization abreast of project progress and promote all your achievements and successes. When you communicate all of the good work that your team is doing, you become an ambassador for the project and put it in the positive light it deserves.

Tips for Optimizing Your Project's Information Flow

✔ Build a simple, easy-to-maintain webpage or portal focused solely on the project. It should contain information about the project's goals and objectives, time frames, milestones, team members, and key achievements, as well as project news. Make it easy to read and navigate, as it will be the first point of call for new starters and many of the project's stakeholders.

✔ Link the webpage to a central document repository that contains all key documents such as the business case, project definition document, project plans, road maps, resource plans, requirements documents, design documents, test plans, estimates, risks and issues logs, steering committee presentations, project reports, newsletters, minutes, project checklists, and procedures. Make the repository accessible to everyone who might need it, and structure the information so that your stakeholders and team members can easily find what they are looking for.

✔ Update the most important artifacts on a regular basis so that you do not have old and stale copies in the repository. Project and resource plans, road maps, budgets, risks and issues, and project reports are the most important documents to keep updated. However, almost all artifacts need to be periodically reviewed to ensure they are still relevant and up-to-date.

✔ Notify people when new documents or artifacts have been uploaded to the repository. Do not assume that people have time to check which new artifacts have been produced. Make it easy for people by informing them. Send them an email highlighting the key decision, change, or update and insert a link to the relevant page.

✔ Send out weekly or bimonthly status reports to everyone who wants to be kept informed. Keep the report short (one or two pages), and make sure all of the information within is precise and accurate. Include a paragraph about the overall status of the project and what has been achieved since the last report. Mention the ten most important risks and issues, and provide updates on budget and schedule.

✔ Include visual effects and graphics in the report to make it more appealing and readable. You could, for instance, insert a time line with key milestone dates and charts or graphs illustrating how far through baseline scope, time, and budget you are. Executives love graphs, but keep them simple so that they are easy to read and understand.

✔ Send out a short, punchy newsletter in addition to your status reports to highlight major achievements and promote your successes. Big achievements deserve special mention. The more you emphasize them and value them, the more others will, too.

✔ Take minutes at all important meetings so that people who are unable to attend can easily stay informed. Taking minutes helps you reinforce what was decided and what actions were agreed upon and by whom. If you struggle to find the time to write up minutes, ask someone else to help out, or take turns writing them. Either way, make sure it happens.

✔ Set up regular and recurring team meetings, and stick to the same time every week. Different types of projects require different types of meetings. Make sure you at least have one central forum where the team can get together to exchange ideas and get updates about what is going on. If you have to cancel (or reschedule) a meeting, give people as much notice as you can—and respect them by arriving at meetings on time.

✔ Set up monthly steering committee meetings to update the sponsor and senior stakeholders. Put together an appealing presentation that highlights the project's key achievements and the main risks, issues, and change requests you need your stakeholders to understand and decide on. This is your opportunity to ask for help and direction, so make it clear what you need them to do. Also include a financial status update and a road map in your presentation that shows how far the project has progressed compared to the original plan.

CONSOLIDATE YOUR SCORES

Well done! You have now completed all ten self-assessments. The next activity looks at how you can consolidate and analyze all of your scores.

Activity: Consolidating Your Self-Assessment Scores

To get a complete overview of how you scored yourself on the ten self-assessments, you will now consolidate your scores in a table format. When you see all of your scores in one table, it is easier to determine what your strongest and weakest points are.

1. Table 2-1 lists all ten self-assessments vertically. The characteristics and tasks associated with each assessment are listed horizontally.

2. Go back to the first spider diagram you completed (on Skills and Knowledge), and transfer each of your eight scores from the spider diagram to the table. That is, if you gave yourself a score of 7 in Knowledge of Client Industry/Sector, write 7 in the first empty cell of the table.

3. Continue filling in all eight boxes alongside Skills and Knowledge with the scores from the spider diagram. When you have transferred all of your scores, add them up and write the total figure in the TOTAL column.

4. Divide the TOTAL score by 8, and write your average score in the AVERAGE column. If you did not score yourself on every item, go back to the spider diagram and rethink how you might do so. If you are still missing some scores, do not use the AVERAGE column, as your average score will have less meaning than it would if you had all eight scores.

5. Continue filling in the table for the remaining nine self-assessments.

	Knowledge of industry	Biz domain knowledge	Solution domain knowledge	Project mgt. best practices	Project mgt. methodologies	Project mgt. tools	QA and testing	Departmental procedures	TOTAL SCORE	AVERAGE SCORE
1. Skills and Knowledge	Score	Score	Score	Score	Score	Score	Score	Score		
2. Project Initiation and Planning	Aims and objectives	Engage stakeholders	Identify initiation team	Capture scope/requirements	Propose/estimate solution	Establish outline schedule	QA approach/controls	Document approach		
	Score	Score	Score	Score	Score	Score	Score	Score		
3. Managing Product Quality	Scope/acceptance criteria	Capture requirements	Traceability matrix	Receive user feedback	QA responsibility	Repeatable dev. process	Repeatable QA process	User acceptance testing		
	Score	Score	Score	Score	Score	Score	Score	Score		
4. Tracking Cost and Schedule	Track actual costs	Track actual work	Track actual time	Revalidate work	Revalidate estimate	Revalidate resources	Adjust plans and schedule	Project reporting		
	Score	Score	Score	Score	Score	Score	Score	Score		
5. Risk, Issue, and Scope Management	Remove blockages	Identify R/I/C	Analyze cause/impact	Identify actions/owners	Log and monitor R/I/C	Work with owner	Get sign-off	Adjust plans and budgets		
	Score	Score	Score	Score	Score	Score	Score	Score		

TABLE 2-1. Self-Assessment Scoring

Continued on next page

Continued

	Inspire/ motivate team	Communicate vision	Listen/value contributions	Challenge individuals	Provide feedback	Grow team members	Deal with mistakes fairly	Monitor stress levels	TOTAL SCORE	AVERAGE SCORE
6. Managing and Motivating the Team	Score	Score	Score	Score	Score	Score	Score	Score		
7. Stakeholder Relationships and Communication	Build relationships	Understand success criteria	Analyze stakeholders	Risks/issues liaising	Hold accountable	Seek feedback	Manage difficult stakeholders	Report progress		
	Score	Score	Score	Score	Score	Score	Score	Score		
8. Self-Management	Stay calm	Be proactive	Value own contributions	Making decisions	Be comfortable saying no	Positive mental attitude	Time management	Take responsibility		
	Score	Score	Score	Score	Score	Score	Score	Score		
9. Leadership Behavior	Share vision	Inspire and provide focus	Be role model	Support / help succeed	Earn respect	Deal with causes	Lead with drive, passion	Delegate effectively		
	Score	Score	Score	Score	Score	Score	Score	Score		
10. Project Stability and Identity	Promote stability	Create sense of belonging	Flexible ways of working	Be an ambassador	Optimize practices	Circulate information	Resolve conflict	Protect from external noise		
	Score	Score	Score	Score	Score	Score	Score	Score		

TABLE 2-1. Self-Assessment Scoring

ANALYZE YOUR SCORES

Look at Table 2-1 and take note of all of the project management capabilities in which you scored yourself 7 or higher. These are likely to be your areas of strength and things you do well. They are also the skills and attributes you need to leverage as much as possible.

Now take a pencil and gently circle the ten capabilities in which you scored yourself the lowest. These are your weakest areas, which are likely to determine the extent to which you can apply all your other attributes and capabilities. Although you are exceptional in some areas, your weakest points will in some ways hold you back and limit your overall success as a project manager.

Questions

- What are your areas of strength? What do you do really well?
- What are your weakest areas, and what are the common denominators between them (if any)?

To create a graphical representation of your scores, transfer your average score for each of the ten project management themes to the spider diagram below.

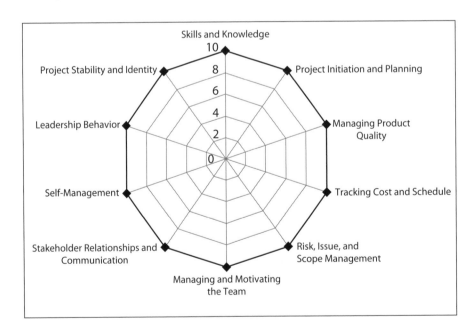

GAP ANALYSIS

Congratulations! You have come a long way!

In Step 1, you looked at what kind of person and project manager you want to become and encapsulated this in a vision and mission statement.

In Step 2, you assessed your current skill set against 80 aspects of project management and personal leadership and identified your strongest and weakest points.

Now it is time to carry out a gap analysis and compare where you are with where you want to be. Go back to Step 1 and review your vision and mission statement. If you would like to make any changes, do so now. Write down the revised vision and mission statement below.

My Vision and Mission Is . . .

Compare your vision and mission statement to the outcome of your self-assessment.

Questions

- What skills and attributes are most important for you to improve (or leverage) in order to progress as a project manager and honor your vision and mission statement?
- What resources do you already have that can help you progress in these areas? That is, what skills, experiences, personal qualities, and support do you have that you can make positive use of?
- What could a natural first step be toward becoming a highly valued and truly successful project management leader and realizing your vision and mission statement?

NOTES

1. This carton is reprinted with permission from www.projectcartoon.com (accessed August 2011).

2. This process of involving the client or end user in the design and development of an application through a succession of collaborative workshops is often referred to as JAD (Joint Application Development).

3. Brian Tracy, *How the Best Leaders Lead* (New York: AMACOM, 2010), 91–92.

360° Feedback:
Seek Feedback from Managers, Peers, and Customers

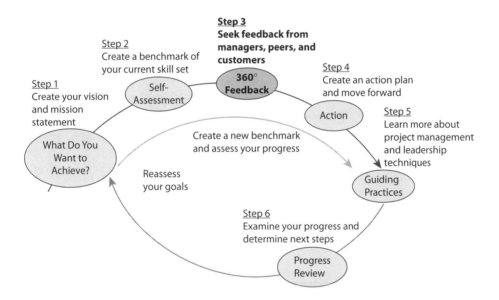

The purpose of Step 3 is to ask others for feedback about what you do well as a project manager and what you do less well. In order to find this out, you need to ask your peers, managers, customers, or business partners to assess you in the same manner in which you just assessed yourself.

Although you may think of this as a daunting task, it could be one of the most defining actions you take. It can lead to remarkable breakthroughs and results, as it will highlight blind spots or weaknesses of which you are not fully aware and which you can now take action to rectify. Receiving feedback will also draw your attention to your hidden potential and talents and in turn increase your self-confidence in areas you had not expected.

There is no rule about who you should ask for feedback. It could be anyone you have worked with professionally and whose opinion you value: coworkers, line managers, business partners, project sponsors, end users, or all of the above. The more people you ask, the more comprehensive a picture you will get of how others rate your performance and perceive you.

After completing Step 3 you will have a clear profile of how others perceive your project management capabilities and you will be able to easily compare it to your self-assessment.

Copy pages 115–126 and distribute them to everyone you want to evaluate you. Select at least four people. You can then transfer their scores into the workbook later.

Carefully explain the purpose of the exercise to your reviewers. If you are new to project management, it may be difficult for people to evaluate your performance in all ten categories. In that case, you might want to ask your reviewers some open-ended questions about how they feel you are performing, rather than using this proposed format.

Ask your reviewers to take you through their responses in person afterwards. This will give you the opportunity to query any comments you might not fully understand. Always remember that there is no such thing as negative feedback. Feedback offers insight into how others perceive you and is an opportunity to understand what you could do to further improve your performance and leverage your strengths.

It is important that you do not automatically take all feedback at face value but that you use your common sense. Look for recurring themes and ignore comments that deviate too much from the norm.

****

360° FEEDBACK FORM: PROJECT MANAGEMENT PERFORMANCE REVIEW

Thank you for agreeing to participate in this 360° review and for contributing to the project manager's professional development. You have been asked to participate because you are in a position to comment on the project manager's performance, and because the project manager values your opinion.

Providing feedback to others is an important part of helping them develop as managers and leaders. It gives them invaluable insight into how their coworkers and business partners view their performance and how they can better use their strengths and potential.

When you provide feedback, others hear your thoughts and suggestions on what they are doing well and not as well. It also shows them that you care about their success and helps motivate them to continue improving.

The following pages contain ten spider diagrams, each of which covers one theme of project management. For each characteristic or task shown on the diagrams, rate the project manager's performance on a scale from 1 to 10 by placing a dot on the corresponding numbered line.

Use the space provided below the spider diagrams to record your comments and make suggestions about things the project manager can do to further develop as a manager and leader—for example, by addressing a weakness or by leveraging a strength and making better use of a capability.

When you have recorded your scores and your comments, please sit down with the project manager and discuss your feedback in person. Bear in mind the following when you provide feedback:

➤ Feedback is as much about stating the positives as it is about stating the negatives.

➤ Be specific about the behaviors on which you are commenting.

➤ Think carefully about what you want to express and how to express it. Explain your comments as clearly as possible.

➤ Take responsibility for your feedback; say "I feel," "I noticed."

➤ Provide a balanced view in your assessment.

➤ Use analogies and examples to illustrate your points.

➤ Make sure the project manager understands your feedback in the way it is intended.

➤ Invite the project manager to comment on and discuss your feedback.

SKILLS AND KNOWLEDGE

1. Record your assessment of the project manager's performance on the spider diagram, using a scale of 1 to 10.

2. For each of the knowledge areas shown in the diagram, envision what good performance (a score of 10 out of 10) looks like. For example, what does a project manager with sufficient knowledge of the client's industry and sector do? Does the project manager you are assessing do this?

3. For each knowledge area, indicate where on a scale from 1 to 10 you believe the project manager's performance is today. When you have provided a score for all eight knowledge areas, please connect the dots.

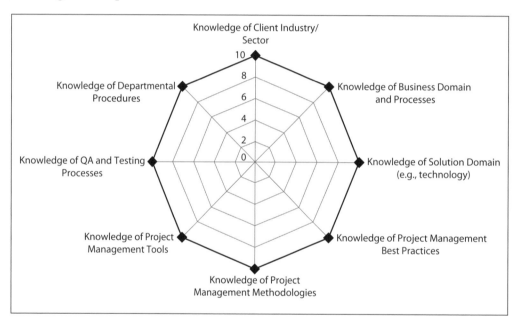

COMMENTS

In the space below, write comments and suggestions that could help the project manager improve his or her skills and knowledge. What should he or she start doing, stop doing, and continue doing?

_____

_____

_____

_____

PROJECT INITIATION AND PLANNING

1. Record your assessment of the project manager's performance on the spider diagram, using a scale of 1 to 10.

2. For each of the duties shown in the diagram, envision what good performance (a score of 10 out of 10) looks like. For example, what does a project manager do when effectively capturing the project's aims, objectives, business case, and benefits? Does the project manager you are assessing do this?

3. For each duty, indicate where on a scale from 1 to 10 you believe the project manager's performance is today. When you have provided a score for all eight duties, connect the dots.

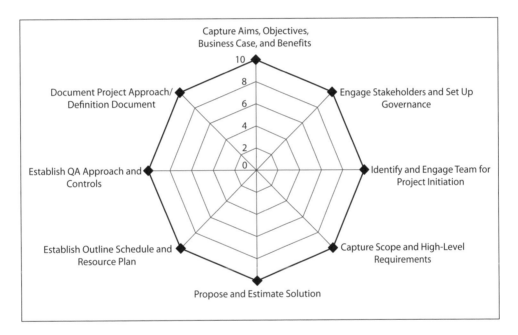

COMMENTS

In the space below, write comments and suggestions that could help the project manager improve his or her project initiation and planning capabilities. What should he or she start doing, stop doing, and continue doing?

MANAGING PRODUCT QUALITY

1. Record your assessment of the project manager's performance on the spider diagram, using a scale of 1 to 10.

2. For each of the activities shown in the diagram, envision what good performance (a score of 10 out of 10) looks like. For example, what does a project manager do when effectively capturing a project's scope and acceptance criteria? Does the project manager you are assessing do this? (Note that the project manager does not necessarily carry out all of the quality activities alone, although he or she remains responsible for them.)

3. For each activity, indicate where on a scale from 1 to 10 you believe the project manager's performance is today. When you have provided a score for all eight activities, connect the dots.

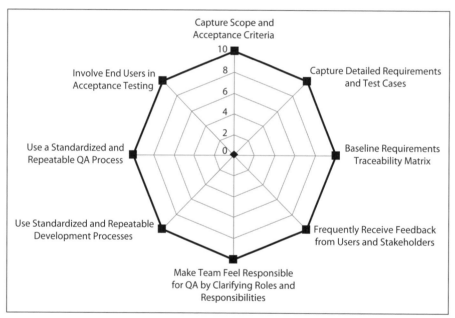

COMMENTS

In the space below, write comments and suggestions that could help the project manager improve his or her quality management capabilities. What should he or she start doing, stop doing, and continue doing?

_____

_____

_____

_____

TRACKING COST AND SCHEDULE

1. Record your assessment of the project manager's performance on the spider diagram, using a scale of 1 to 10.

2. For each of the duties shown on the diagram, envision what good performance (a score of 10 out of 10) looks like. For example, what does a project manager do when effectively tracking actual costs versus planned costs? Does the project manager you are assessing do this?

3. For each duty, indicate where on a scale from 1 to 10 you believe the project manager's performance is today. When you have provided a score for all eight duties, connect the dots.

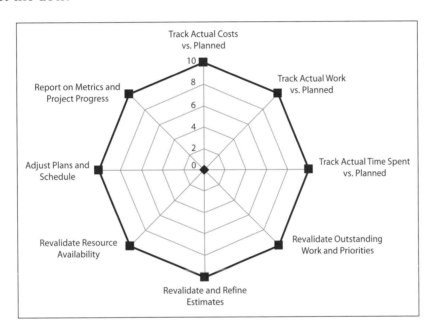

COMMENTS

In the space below, write comments and suggestions that could help the project manager improve his or her tracking capabilities. What should he or she start doing, stop doing, and continue doing?

_____

_____

_____

_____

RISK, ISSUE, AND SCOPE MANAGEMENT

1. Record your assessment of the project manager's performance on the spider diagram, using a scale of 1 to 10.

2. For each of the duties shown on the diagram, envision what good performance (a score of 10 out of 10) looks like. For example, what does a project manager do when proactively working to remove project blockages? Does the project manager you are assessing do this?

3. for each duty, indicate where on a scale from 1 to 10 you believe the project manager's performance is today. When you have provided a score for all eight duties, connect the dots.

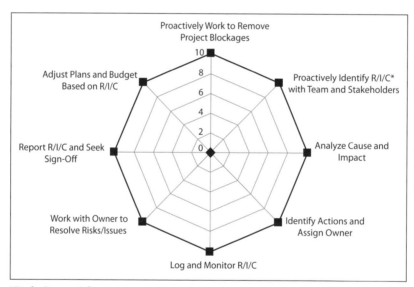

*Risks/issues/changes

COMMENTS

In the space below, write comments and suggestions that could help the project manager improve his or her risk and issue management capabilities. What should he or she start doing, stop doing, and continue doing?

_____

_____

_____

_____

MANAGING AND MOTIVATING THE TEAM

1. Record your assessment of the project manager's performance on the spider diagram, using a scale of 1 to 10.

2. For each of the responsibilities shown in the diagram, envision what good performance (a score of 10 out of 10) looks like. For example, what would a project manager who is fully able to inspire and motivate the team do? Does the project manager you are assessing do this?

3. For each responsibility, indicate where on a scale from 1 to 10 you believe the project manager's performance is today. When you have provided a score for all eight responsibilities, connect the dots.

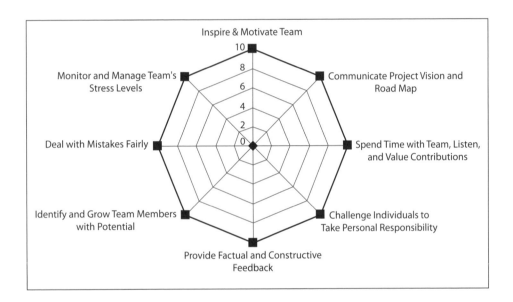

COMMENTS

In the space below, write comments and suggestions that could help the project manager improve his or her team management capabilities. What should he or she start doing, stop doing, and continue doing?

_____

_____

_____

_____

STAKEHOLDER RELATIONSHIPS AND COMMUNICATION

1. Record your assessment of the project manager's performance on the spider diagram, using a scale of 1 to 10.

2. For each of the competencies shown on the diagram, envision what good performance (a score of 10 out of 10) looks like. For example, what would a project manager who is able to build strong relationships with the project's stakeholders do? Does the project manager you are assessing do this?

3. For each competency, indicate where on a scale from 1 to 10 you believe the project manager's performance is today. When you have provided a score for all eight competencies, connect the dots.

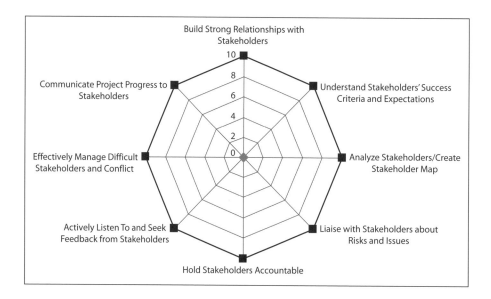

COMMENTS

In the space below, write comments and suggestions that could help the project manager improve his or her stakeholder management capabilities. What should he or she start doing, stop doing, and continue doing?

_____

_____

_____

_____

SELF-MANAGEMENT

1. Record your assessment of the project manager's performance on the spider diagram, using a scale of 1 to 10.

2. For each of the capabilities shown in the diagram, envision what good performance (a score of 10 out of 10) looks like. For example, how does a project manager who is able to stay calm in stressful situations behave? Does the project manager you are assessing do this?

3. For each capability, indicate where on a scale from 1 to 10 you believe the project manager's performance is today. When you have provided a score for all eight capabilities, connect the dots.

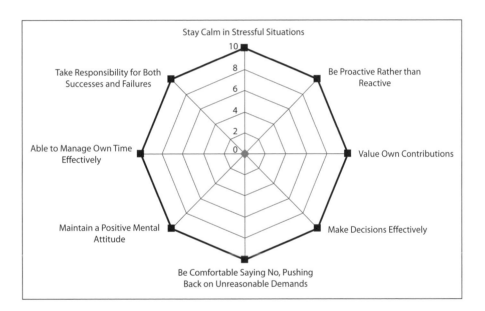

COMMENTS

In the space below, write comments and suggestions that could help the project manager improve his or her self-management capabilities. What should he or she start doing, stop doing, and continue doing?

LEADERSHIP BEHAVIOR

1. Record your assessment of the project manager's performance on the spider diagram, using a scale of 1 to 10.

2. For each of the responsibilities shown in the diagram, envision what good performance (a score of 10 out of 10) looks like. For example, what should a project manager do to effectively share the project's vision, plans, and roles? Does the project manager you are assessing do this?

3. For each responsibility, indicate where on a scale from 1 to 10 you believe the project manager's performance is today. When you have provided a score for all eight responsibilities, connect the dots.

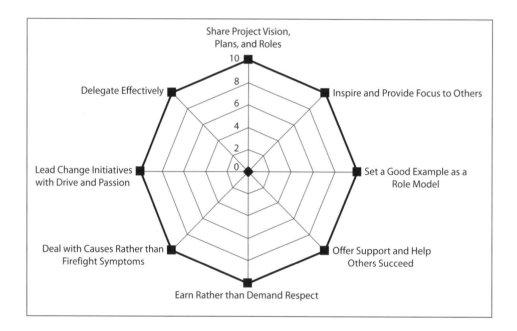

COMMENTS

In the space below, write comments and suggestions that could help the project manager improve his or her leadership capabilities. What should he or she start doing, stop doing, and continue doing?

_____

_____

_____

_____

PROJECT STABILITY AND IDENTITY

1. Record your assessment of the project manager's performance on the spider diagram, using a scale of 1 to 10.

2. For each of the responsibilities shown on the diagram, envision what good performance (a score of 10 out of 10) looks like. For example, what could a project manager do to effectively promote project stability and order? Does the project manager you are assessing do this?

3. For each responsibility, indicate where on a scale from 1 to 10 you believe the project manager's performance is today. When you have provided a score for all eight responsibilities, connect the dots.

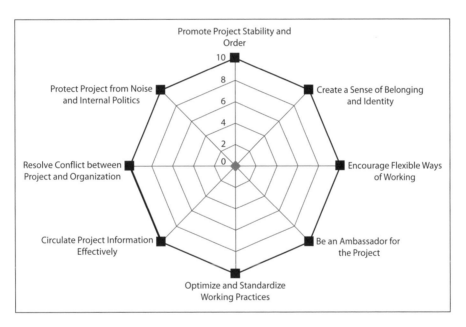

COMMENTS

In the space below, write comments and suggestions that could help the project manager improve his or her capabilities in this area. What should he or she start doing, stop doing, and continue doing?

_____

_____

_____

_____

CLOSING COMMENTS

➤ Please provide any overall comments and suggestions you have that could help the project manager improve his or her performance.

➤ What would you say the project manager's most outstanding talent or gift is?

➤ In what ways could the project manager better leverage his or her strengths and potential?

_____

_____

_____

_____

_____

_____

_____

_____

_____

_____

Thank you for taking the time to fill in this 360° feedback form.

Your feedback is invaluable in helping others better understand how they can work to further improve their performance and leverage their strengths.

Please sit down with the project manager and explain your views and comments so that your feedback will be received in the way it is intended.

Be as precise and specific as you can, and give concrete examples of excellent (and not so excellent) performance. The more specific you are, the more accurate and helpful your feedback will be. Provide a balanced view and mention areas for improvement as well as areas of strength.

****

INCORPORATE 360° FEEDBACK INTO YOUR WORKBOOK

Activity: Incorporating 360° Feedback into Your Workbook

To get a complete overview of how your managers, coworkers, customers, or business partners rated you, transfer all of their scores into this workbook.

1. Gather all of your completed 360° feedback forms.

2. Take the first feedback form and look at the first topic, Skills and Knowledge. Choose a colored pen and copy the ratings from the feedback form onto the spider diagram in the workbook.

3. Continue copying the scores from the first feedback form into the book for the next theme, Project Initiation and Planning. Do the same for the remaining eight themes.

4. When you have copied all of the scores from one reviewer into the workbook, repeat the process for the remaining sets of feedback forms you have received. Choose a different colored pen for each reviewer. What you will end up with is several colored webs for each project management theme. (The diagram below uses different shapes to signify different reviewers.)

Skills and Knowledge

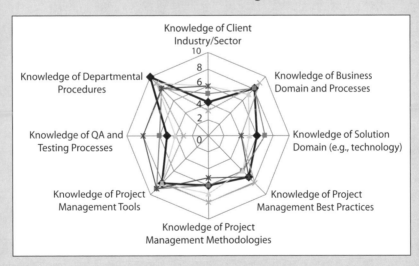

5. In order to easily compare all of your reviewers' ratings to how you scored yourself, calculate the *average* rating for the first knowledge area in the diagram. In the example above, Tim has received the following ratings from his reviewers on Knowledge of Client Industry/Sector: 4, 5, 6, 3, 6. His average score is, therefore, 5.

6. Continue calculating the average score for each of the remaining knowledge areas shown on the diagram, and note them. The boxes with the numbers in the diagram below represent Tim's average scores.

7. Calculate your average score for each activity or competency within the remaining nine project management themes, and clearly mark them in the workbook.

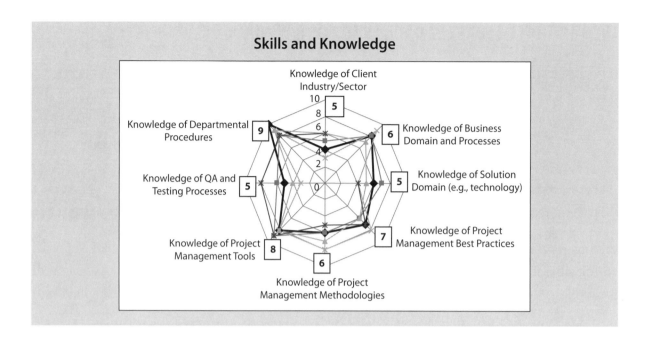

CONSOLIDATE YOUR SCORES

Activity: Consolidating Your 360° Review Scores

To get a complete overview of how your managers, peers, customers, or business partners rated you, you will now summarize and consolidate your average scores in a table format. When you see all of your average scores in one table, you can directly compare your 360° feedback ratings to your own scores from the self-assessment.

1. Look at Table 3-1. It is identical to the one in which you recorded your self-assessment scores. All ten project management themes are listed vertically, and the competencies or activities associated with each theme are listed horizontally.

2. Go back to the first spider diagram from the 360° review, Skills and Knowledge, and look at the average scores you calculated. Now copy each of the average scores into the table. (To illustrate, because Tim's average score for Knowledge of Industry/Sector was 5, he would write a 5 in the first empty cell of the table.)

3. Continue copying all of your average scores from the Skills and Knowledge diagram into the table. When you have transferred all of them, add up the ratings and write the total figure in the TOTAL column.

4. Divide the TOTAL score by 8 and write this average in the AVERAGE column. (You now have an average of an average score.)

5. Continue filling in the table for the remaining nine project management themes. If your reviewers did not provide scores for certain competencies or activities, you need to be mindful about how much weight you give to the AVERAGE figures. Use your common sense and complete the table the best you can with the ratings you have received.

ANALYZE YOUR SCORES

Look at Table 3-1 and compare the scores and comments you received with your self-assessment.

➤ How does the 360° feedback from peers and managers compare to your self-assessment?

➤ What blind spots came to light?

➤ What do others believe your most outstanding talent or gift is?

➤ What are the main conclusions you have drawn from the feedback?

_____

_____

_____

_____

_____

_____

_____

_____

_____

_____

_____

_____

	Knowledge of industry	Biz domain knowledge	Solution domain knowledge	Project mgt. best practices	Project mgt. methodologies	Project mgt. tools	QA and testing	Departmental procedures	TOTAL SCORE	AVERAGE SCORE
1. Skills and Knowledge	Score	Score	Score	Score	Score	Score	Score	Score		
2. Project Initiation and Planning	Aims and objectives	Engage stakeholders	Identify initiation team	Capture scope / requirements	Propose / estimate solution	Establish outline schedule	QA approach/ controls	Document approach		
	Score	Score	Score	Score	Score	Score	Score	Score		
3. Managing Product Quality	Scope/ acceptance criteria	Capture requirements	Traceability matrix	Receive user feedback	QA responsibility	Repeatable dev. process	Repeatable QA process	User acceptance testing		
	Score	Score	Score	Score	Score	Score	Score	Score		
4. Tracking Cost and Schedule	Track actual costs	Track actual work	Track actual time	Revalidate work	Revalidate estimate	Revalidate resources	Adjust plans and schedule	Project reporting		
	Score	Score	Score	Score	Score	Score	Score	Score		
5. Risk, Issue, and Scope Management	Remove blockages	Identify R/I/C	Analyze cause/ impact	Identify actions/ owners	Log and monitor R/I/C	Work with owner	Get sign-off	Adjust plans and budgets		
	Score	Score	Score	Score	Score	Score	Score	Score		

TABLE 3-1. 360° Review Scoring

Continued on next page

Continued

	Inspire/ motivate team	Communicate vision	Listen/value contributions	Challenge individuals	Provide feedback	Grow team members	Deal with mistakes fairly	Monitor stress levels	TOTAL SCORE	AVERAGE SCORE
6. Managing and Motivating the Team	Score	Score	Score	Score	Score	Score	Score	Score		
7. Stakeholder Relationships and Communication	Build relationships	Understand success criteria	Analyze stakeholders	Risks/issues liaising	Hold accountable	Seek feedback	Manage difficult stakeholders	Report progress		
	Score	Score	Score	Score	Score	Score	Score	Score		
8. Self-Management	Stay calm	Be proactive	Value own contributions	Making decisions	Be comfortable saying no	Positive mental attitude	Time management	Take responsibility		
	Score	Score	Score	Score	Score	Score	Score	Score		
9. Leadership Behavior	Share vision	Inspire and provide focus	Be role model	Support / help succeed	Earn respect	Deal with causes	Lead with drive, passion	Delegate effectively		
	Score	Score	Score	Score	Score	Score	Score	Score		
10. Project Stability and Identity	Promote stability	Create sense of belonging	Flexible ways of working	Be an ambassador	Optimize practices	Circulate information	Resolve conflict	Protect from external noise		
	Score	Score	Score	Score	Score	Score	Score	Score		

TABLE 3-1. 360° Review Scoring

REFINE YOUR GAP ANALYSIS

Compare the feedback you received from your peers, managers, customers, or business partners to the gap analysis you carried out at the end of the self-assessment.

What new insights do you now have, and how do they apply to the skills and attributes you most need to improve, or leverage, in order to progress as a project manager?

Remind yourself of what your vision and mission statement is, and take time to refine the gap analysis.

My Vision and Mission Is . . .

Questions

- What skills and attributes are most important for you to improve in order to progress as a project manager and honor your vision and mission statement?
- Which capabilities and strengths could you better leverage?
- What resources do you already have to help you progress in these areas (e.g., skills, experience, personal qualities, support), and what could a natural first step be?

Action: Create an Action Plan and Move Forward

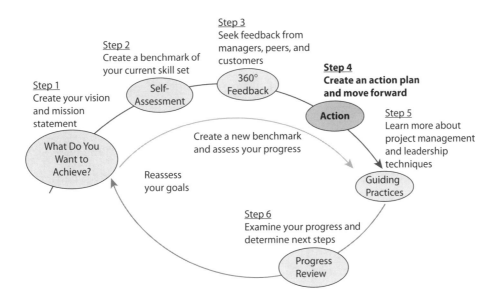

By now you know what your vision and mission is and what kind of project manager you want to become. You know what your strengths and weaknesses are, and you know how others perceive you. You also have a really good understanding of what you need to do to become a highly valued and truly successful project management leader and fulfill your ambitions.

In order to move forward, you must take action. I can help you become aware of what your vision and mission is and what you need to do to accomplish it, but nothing will happen unless *you* are proactive and are committed to making a change.

The purpose of Step 4 is to create a tangible action plan that you can actually implement. To do this, you need to look back through the workbook and consolidate everything you have learned. The key is to determine what you *will* do and by *when* you will do it so that you can start to fulfill your ambitions and live up to your vision and mission statement.

When you put together your action plan, it is important that you do not overcommit yourself and that you create a realistic plan. Setting sensible and pragmatic goals is the first step in achieving them. The purpose of creating an action plan is not to make you a gold medalist overnight, but to gradually help you move toward your goal. Focus on the direction you want to move in, and start off by taking small steps. Creating stepping stones in the path to your goals will generate momentum. This will increase your confidence and in turn make you take more action. As long as you keep moving in the right direction, you are bound to achieve your goals sooner or later.

After completing Step 4 you will have a concrete plan with actions and dates that you can start to implement.

ACTION PLANNING

It is time to record the steps you will take toward becoming a highly valued and truly successful project management leader.

Before you do so, please remind yourself of your vision and mission (Step 1) and the gap analyses you performed at the end of Steps 2 and 3. Think about the following questions:

➤ What do you want to achieve as a project manager, and who do you ultimately want to be?

➤ What do you need to do in order to honor your vision and mission statement?

➤ Which personal and professional skills and attributes do you need to leverage or improve?

➤ What do you need to start doing or stop doing?

➤ Which limiting factors do you need to get rid of?

Set your standards high: decide to be the best at what you do. The top people in every field got there by continually working on themselves and by taking action. You can do the same.

Have you ever asked yourself why you are not already the best at what you do? The reason is probably not lack of talent or experience—rather, you have not yet *decided* to be the best! So decide now that you want to fulfill your ambitions and be excellent at what you do. Decide that you want to become one of the top project management leaders within your field.

Action Plan

Date:_____

1. Select the three most important areas for improvement (goals) you need to work on right now as a project manager. List them below.

Goal 1: _____

Goal 2: _____

Goal 3: _____

2. Define what "10 out of 10" looks like for each of the three goals or development areas. How will you know when you have reached each of these goals? What will you be doing and feeling, and what will you have?

Goal 1: _____

_____

_____

Goal 2: _____

_____

_____

Goal 3: _____

_____

3. Prioritize your goals in terms of importance. Which one will have the biggest positive impact on your current performance once you start working toward it?

Priority 1: _____

Priority 2: _____

Priority 3: _____

4. On a scale of 1 to 10, how would you rate your performance within each of the three areas for improvement? Record your score below.

Rating for area 1:
_____

Rating for area 2:
_____

Rating for area 3:
_____

5. What do you need to do to move just one step closer to your top three goals?

Next step for Goal 1:
_____

_____

Next step for Goal 2:
_____

_____

Next step for Goal 3:
_____

_____

6. Who or what can help you with these next steps?
_____

_____

_____

_____

7. For each of the next steps you have identified, set a date and a time for when you will take the action.

    Set time aside for these actions now. Schedule them in your personal planner and visualize yourself working on them at the scheduled time. Make sure the time frames you have scheduled are realistic and take into consideration your other commitments.

Date/time frame for Action 1:
_____

Date/time frame for Action 2:
_____

Date/time frame for Action 3:
_____

8. For each of the actions you have identified, ask yourself how committed you are to carrying them out.

What could get in your way?

What do you need to do to avoid any roadblocks?

What do you need to commit to in order to follow through with the actions?

_____

_____

_____

9. How will you reward yourself once you have carried out the actions?

_____

_____

_____

10. Set a date for when you will review this action plan. On that date, you will go back and revisit this sheet and create a new set of ratings for your three chosen development areas. You will compare those ratings to today's—and you may be astonished at the progress you have made. Schedule the review in your calendar now.

Date for Next Review:_____

Visualize yourself as the project manager you want to become. See yourself as a "10 out of 10" in the three areas for improvement you have identified. Keep this image in mind, and make a decision to carry out your actions by the date you have set.

DRAW YOUR GOAL MAP

Making simple drawings to illustrate your vision and mission statement, overall goals, and chosen actions can have a profound impact on your subconscious mind and your ability to achieve what you set out to do. This is because images appeal to the right side of your brain, while words appeal to the left side of your brain. Engaging both sides of the brain gives you the best conditions for working with and reaching your goals.

Use the template in Figure 4-1 to write and draw the key elements of your vision and mission statement, your goals (development areas), and the actions you will take to achieve them. Use symbols, images, and keywords that best illustrate your mission and goals. Use as many colors as you want.

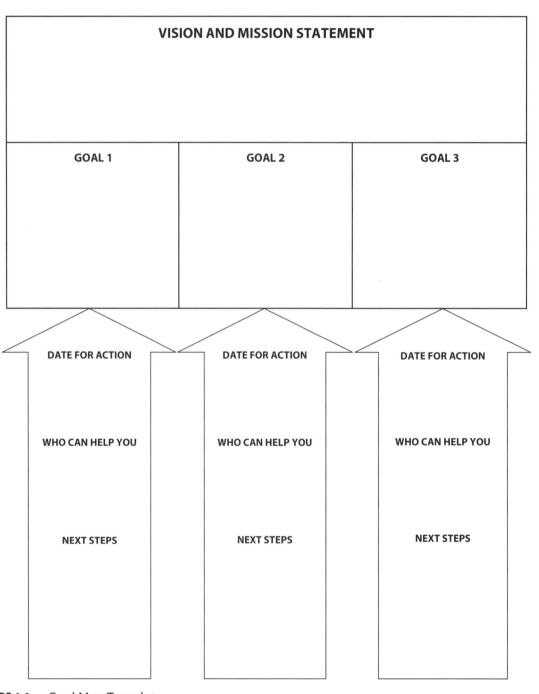

FIGURE 4-1. Goal Map Template

TAKE ACTION AND CREATE STEPPING STONES FOR SUCCESS

All you need to do now is to focus on your actions. It is when you apply your skills and knowledge in your day-to-day work that you learn, grow, and develop. So take action, observe the results, and learn from them. Try out new techniques, adopt new attitudes, spend your time more effectively, and feel good about yourself. You are being proactive and taking steps to grow as a person, leader, and project manager.

If the actions you have chosen require you to block out big chunks of time (e.g., to acquire a new skill), then be realistic about how much you can achieve during a specific time frame. It is better to start with modest goals and over-deliver than to set unrealistic targets that you miss.

> *Achieving your goals is all about creating small successes that you can build on. Create stepping stones, and keep moving in the right direction. That is all you need to think about. One step in the right direction will automatically lead to the next.*

To maintain momentum and keep yourself on course, share your actions with someone you trust and ask him or her to have regular review sessions with you. If you have a mentor, work with him or her as much as you can. Otherwise, ask a friend or a coworker for guidance, and make sure you emphasize the importance of the role. He or she should be there to support and motivate you when you need it.

If some of your goals are ongoing (e.g., something you do every day or every time you interface with a specific person), then create reminders to help you establish a new routine. You can do this by writing sticky notes, using an electronic reminder system on your computer, wearing something around your wrist, or doing anything else that will remind you of your actions. Make it as easy as possible to create a new habit, and remember to promise yourself small rewards when you make progress.

Fully commit yourself to your action plan. Keep visualizing the end goal and remind yourself why you want to change and what the benefits are. Let the "new you" be the first thing you think about in the morning and the last thing you think about at night.

Close your eyes and visualize who you want to be. Then act as if you are already that person.

Watch yourself as you start to feel more confident and move closer to success. And do not worry if some things do not turn out as expected. Be resilient. Keep refining your ways until you find what works for you, your team, and your project.

Guiding Practices: Learn More about Project Management and Leadership Techniques

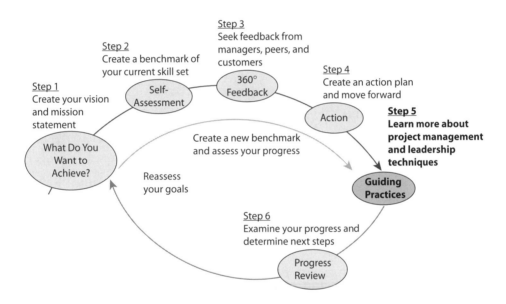

The purpose of Step 5 is to provide you with further background information, guiding practices, and exercises to help you move forward even faster.

On the subsequent pages, you will find information and exercises on everything from project initiation and scope management to team motivation and stress management. Focus your attention on the areas in which you need to improve the most. Think about new techniques and tools you want to apply in your work.

The aim is not to tell you how you *should* do things, but rather how you *could* do things. Focus on the outcomes you desire and what you want to achieve in any given situation. This workbook will give you enough information and examples to help you find the *how* and enable you to optimize the way you work.

After completing Step 5 you will have learned and internalized new methods that will help you reach your goals even faster. I will ask you to make a note of your key learning points and summarize what you will do to incorporate them into the way you currently work.

WHAT CAUSES POOR PROJECT DELIVERY AND FAILURE?

In order for you to become as effective and successful a project manager as possible, you must learn to avoid some of the most common project pitfalls. The first step is to understand why a large percentage of projects are late, come in over budget, or fall short of delivering the products they were designed to produce. The second step is to address the underlying causes for failure so that your project has every chance of succeeding.

Exercise: Project Failure

1. Take a step back and think about all of the different projects you have been involved in to date. Make a note of them on a separate piece of paper.

2. As a fun exercise, imagine that your mission is to sabotage these projects and to make them fail. How would you do that? Brainstorm all the things you could do (or omit doing) and put your thoughts down on paper.

3. Have you ever known someone to knowingly or unknowingly sabotage a project?

4. How many of the projects you have been involved in have not been delivered on time, on budget, or to the required quality? Why did they derail?

Many factors can contribute to project failure, and often there is more than one factor at play. Here are some of the most common reasons projects fail. The list is not definitive, so feel free to add to it.

➤ **Lack of solid business case and strategy.** Sometimes, projects are kicked off even though the business case or business strategy is weak or incomplete or has not been fully thought through. This may be especially common on internal projects. If the business case and rationale behind your project are not robust and clear, the project will be much more prone to changes or cancellation if, for example, a new business owner joins, business priorities change, or the project turns out to require more resources than anticipated.

➤ **Lack of executive direction and buy-in.** The project's steering committee is responsible for executive decision-making and for providing high-level direction. This is the group to which you escalate issues that you cannot deal with on your own. If this group is not supportive of the project, does not accept ownership and responsibility, or does not allocate the necessary time and energy, your project is likely to suffer or even fail as a result.

➤ **Lack of end user involvement.** Users can be very busy people with regular day jobs. They are not always given sufficient time to devote to the project. Without involvement from the end users (or their representatives), requirements specification, user testing, and product quality are likely to suffer, and the user community may feel less committed to the end product. If the users are not sufficiently committed or if they cannot clearly articulate what they want, you will have limited ways to ensure the quality of your deliverables.

➤ **Failure to adequately identify and document requirements.** Some projects have high-level, vague, or poorly documented requirements. If design or build work is kicked off too early, without the core business requirements having been adequately identified, documented, and agreed on by the client, your project has every chance of producing the wrong product and consuming more time and money during testing and rework phases than planned.

➤ **Inadequate focus on QA and testing.** In order to successfully complete a project and deliver its products and benefits in line with the client's expectations, you must use a structured approach to QA and testing. Projects can and do fail if this is not done. It is not enough to trust that your team will correctly develop what the users have specified or to leave testing until the last minute. Skipping certain types of testing and going straight to user acceptance testing also can be a recipe for failure.

➤ **Poor planning and estimation processes.** A project that is poorly planned and estimated is risky, difficult, and can lead to project failure. Without a decent plan and estimate, resources cannot be managed and organized, risks cannot be mitigated, dates and budgets cannot be forecasted, effective reporting cannot take place, and the measures of success will be flawed from the outset.

➤ **Lack of success criteria.** If your project's success criteria are too vague or are not properly understood or formalized, your project is likely to fail. You simply cannot hit a target if you do not know what that target looks like and what is expected from you. The same often holds true if you have not defined what the success criteria are for each stage of your project or for go-live.

➤ **Failure to effectively manage changes to scope.** Incorporating necessary scope changes into a project is often a prerequisite for delivering a fit-for-purpose product. Problems may arise when scope management is too informal or, on the contrary, overly formal. If scope is not controlled, changes will creep in unnoticed, and budget, schedule, and quality may be adversely affected. However, if management of scope is too rigid, there will be insufficient flexibility to accommodate requests for changes, which in turn could end up jeopardizing the quality of the end product.

➤ **Poor risk and issue management.** A project is often a hugely complex undertaking with lots of interdependencies, assumptions, and constraints. Circumstances change, new risks are identified, and some of them turn into issues that may prevent your project from progressing. If you are not able to effectively manage risks and issues and make decisions about how to progress when circumstances change, your project will likely suffer severe consequences.

➤ **Inadequate resources.** A project can fall apart quickly if the team is not sufficiently skilled or if certain key roles on the project cannot be filled due to an ineffective hiring process or limited talent in the market. In addition, team members might leave the project if they feel neglected or unappreciated, which in turn could jeopardize the execution and success of the project.

➤ **Poor definition of roles and responsibilities.** If a project is to operate effectively, everyone must know not only what their own roles and responsibilities are, but also what the other players are doing—or not doing. If roles and responsibilities are unclear, people will be less effective and accountable and will become frustrated, and tasks will fall through the cracks. You will not be able to plan, communicate, and manage effectively.

➤ **Too long or unrealistic time frames.** When project time frames become too long, the project can lose momentum, or you can end up delivering products and services that are no longer of any benefit to the customer and organization. On the other hand, senior managers may set unrealistically short project time frames in an attempt to speed up delivery, without considering the volume of work that needs to be done. As a result, the project is delivered late, or a significant number of features must be cut out.

➤ **Poor leadership and ability to focus the team.** As a project manager, your role includes an obligation to liaise with the customer, fully understand the goals and objectives of the project, set the course, and keep the team and stakeholders focused on the end deliverables. If you do not fully understand or believe in the end product, do not engage the stakeholders, or do not have sufficient experience or willingness to lead a project, you will not be able to inspire, motivate, and focus the team, and your project is likely to suffer as a result.

➤ **Poor or delayed decisionmaking.** A project can only be managed effectively if decisions are made in an informed and timely fashion. Problems can arise when you delay making a decision for fear of making the wrong one or when you rely too heavily on obtaining consensus. You may depend on the expertise of others before making a decision, but if you rely too much on decisionmaking by consensus, your project could fail while you wait for everyone to reach agreement. The best design or solution is often the result of analysis, not consensus.

> **Questions**
>
> - Which of the above reasons for failure or warning signs are most evident on your current project?
> - What would the short-term, medium-term, and long-term consequences be if nothing were done about these warning signs?
> - What can you do to start addressing these potential problems and avoid the risk of failure?

The next section, Guiding Principles for Project Management Success, explains how you can address the underlying causes for failure and lead your project to success.

GUIDING PRINCIPLES FOR PROJECT MANAGEMENT SUCCESS

Project management knowledge, tools, and processes are not enough to make your project succeed. You need to get away from your desk and get your hands dirty. Liaise with the team, users, and stakeholders, and actively focus them on the objectives and outcomes of the project. Work to remove blockages and build effective personal relationships.

One of the worst things you can do is to assume that everything is OK—that product quality will come automatically and that your team is happy and motivated. Instead, you need to be positively skeptical: constantly ask if you have *proof* that things are working well. Be proactive and investigate the true state of your project. Ask yourself the following questions:

➤ How do I know that my team is motivated and fully embraces the objectives of the project?

➤ How do I know that what we are developing is what the users want and need?

➤ How do I know that risks are being effectively identified and mitigated?

➤ How do I know that my customer is happy with the way the project is progressing?

➤ How do I know that we will hit the projected deadline and deliver the project within budget?

To become a highly valued and truly successful project management leader, you need to adopt a curious and positive mindset, and you need to keep your finger on the pulse of your projects at all times.

Exercise: Project Success Factors

Think about a project you have been involved in that worked out really well.

1. What factors contributed the most to its success?
2. What tools, technique, talents, and abilities did you successfully make use of?
3. Compile a list of the ten most important factors in project success.

Below, I have summarized some of the factors that contribute the most to successful project delivery. Read through them, and note the principles that you could make better use of to enhance project control and, in turn, your value as a project manager. Rate how effectively you make use of each principle today.

While most of the factors below are directly under your control as a project manager, some of them are not. For example, in most cases, you cannot completely control senior stakeholders' buy-in, organizational hiring policies, or the line management of project staff who do not report to you. When you do not have direct control, you will need to influence others to reach a resolution.

Begin with the end in mind

To successfully deliver a project, you must know the project's end game. Confirm that the project has a valid and sound business case, define its scope, and really understand the end product and its purpose. Often, the business case will have been written by a senior executive before you get involved in the project. But although you may not be the owner of the business case, you are obligated to ensure that a business case exists and that it is sufficiently detailed and sound. Ask to see it, and ask questions if you feel it is too weak.

Investigate whether any existing business processes need to change as result of the project, and clarify what needs to happen for the end product to be successfully transitioned into the client's business. Identify all the main stakeholders, and determine how the project's benefits will impact each of them. Get agreement from the stakeholders about how to define and measure the end goal, and confirm that the products you plan to deliver at each stage of the project will actually fulfill the business needs and provide the expected benefits.

> ➤ To what extent do you begin with the end in mind? (Give yourself a score between 1 and 10.)

> ➤ Do you fully understand your project's end product, its purpose, and the business case?

> ➤ Have the project's in-scope and out-of-scope items been clearly defined?

Win the support of your stakeholders

To deliver a project effectively and successfully, the project sponsor and steering committee must have the authority to determine the project's direction and to approve project deliverables, spending, and resources. They must live up to this responsibility by being active participants who provide support and guidance when needed. Build strong relationships with your stakeholders and win their support by spending time with each person individually, striving to understand their concerns and viewpoints. Provide stakeholders with the information they need and in a format they want.

> *Give your stakeholders regular project updates, and never be afraid to disclose risks or issues or to ask for help. The true test of a confident project manager is having the courage to be open and ask for help.*

Involve your stakeholders in the project as much as you can, and hold them accountable for actions they take on. Ask them to help define and sign off on key deliverables and to make decisions and resolve urgent issues that you cannot handle on your own.

When you involve your stakeholders and make them take ownership, they become part of the solution. They will feel responsible for the project's success and will do everything they can to make sure it happens.

> ➤ To what extent are you winning the support of your stakeholders?

> ➤ How good are you at highlighting issues and asking senior stakeholders for help?

> ➤ To what extent do you hold your stakeholders accountable for their actions and responsibilities?

Understand and focus on project success criteria

Project success generally means that products are delivered on time, within budget, and at a level of quality that is acceptable to the client. It is essential for you to establish what the project's success criteria are and keep the team's attention focused on achieving them. You must understand the parameters and constraints that apply to the project and how they apply to each stage of the project and for go-live.

Put yourself in the shoes of each stakeholder, and figure out what it would take for each of them to say that the project was a success at each major stage. Then confirm that the stakeholders' success criteria are congruent with the project's measurable objectives. Bear in mind that not all success criteria can be top priority, so ask the project sponsor to set clear priorities.

➤ To what extent do you understand and focus on the project's success criteria?

➤ Are the criteria specific and measurable, and do they have relative priorities?

Focus on product quality

The key to successful delivery and quality management is carefully defining scope, detailed requirements, and acceptance criteria by liaising closely with the end users and continually confirming that the products you are developing match these criteria. Establish a close working relationship with the client and users, and keep them involved throughout the project. Paint as comprehensive a picture as you can of the finished deliverables. Avoid vague descriptions at all costs; illustrate the end product using models, prototypes, or storyboards; and use requirements documents to clarify the details. Make sure everyone agrees with the vision you are defining for the deliverables.

When everyone knows what the finished deliverables will look like, plan to carry out comprehensive tests involving independent testers, if possible, as well as end users. Test and verify functionality continuously throughout the project, and set aside time in your schedule for rework after each test activity.

➤ To what extent is your team focused on product quality?

➤ Are the requirements detailed enough, and have the users been sufficiently involved in defining them?

➤ How have you modeled or illustrated the finished deliverables?

➤ What is your process for continuously confirming that what you are developing matches the users' needs and requirements?

Get the best people involved, and value your team

Delivering a successful project is heavily dependent upon having a successful team. Retain the most driven, experienced, and best-qualified people, and focus on helping them thrive.

Show them you value them, protect them from internal politics, and give them the training, tools, and working conditions they need to apply their talents. Find out what motivates each individual, and find a way to tap into his or her hidden potential. Make sure that working on the project is a worthwhile experience for everyone involved.

At a more practical level, cross-train staff, facilitate knowledge sharing, and plan for succession. Ring-fence resources when possible so that you do not have to share them with other projects. If your team members must work on several projects, fight for their time, and ask senior managers to set project priorities to avoid conflicts.

➤ Do you have the best possible people on your project?

➤ In what ways do you value and motivate your team?

➤ What are you doing to ring-fence resources and avoid resourcing conflicts?

Be proactive in the identification and resolution of risks and issues

You must stay on top of risks and issues so that they do not get out of hand and inadvertently affect project quality, time, and cost. The importance of this part of your job cannot be overemphasized. Be proactive and continuously identify and mitigate risks by spending time with each team member and stakeholder. Ask them what is worrying them, discuss different scenarios, and brainstorm events and factors that could jeopardize the success of the project. Then carry out root cause and impact analysis and identify options for how you can best move forward.

Secure buy-in and support from your stakeholders, and ask for guidance and direction when you need it. Some problems can only be resolved at a steering committee level, so do not hesitate to share them with executives. Always encourage open and honest communication, and do not assign blame for issues that arise.

➤ To what extent do you proactively work to identify and resolve risks and issues?

➤ How actively do you involve the team and stakeholders in the risks and issues process?

Deliver tangible benefits gradually

Usually, projects have a greater chance of success the earlier you start to deliver real benefits to the customer and end users. The traditional way of delivering a project, in which products are tested and delivered toward the end of the project, can be risky. If possible, use an iterative approach, which breaks this pattern and enables you to build, test, and deliver functionality gradually.

Split a large project into smaller projects or phases with clear milestones and deliverables. Focus on the highest-value and highest-risk items first. Plan for early successes, and closely track your milestones. You want to have fast-moving deliverables so that you can experience the rewards of hitting smaller milestones.

Good news on project progress is also something that should be delivered gradually. Instead of giving a lot of positive reports one month and none the next, consider managing the flow of positive information so that there is always a little piece of good news on which to report.

> ➤ Do you deliver products, news, and benefits gradually?

> ➤ Is your project sufficiently iterative to promote quality and minimize overall risk?

Provide good estimates, and build sufficient contingency into the schedule

You will recall that it is essential to project success that your project starts off on the right foot and that you have a good understanding of how much it is likely to cost and how long it is likely to take to complete. Use a variety of estimation techniques and tools and involve team members and senior managers in the estimation process.

Break large tasks and products into smaller and much more detailed tasks; this will make it easier to develop accurate estimates. Build in sufficient contingency and remember to factor in all phases, roles, and activities. Convert estimates of effort into actual person-hours of duration and account for the fact that no team is ever 100 percent effective. Push back on sponsors and managers who want you to commit to a delivery date that is not feasible. Provide best-case and worst-case costs and dates, not just one figure. This will give you more leeway and will increase your chances of delivering within the agreed parameters.

> ➤ Have you provided good and realistic estimates for your project?

> ➤ What have you done to build sufficient contingency into your estimates and schedule?

Have realistic, transparent, and up-to-date plans

Regardless of whether you use a traditional or iterative project methodology, realistic project planning is a must if you want to succeed. An effective project plan is much more than just a schedule of work. It must be based on clear requirements and sound estimates—and it should explain, in plain English, what is to be accomplished and delivered, what methods and resources will be used, how quality will be measured, and when the products will be delivered. The plan should contain frequent milestones that will allow for gradual delivery of benefits to the users, and the progress of these milestones should be tracked and reported.

The planning process must continue throughout the project and be adjusted to account for progress and approved changes to scope. If applicable, keep a detailed plan of work for the near future and an outline of a plan for the far future. There may be little point planning in detail for what will happen in three months' time, as things will change. Just adjust and add more detail to your outline plan as you move forward.

Involve the entire team in the planning process, and make sure everyone has access to the plans. A perfect plan has little value if no one knows about it.

➤ How realistic, transparent, and up to date are your project plans?

➤ Do your project plans address project scheduling and include descriptions of scope, acceptance criteria, QA, resource planning, and controls?

Provide metrics and honest project reporting

Metrics are vital indicators for keeping projects on course. They enable you to accurately report on project progress and help you spot trends that you might otherwise overlook.

Key metrics include *cost ratio,* a measure of actual costs versus planned costs, and *effort ratio,* a measure of actual progress (or effort) versus planned progress. These metrics (often referred to as earned value) let you know where you are versus where you should be. Compare your cost metrics to your effort metrics to see if you are making progress at the same rate you are spending money. (Note that the two do not necessarily need to line up exactly.)

Always include these metrics in your status reports, along with an honest explanation of current risks and issues. At steering committee meetings, make sure you highlight problem areas so your stakeholders can help you resolve them.

➤ To what extent do you make use of project metrics?

➤ How honest and accurate are your project reports?

Establish clear controls and sign-off points

To successfully manage any project, it is important to establish clear controls for effectively managing cost, time, and quality. Make sure invoices and time sheets are signed off and costs are accurately tracked. Get your stakeholders to sign off on the project definition document and ensure requirements specifications are signed off before development begins.

Have a clear process for prioritizing, planning, and assigning new work items and never assume a task has been completed until its quality has been independently verified and signed off. If you run an agile project, have clear start and end points for your iterations. Clearly define sign-off points between various project phases, and make sure everyone knows what the criteria are for closing down one stage and moving to the next. For recurring tasks and activities, develop checklists, templates, and lightweight procedures to help your team better complete the work.

➤ To what extent have you established clear controls and sign-off points around scope, quality, cost, and time?

➤ Are people adhering to these controls?

Monitor and control changes

To manage a project well, you must embrace and control change at all levels. Circumstances external to the project change, users' needs change, dependencies change, and people change jobs. The reason it is so important to stay on top of changes is that the contract or baseline (as documented in the project definition document) for the product you have committed to delivering must be aligned with what you are actually going to deliver.

When something changes, do not resist; analyze the cause and the impact of the change on existing budget, schedule, and quality. Log all change requests, and never start any significant new work until the steering committee has approved it. Renegotiate the contract (i.e., the parameters in the project definition document) when material changes occur, even if you feel uncomfortable doing so.

➤ Do you monitor and control changes in an effective manner?

➤ Do you ask the steering committee to approve all material changes to scope, budget, and time?

Focus on project organization and communication

If a project is to have the best chance of succeeding, you must establish and formalize roles and responsibilities and communicate these to everyone in an effective manner. Clearly explain team members' and stakeholders' roles and what is expected from them. Clarify the purpose of key forums, such as the steering committee, as this will help ensure that your sponsor and senior stakeholders live up to their assigned responsibilities.

Write a communication plan that details the different types of project information, who will receive this information, and how often. Base the plan on feedback from your team and stakeholders so that you can tailor communications to their individual needs.

➤ To what extent do you focus on project organization and communication?

➤ Do all team members and stakeholders know who does what and understand the flow of communication?

Continuously review and improve your approach

Highly valued and truly successful project management leaders continually seek to improve the way they run their projects. Regular project reviews provide opportunities for you and your team to reflect on how the last iteration or phase went: What worked well and what do you need to improve on going forward? Encourage honest feedback and create a climate in which team members feel safe reporting how they think the project is being run and managed. Listen to comments and new ideas with an open mind. Ensure that these reviews do not become a forum for assigning blame for previous problems. Instead, keep asking, What can we learn from our mistakes, and what can we do to avoid this problem going forward?

Review your tools, techniques, and processes and how you interact with one another. Look at the project's success criteria: Are you within budget, are you on time, and is the quality of your products as expected? Seek feedback from the sponsor, end users, and senior stakeholders. Do a final review when you close down the project, and write up a report on your findings. Circulate it to senior management to help improve future project delivery.

➤ Do you continually review and improve your approach to managing projects?

➤ Do you actively encourage feedback from all parties so that you can learn from past issues and mistakes?

Be the best you can in all that you do

To be a truly successful project manager, you must love what you do and strive to set a great personal example for others to follow. When you are passionate, positive, and proactive, others will notice your example and want to follow. Strive for personal effectiveness and consistently focus on those things that matter the most to the well-being of your team and to the success of your project.

Remember that less is more, so keep things as simple as you can. For instance, plan things in detail for only the immediate future. Delegate tasks that will help grow and motivate the people you are delegating to, and give people the support they need to succeed. Make decisions that are consistent, well-thought-out, and based on analysis rather than consensus.

Proactively identify and resolve risks and issues and think of yourself as the project's champion and ambassador. Maintain a positive attitude and never make a commitment you cannot keep. Be honest and approachable, and always treat others the way you want to be treated.

➤ To what extent do you strive to be the best in everything you do?

➤ Do you try to set a great personal example?

➤ To what extent do you help grow and motivate others?

➤ Are you passionate, positive, and proactive in your work?

Questions

- How did you rate your current use of each of the above principles of success?
- Which of the principles do you need to make more use of in your daily work?
- How can you start doing that?

PROJECT SUCCESS CRITERIA

Now we will look at the importance of extracting and validating your stakeholders' success criteria on an ongoing basis. Doing so will increase your chances of delivering your project in line with expectations and help you avoid the perception of failure.

Test Yourself

- What are success criteria, and why are they important to projects?
- Name three examples of success criteria from your current project.

To successfully deliver your project and satisfy *all* of your stakeholders' needs and requirements, you need to elicit and understand all of their success criteria. That means *understanding all of the conditions that must be met for the project to be considered successful.*

While this may sound like common sense, it is not always common practice. As you will see, capturing success criteria is further complicated by the fact that the customer will probably not verbalize all of the project's success criteria, and your stakeholders may not be fully aware of all of the factors that influence their definition of project success.

Questions

- Think about the project you are currently working on. What are the most important success criteria for this project, according to the sponsor? On what will the project's success be judged?
- Have these success criteria been openly stated, prioritized, documented, and circulated to all parties (e.g., in your project definition document)?
- How confident are you that these are the *only* criteria on which your project's success will be judged? That is, could other factors come to light once the project has been delivered?

When judging whether a project was successful or not, we look at whether the stated goals and objectives were met and whether the project was delivered within the agreed parameters. These goals and objectives are typically documented in the project definition document.

The assessment of whether a project is successful or not usually happens during the last phase of the project—the closeout or closedown phase. In this phase, you officially ask your stakeholders to accept delivery of the products and to agree that the project can be closed down. This is also the phase in which you review the project and assess to what extent the project was a success and whether it met its objectives.

Traditionally, projects are said to succeed when they are delivered on time, on budget, and to the required quality. This means that they satisfy the user's requirements and deliver the outcomes and benefits presented in the business case. Note that *quality* refers to the finished product. Were all in-scope features delivered, and were they fit for purpose?
A project's success criteria might include:

➤ Specific, measurable business benefits that represent dollar savings—for example, an annual head-count savings of $200,000 after implementation of a project to automate an order-handling process.

➤ The delivery of specific products that contain certain measurable features—for example, an enhanced system that can process 1,000 orders per minute, meets all high- and medium-priority requirements, and has passed user acceptance testing.

➤ Delivery on a specific date or within a certain time frame—for example, on October 1, 2013.

➤ Delivery within a certain budget—for example, $1 million.

It is your job as a project manager to elicit the success criteria from the sponsor and main stakeholders and to get consensus from the steering committee regarding their relative priority. Relative priorities are important because you will probably have to make trade-offs as the project progresses.

If, for instance, you are working to a fixed budget that cannot be exceeded, and costs are increasing unexpectedly, you have to either cut back on scope or quality or save on execution costs in order to stay within budget. Cutting back on execution costs, for example by finding cheaper resources or materials, could affect the project's time frame; the project may take longer to complete.

If, on the other hand, time and quality are the most important success criteria, it might be difficult to operate within a fixed budget. Imagine that a quality issue is identified and that it has to be fixed within the original time frame specified for the delivery. To do this, your

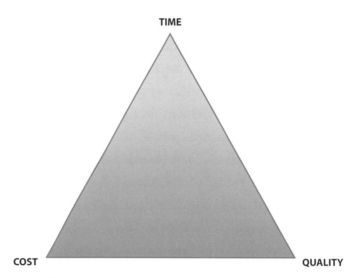

FIGURE 5-1. Time-Cost-Quality Triangle

only option may be to recruit more resources (and increase cost) to get the work done on time. In other words, something will have to give, and that something will be the factor of least importance to the project sponsor and the stakeholders.

The time-cost-quality triangle in Figure 5-1 illustrates the interdependent relationship between these three parameters.

Depending on the nature of your project, factors other than time, cost, and quality may matter to its success; for instance, *how* the project arrived at its end goal. Imagine a project that delivered real benefits on time, but that was executed in a haphazard way, with poor communication and a lot of disputes. Would your stakeholders perceive that project as successful?

> *To uncover the criteria that will really affect how your project will be judged, ask each of your stakeholders what would make them perceive the project as a success. Some people may give you a textbook answer, so challenge their response and dig deeper.*

Remember that the success of your project will ultimately be measured by whether your sponsor and stakeholders *feel* they got the benefits they wanted in a way they expected. So, to avoid the perception of failure, not only do you need to clearly define the objective success criteria (such as time, cost, and quality), but you also need to turn any subjective and qualitative feelings and statements into quantitative and measurable conditions. Only when you quantify all objectives and success criteria will you truly know what is expected of you.

When analyzing the success criteria, make sure they relate back to the project's purposes and that they are as specific and measurable as possible. That will make it easier for you to deliver against them.

Be careful not to consider only concrete project outcomes, such as particular functions, products, or devices. The real success criteria may be related to whether the customers are satisfied or whether the business generates extra revenue as a result of your project. To ensure you capture all of the success criteria, concrete and otherwise, elicit and document the acceptance criteria for each phase or stage of the project. These could include specific criteria that determine when the initiation phase is complete, when the product is fit to be released or delivered, and when the entire project is complete and can be closed down.

Make sure that you always highlight the assumptions that serve as the basis for the success criteria to the members of the steering committee. This will help them appreciate the complexities of the project and the challenges of your role. In a more practical sense, it will also enable the steering committee to approve changes to the project's constraints and acceptance criteria, if required. As an example, imagine that you have agreed with your customer that they will provide you with certain resources to help you deliver a certain product at a certain time and cost. If the customer does not provide these resources per your agreement, you must raise this as an issue to your steering committee so that you can adjust your constraints (e.g., cost constraints) to account for this change.

However, do not assume that you are safe just because you highlighted the assumptions. The best way to address them is to treat them as risks and to mitigate them to the best of your ability.

Judging whether a project was a success is not always a straightforward or logical matter. On the one hand, there are clear successes: a high-quality product is delivered in line with business needs and on time and budget. On the other hand, there are clear failures: for instance, quality is so poor or the delivery so late that the product becomes useless or financially infeasible. In between these extremes, there is a vast grey area of projects that meet some but not all of their success criteria. If the outcomes and benefits of your project exceed expectations, the project could be perceived as a success even if it was delivered late or over budget. However, the opposite could also be true. You may have delivered a great project, but if the project sponsors, stakeholders, or users somehow think your project has failed, then it has.

To guard against the perception of failure, spend time with your stakeholders and understand what matters to them. Feel what they feel and see what they see, and do your best to honor their expectations.

Another great way to guard against the perception of failure is to involve your stakeholders as much as possible and make them take ownership. When you make them feel as if they are part of the team and part of the solution, they will have a stake in the project. Consequently, they will feel more responsible for the project's successes and failures and will want to work with you to make the project succeed.

On a final note, make sure everyone knows about all of the good stuff you are actually delivering. Promote your project, and celebrate and communicate every little success along the way. Be an ambassador for the project—for instance, by sending out catchy newsletters or gathering people for celebratory drinks or snacks, if appropriate. Do not let false modesty deter you; that could give people the impression that the project is not delivering anything.

Exercise 1: Envisioning Project Success

1. Take a minute to imagine the end state of the project you are currently working on.

2. Imagine that the project has been successfully delivered and that all stakeholders are satisfied. Not only have the objective success criteria (such as time, cost, and quality) been met, but the project is also perceived as a success. The stakeholders are happy about the way the project was led and managed.

3. What would need to happen on your project today in order for everyone to eventually be able to say that it was a success?

_____

_____

_____

Exercise 2: Documenting and Rating Success Criteria

Let's explore a structured approach for identifying all of the success criteria on your project.

1. In the table below, list all of the stakeholders of your project in the left-hand column. Include everyone who has a vested interest in the project, directly or indirectly. This includes everyone on the steering committee, users, vendors, department heads, team members, and yourself. List the most important stakeholders with the most influence first.

2. Write down each stakeholder's success criteria—the things that would make each stakeholder see the project as a success. Do not focus only on objective measures (such as quality or time); also think about the subjective measures each stakeholder cares about. What would make them *feel* that the project is successful? Use one line for each success criterion.

3. When the list is complete, provide a relative rating for each success criterion you have entered. Rate the criterion that you believe is of the highest importance to the project #1; rate the second-most important #2, and so on.

STAKEHOLDER	SUCCESS CRITERIA	RELATIVE RATING
Sponsor	*Project should ideally be delivered on October 1, but must be delivered no later than November 10.*	
Sponsor	*Project should ideally be delivered within a budget of $1 million, but the budget must not exceed $1.1 million.*	
User Group A	*Solution must comply with government rules and regulations as outlined in compliance document A1.*	
Program Manager	*Project must employ an agile development methodology in line with stated department procedures.*	

Questions

- What can you do to verify that the success criteria you just listed are in fact the true success criteria? Who would you need to talk to?
- What would need to happen to get the steering committee to agree to a relative priority for the success criteria?
- What are you doing to guard your project against the perception of failure?

MANAGING RISKS AND ISSUES

Risk and issue management is a fundamental part of a project manager's job. It is an activity that needs to be attended to weekly, or sometimes even daily or hourly – and it is a discipline that really puts your positive and proactive mindset to the test.

> *The effective management of risks is all about being proactive; you need to identify and tackle potential concerns before they turn into problems.*
>
> *The effective management of issues requires you to stay focused and calm while deciding on the best option for moving forward.*

As a project manager, you are ideally positioned to catch and address potential or real blockages so that the project can continue as planned. But this is not a mechanical process to be carried out on a spreadsheet while sitting behind your desk. It is something you need to do in close cooperation with your team and stakeholders if you want to succeed. Although you are responsible for the facilitation and management of the risks and issues process, you cannot and should not do it in isolation. When you involve your team and stakeholders, not only do you improve the quality of the process, but you also help promote a shared sense of responsibility for the project's successes and failures.

Test Yourself

- How would you describe the difference between a risk and an issue?
- What steps would you say are involved in managing a risk?

A **risk** is a potential threat or opportunity that could affect the success of your project and that has not yet occurred. It has some probability of occurring in the future. If it occurs, it could have a material impact on your project's success criteria (e.g., time, cost, quality). The possibilities that key team members will leave the project or that your proposed solution will not meet the customer's performance expectations are examples of risks.

An **issue** is an actual problem that is currently affecting the project—for example, a key team member *has* left the project with no one to take over his work, or your solution has been proven to not meet the customer's performance criteria. Those are real issues. Risks can turn into issues if not fully mitigated.

The process for managing a risk is different from that for managing an issue. First, let us look at how to manage a risk.

RISK MANAGEMENT

The importance of proper risk management cannot be overemphasized. Proactively identifying and mitigating risks means that fewer issues will arise on your project. It is always much easier and more effective to manage a risk than an issue. As Tim Lister and Tom DeMarco put it, "Risk management is how adults manage projects."[1]

The key to good risk management is to discipline yourself to take some time out on a regular basis, on your own and with your team and stakeholders, to assess everything that could impede the success of the project. You need to understand the nature of each risk you identify and its potential impact, and then determine how to best deal with it. You also have to assign an owner to each risk and follow up on any agreed-upon actions to reduce the probability of the risk materializing.

The first step in risk management is to *identify* all possible risks. Think through everything you are supposed to deliver, and identify everything that could go wrong on your way to achieving a successful outcome. Consider your success criteria, assumptions, and dependencies. Set up workshops with your team and stakeholders to identify and add more risks you did not think of yourself. You will not be able to identify all possible dangers to your project on your own.

To identify your project's risks, brainstorm and review standard risk lists and lessons learned from other projects. Some of the risks you think of will be specific to your project, while others will be generic risks that affect all projects—for example, user unavailability at the time of user acceptance testing. Pay equal attention to both sets of risks, because they could *all* turn into issues if not properly mitigated. Do not make the mistake of deliberately omitting certain risks because they are too precarious to discuss or for other reasons. Remember, it is always easier to manage a risk than to wait until it becomes an issue.

Also, consider that risks can be positive, like an early delivery or the opportunity to employ new technology. You need to determine ahead of time how you would handle and take advantage of such situations.

As you identify your risks, add them to your risk register (see Figure 5-2). Assign each a unique reference number, note the date you logged it and the category in which it fits, and briefly describe it.

Risk Log/Register									
Reference Number	Date Registered	Category	Risk Description	Probability	Impact	Owner	Risk Response	Actions	Risk Status
1		Resourcing	Risk that lead architect may leave project	High	Medium				Open
2		Budget	Risk that allocated budget may not be sufficient to complete project.	Medium	High				Open

FIGURE 5-2. Sample Risk Register

You can use the category field to filter the register for risks in the same category—for example, resourcing, budget, or a specific vendor or user group.

Step 1: Create and Complete a Risk Register

1. Choose a project you are working on.
2. Create a risk register for that project, for instance in a spreadsheet, that you can use to log all of the risks you identify. Include fields for a unique reference number, date, risk category, description, probability, impact, owner, risk response, actions, and status.
3. Brainstorm all current risks on your project with the project's key team members and stakeholders. Identify risks related to requirements, scope, technology, resources, materials, budget, quality, stakeholders, suppliers, testing, rollout, business processes, legislation, and any other elements you can think of. Include *everything* that could potentially become an issue for your project.
4. Spend time identifying positive risks as well as negative ones. Positive risks are opportunities which you need to prepare for and take advantage of.
5. Add all identified risks to your risk register.

The second step in risk management is to analyze the risks you have identified. To do this properly, consider the root cause of each risk. Keep digging until you find the ultimate source of a risk. This will make it much easier for you to determine how best to deal with it and mitigate it. For example, perhaps there is a risk of key team members leaving the organization. You might think that the best way to deal with this is to cross-train staff and line people up to fill the vacancies. While that is definitely a good idea and will help lessen the impact of the risk, you will really only be able to mitigate the probability of this risk by investigating why the team members might leave.

Carry out a thorough analysis of your risks, and identify their ultimate source. Get to the root cause and take action at that level.

In addition to carrying out a root cause analysis, it is equally important to analyze and understand the potential impact of each risk. What will happen if this risk materializes? How will it affect time, cost, quality, business benefits, and resourcing of your project?

Step 2: Conduct a Root Cause and Impact Analysis

1. Explore the root cause of each risk you have identified. To get to the root cause, keep asking why, why, why.
2. Analyze the impact of each risk on time, cost, quality, business benefits, and resourcing.
3. Add this information to the description field of your risk register.

Once you understand the nature of a risk—its root cause and potential impact—the next step is to determine the *probability* of the risk happening as well as the *level* of impact if it does happen. In other words, you need to assess how serious this risk is.

Assign a high, medium, or low rating for the probability of a risk and a separate rating for the impact. You might use the following rating system:

High probability: almost certain to occur
Medium probability: likely to occur
Low probability: unlikely to occur

High impact: would stop the project
Medium impact: would cause serious delays or rework
Low impact: would cause minor delays or rework

To help you carry out this step, refer back to the impact/probability matrix (Figure 2-6). It gives you a visual overview of the risk categories that might apply to the risks you have identified.

As mentioned, a risk with high impact and low probability is more serious than a risk with high probability and low impact.

Step 3: Determine Probability and Level of Impact

1. Determine if each risk has a high, medium, or low probability of occurring.
2. Determine the level of impact of each risk (also high, medium, or low) if it were to occur.
3. Add this information to the appropriate fields of your risk register.

Now focus on the risks with the highest probability and highest impact and determine what the risk response should be. What is the best strategy for addressing each risk, and what actions must be taken to lower its probability and lessen its impact? Encourage your team to provide feedback, and listen to their suggestions. Actions, as logged in your risk register, should include what needs to be done, who is to do it, and the date by when it should be completed.

Some high-risk items may require that you add tasks to the project plan to fully mitigate the risk (for instance, you might decide to build a prototype to mitigate the risk of using new technology). If these tasks affect your plan negatively by pushing out agreed-upon milestones, but you still deem them to be worthwhile activities, make sure you raise them to the steering committee for approval.

Sometimes the only thing you can do is to accept a risk and prepare a plan B (i.e., a contingency plan) in case it materializes. In that case, make sure everyone understands that the risk is outside your control and that there is nothing you can do to prevent it. An example of a risk you cannot control is the implementation of new government legislation that would change the requirements of your project. You may not be able to alter the probability of this happening, but you may be able to lessen its potential impact by anticipating new legislative features in your project.

Note that where risks are positive you need to consider actions that can increase rather than decrease their probability of happening. Embrace the opportunities that present themselves by preparing a plan which support them and exploit them.

Step 4: Determine Risk Responses

1. For each of the risks you identified, determine what the risk response should be. What can be done to lower the probability and lessen the impact of negative risks? Where risks are positive, what can be done to increase their probability and impact?
2. Add your findings to the risk register.
3. Assess whether any of your risk responses impact your project to such an extent that you need them to be signed off by the steering committee. If so, add them to the agenda for the next steering committee meeting.

Next, you need to assign an owner to each risk. The owner should be the person who is best suited to take mitigating action and monitor its progress. It could be anyone from within the team or steering committee—as long as he or she accepts responsibility.

Although you are responsible for facilitating the risk management process, you should not be the owner of each individual risk. Who you end up assigning as the owner depends entirely on the nature of the risk and who is best placed to deal with the risk response and mitigating actions.

Some risks, such as items external to the project or organization, or anything that relates to the business case, are best dealt with by the sponsor or business owner. Deal with as many of the medium-impact and medium-probability risks as you can at a team level, and escalate the remainder to the steering committee for ownership and resolution. Use your sense of judgment. Some risks are simply too significant to be left to the team to monitor.

Secure ownership from the best-suited executives, and hold them accountable for actions they have committed to, just as you would a team member. When you ask an executive to deal with a risk, you make him or her share the responsibility and ownership for the project. Do, however, make sure that you do not overwhelm senior executives with bad news or items you want them to resolve all at once. Give them an early heads-up, and manage their expectations before you ask them to take action and own a specific item.

Step 5: Assign Ownership of Risks

1. Assign an owner to each risk. The owner should be the person who is best placed to deal with the risk and monitor it.
2. Let the risk owners know that you have assigned them a risk, and get their buy-in.
3. Come to agreement with the risk owners about the actions that need to be taken and by when.

The final step is to continually monitor the risks you have identified along with the agreed-upon actions.

Schedule regular risk reviews with your team and stakeholders to talk through outstanding actions, remove risks that have passed, and identify new ones. Also, be aware of any changes to the nature of a risk.

Remember to always mention your main risks and mitigating actions in your progress reports and to highlight them during steering committee meetings. Not only will this show your stakeholders that you are being proactive, but you might also get valuable feedback that will help you do an even better job of managing and mitigating the risks.

Step 6: Monitor Risks

1. Set aside time, at least once a week, to review your risk register and to monitor the progress of all logged items.
2. Hold risk owners accountable for any outstanding actions.
3. Schedule follow-up meetings with your team to identify new risks and to review previous actions and risk descriptions.

4. Ensure all risks with medium-to-high impact and probability are listed on your status report.

5. Encourage discussion of the top ten risks at the steering committee meetings for executive direction and input.

ISSUE MANAGEMENT

As discussed, an issue is a specific problem that is affecting your project in a negative way right now. Perhaps a supplier has failed to deliver on time, or you have identified unexpected problems in the solution you have built for the customer. Large projects may encounter many problems, and your ability to deal with them effectively could make or break your project.

Issue management has many similarities to risk management. You need to liaise with the team when you analyze the impact of an issue and when you determine the best possible resolution for it. You also need to identify an owner and a plan of action—all of which is similar to dealing with a risk.

But there are some differences. In particular, the urgency is greater when addressing an issue. To resolve an issue effectively, you need to move fast to understand the problem and how it impacts your project. What possible solutions are there, and how would each of them affect cost, time, and quality? You often have to make a quick but informed decision, and you may need to escalate to the steering committee for advice and approval.

Some issues can be very serious and politically challenging, and your reputation, as well as your sponsor's, may be at stake. This is when you really need to leverage your good stakeholder relationships and be as open as possible. Your reputation will be in jeopardy if senior executives think you are hiding major issues.

> *When faced with a major issue, you need to show strength, determination, and good negotiation skills. Maintain a calm and positive attitude and think strategically.*

When presented with an issue, avoid making reactive, knee-jerk decisions just so it looks as if you are doing something. Gather the most capable team members to brainstorm the impact of the issue and ways of resolving it. Take your time, seek information, *then* make an informed decision. Be mindful, however, that you do not delay making a decision out of fear of making the wrong one or because you want consensus. Remember, good decisions tend to be based on analysis rather than consensus.

Bear in mind that issues are not necessarily big or catastrophic—especially when you manage to catch them before they get out of hand. As with risk management, you need to spend time with people to find out what is going on and what is holding them back. This is by far the best way of identifying issues before they spiral out of control.

Once you have identified an issue, however big or small, add it to your issue log (similar to your risk register). Thoroughly analyze its impact on time, cost, and quality, and brainstorm options for resolving it with your team. Rate the impact of the issue low, medium, or high, and assign an owner who is best placed to deal with it. As with a risk, the owner could be a team member or a senior executive, depending on the issue's nature, seriousness, and urgency.

Some issues have trivial resolutions, while others require a change of plan and approvals from the steering committee before you can move forward. Be as transparent as you can about the status of an issue with everyone involved, and follow up on the action plan until the issue has been resolved.

Once you have taken action and dealt with the urgency of the situation, you can start to ask *why* the issue came about in the first place. Look at its root cause and what you can do to prevent a similar issue from arising in the future.

Exercise: Managing Your Project's Issues

1. Spend as much time as possible with your team, and log all of the issues you come across. List anything that is preventing your project or any of your team members from moving forward, however big or small.

2. Carry out a thorough impact analysis of each issue with the appropriate people. How is this problem affecting your plan, team, budget, deliverables, and milestones? What are the negative (or positive) consequences of this issue?

3. Brainstorm options for resolving the issue and discuss what each of the options entails. The best resolution is one that addresses all of the negative consequences of the problem.

4. Decide on concrete action steps and who is to take action. Formally agree on who the owner of the issue is, and schedule the actions you have agreed on.

5. Follow up and confirm that action is being taken and that the issue is being resolved.

6. Bring all major issues to the attention of your key stakeholders, and ask for direction and approval where necessary. You may need to schedule an emergency steering committee meeting if an issue is urgent and large enough to potentially derail your project.

7. Update your issue log and status report so that everyone involved is aware of current issues, agreed-upon actions, and ownership.

8. Examine *why* the issues occurred and what you can do to prevent similar problems from happening again. Investigate causes *after* you have taken action to resolve an issue, or you could end up blaming someone without addressing the real problem.

INITIATING AND PLANNING A PROJECT

Use the guiding principles below if you are just about to start a new project and are unsure about what to do, or if you want to find out if there is anything you ought to have paid more attention to when you started the project you are currently managing.

As we have touched upon previously, starting your project off on the right foot is half the job done. If you do not know what you are developing, who you are developing it for, and how you will go about developing it, you will not be able to deliver a successful project.

Test Yourself

- What is the project initiation phase?
- Which activities normally take place during the initiation phase?
- What is a project definition document, and what information does it typically contain?
- At what point can you close the initiation phase and move into the execution, build, or construction phase?

The **project initiation phase** is the first major phase of the project, where the project's aims, objectives, scope, costs, and approach are established. This is where you define the ground rules and lay the foundation for everything that is to come later.

Note that this phase may have a different name depending on the methodology you use. I have used the term *initiation phase* to cover any project activity that aims to formally define the project before it enters into its execution, construction, or build phase.

During the initiation phase, project managers typically engage in the following activities:

➤ Understand the business drivers, objectives, and constraints for the project, and formulate the business case (if this has not already been done by the project sponsor)

➤ Liaise with the customer, domain experts, and users to understand and analyze the project's scope

➤ Identify and build a team of people who can help initiate the project

➤ Identify the stakeholders and secure their buy-in

➤ Work with the team to propose and design a target solution

➤ Demonstrate or prototype the proposed solution

➤ Carry out preliminary estimates and planning

➤ Define the steering committee, and project roles and responsibilities

➤ Identify and analyze key risks and issues

➤ Agree on a QA approach, and formulate project controls

➤ Formally document the project "contract."

The "contract" can be the project definition document, the project management plan or the initiation document. The purpose of each of these documents is the same: they represent an agreement with the sponsor, customer, and key stakeholders about what is to be delivered, to whom, by when, for how much, and how you intend to go about delivering it.

The written contract is a tangible outcome of the initiation phase. The goal is to get the contract approved so that you can move on with the actual execution and delivery of the project. In order to get to the point at which all parties agree on the terms of the contract, you and your team need to carry out a great deal of analysis and design work and possibly also perform demonstrations or prototyping.

Note that the contract or project definition document needs to be reviewed at regular intervals throughout the project to account for changing circumstances and to update it with further detail.

Exercise: Initiating Your Last Project

1. Take some time to think about the last time you started a new project. Write down the name of the project.

- How did you go about starting it?
- What were the first things you did?
- Was it a relatively formal or informal process?
- Did you have a lot of say in how the project was kicked off and who was involved?
- Did you formulate the business case, or was it written by someone else?
- How much time did you spend understanding the project's scope and objectives and what it was all about?
- Who helped you analyze the requirements and initiate the project?
- Did you engage the main stakeholders right from the start?
- Were you pleased with the way the project was estimated and planned?
- Did you carry out any prototyping during the initiation phase?
- Were you satisfied with the quality of the project definition document you wrote?

2. From that experience, what would you say your biggest lessons learned were? What worked well and what not so well?

3. If you had to do it again today, what would you do differently?
4. Take a minute to write down how you would go about initiating a project today.

_____

_____

_____

There are different ways of kicking off a project, and different terms are used, depending on the methodology, to describe what should be done and how it should be done. I have kept these guiding practices as generic as possible and highlighted the main things for you to consider and investigate when starting a new project. Keep in mind that this is by no means a definitive list or a fail-safe recipe. All projects, circumstances, and organizations are different, and what applies to one project might not apply to another.

> _Always use your common sense and think about the outcome you are aiming for. Do not let jargon or overly complex procedures get in your way. Keep things simple; most of the time, less is more._

As you go through the guiding practices, identify to what extent you used that principle last time you kicked off a project. Do not worry if you find gaps that may impact your existing project. Simply make a note of them and identify ways in which you can start rectifying them, even if you are currently halfway through the execution phase.

Note that I use the terms _customer, client, business owner,_ and _sponsor_ interchangeably to describe the person who is the ultimate decisionmaker and beneficiary of the project.

Plan your work

Before you get too far into the initiation phase and start engaging in lots of activities, take time to consider what this phase is all about and what you want to achieve. Create a list of the tasks you need to embark on during this first phase of the project. Make a note of all of the people you need to talk to, the artifacts you need to get hold of, the resources you need allocated, the questions you need answered, the analysis you need to do, the documents you need to write, and the sign-offs you need to obtain. Prioritize your list and create a mini plan for the initiation phase. Run this plan past your manager and other stakeholders. Not only will that help you sanity-check the plan, but it will also help you start building relationships and promoting the project. Periodically review the plan, and add new tasks as they arise.

✔ Do you know exactly what you want to achieve during the initiation phase?

✔ Have you created a plan for the things you need to do during the initiation phase?

Understand the business case and constraints

As a project manager, you will often get asked or appointed to run a project after the decision has been made to initiate it. This decision could be based on the sponsor or business owner having carried out a cost-benefit analysis or developed a business case stating why the project is important and outlining the expected benefits and costs. If that is the case on your project, ask to see the business case and question anything you do not understand. Your main concern is to confirm that the business case is sound and that you have a clear mandate to initiate the project.

Sometimes business cases do not discuss financial and non-financial benefits in enough detail, or there is an incorrect assumption that execution costs will be much lower than they really will be. Thoroughly examine the constraints as described in the business case, and beware of situations where budget and schedule are predetermined and/or overly optimistic. Your team needs to further investigate any assumptions or constraints regarding scope, cost, and time listed in the business case before you commit to delivering the project within these constraints.

As the project manager, you need to provide your own project estimates based on the requirements presented to you. As you start to build up a better understanding of what the project is all about, your job should be to work with the sponsor to refine the business case and ensure that it provides a realistic view of expected benefits and costs.

If for some reason a business case does not already exist, it may be up to you to pull it together and to get it approved. What is important is that there is a business case as well as a clear commitment and mandate to initiate the project.

✔ Does a sound business case exist?

✔ Is there a clear mandate for you to initiate the project?

✔ Do you understand the parameters and constraints of the project?

Engage the stakeholders and form a steering committee

Early on in the initiation phase, it is important that you take the time to understand who the main stakeholders are and the interests they have in the project.

Engage with everyone who has a vested interest, including potential vendors, your manager, user groups, the sponsor, and executives who may have to supply resources. Meet with them and hear what they have to say. Find out which parts of the business they represent, what outcomes they are looking for, how realistic their expectations are, if they have a personal interest in the project's successful completion, what risks and issues they foresee, how they define project success, and how they prefer to be communicated with during the project. Also, ask them who else you should be talking to at this stage of the project. Record all of the information you gather, and slowly start to build up your stakeholder analysis (See Stakeholder Management).

Start forming the steering committee, so that you have a forum in which to discuss ideas and resolve escalated risks and issues. This is the body you report to and which ultimately decides what needs to be done and what the success criteria are. It is imperative that the people who comprise the steering committee are experienced and supportive and that you establish an open and trustworthy relationship with them right from the start. Make their roles and responsibilities clear so that they know what you expect from them.

✔ Have you engaged all of the project's main stakeholders?

✔ Do you understand what each stakeholder wants to get out of the project?

✔ Have you set up a steering committee, and have you established clear roles and responsibilities for each of its members?

Caution

As you get involved in a project, you may come under pressure from the sponsor or executives to skip the initiation phase and start building the solution right away. However, it is imperative to project success that investigative work is carried out and that a firm agreement is established before you start committing resources and executing the project. Initiating a project is all about getting the foundation right. You need to understand the scope and characteristics of what the customer wants, then analyze how you can best go about delivering it. Only then can you create a contract or agreement between you and the client that you can comfortably sign off. No one should ask you to engage external vendors or start building the solution until your contract has been agreed upon.

When dealing with external customers, this step seems obvious. There would be a phase in which you put together and agree on a proposal before you start the actual work. But when your customer is internal, the phases sometimes become blurred. An urgent request to start a project comes down from the sponsor or business head, and the pressure is on to get the work done as quickly as possible. Stick to your guns and establish a firm agreement on what exactly is to be done and within what parameters before you move forward. If you rush into the execution phase too soon, you may come to regret it when you realize that the project is shaky due to unclear requirements, lack of acceptance criteria, or a fundamental design flaw.

Identify and build the initiation team

Before you progress too far into the initiation phase, you need to identify and put together a team that can assist you during this initial phase. The people you choose must be able to help you analyze the project's scope and requirements as well as help you plan, estimate, and prototype the proposed solution.

You may not always be able to choose who to work with, but when you can, aim to engage people who want to be on the project and who have the necessary skills and time available to focus on the job. Set high standards: choose the most experienced and proactive people.

The types and numbers of people you need at this stage will depend on the nature of your project and whether you plan to run demonstrations and create prototypes and proof of concepts during initiation. Some of the team members who get involved at this stage may or may not carry on into the construction or execution phase. Remember that although you fully expect the project to be executed, in theory you do not know for sure that it will be until initiation is complete and the next stage of the project has been approved.

✔ Does the team involved in the initiation phase have the necessary experience, skills, and attitude to do what you want to achieve?

Understand the project domain, objectives, and scope

Most of the work in the initiation phase is concerned with understanding what needs to be built and delivered. You need to understand the outcomes the customer and users are looking for and the products you need to deliver to generate the desired business benefits. Begin with the end in mind and work backwards. Clearly define what is in and out of scope and break products and deliverables into their constituent parts.

Use text, diagrams, and illustrations to capture the collective scope and to verify that you have understood it correctly. Every time you come across a new feature, document it and determine its acceptance criteria. The requirements of a feature really come to light once you ask a user to specify the tests he or she would carry out to verify that it was built correctly.

Inquire about non-functional requirements, such as maintainability, scalability, and performance. It may, for instance, be relevant to find out how many people are likely to use the product at any one time and the volume the solution is expected to handle per minute, hour, or week. Also investigate how the solution will be supported and maintained after project completion.

Do not be afraid to ask basic questions. What seems obvious to the users and domain experts may be new and complicated knowledge to the project team, so ask away. If you are dealing with a particularly complex domain, consider taking a relevant course or spending time with the customer to get up to speed.

Get into the heads of your customer and users. Knowing what they know and feeling what they feel could make the difference between success and failure.

During the initiation phase, you may not be able to analyze all requirements in great detail, and in most cases, you should not have to. Remember that this phase is about establishing the baseline and understanding the risks. You need to know enough to comfortably propose a solution, estimate it, and provide an outline schedule. To do this well, you must explore all core requirements and look in particular at the risky parts of the project.

✔ Are the users and domain experts able to articulate what they want, and have they provided you with measurable acceptance criteria?

✔ Do you and the team understand the project's scope and requirements, and have they been documented and signed off?

✔ Do your team members have sufficient business knowledge to be effective in their roles?

Propose a solution to the client's problem

Proposing a solution to the client's problem and producing a high-level design for that solution is one of the most challenging aspects of the initiation phase. This is where your designers and architects come in. The questions that need to be answered here are: What are you going to do to satisfy the customer's needs? What technologies, materials, and design principles are you going to use?

Identify and discuss different solutions and their pros and cons. Compare them to the customer's success criteria, and make sure that all of the users' high- and medium-priority requirements are satisfied. Some of your proposed solutions may be more cost-effective than others but deliver a lower-quality product. Others may deliver just what the users want but be associated with higher risk—for example, a solution involving the use of new, untested technology or materials. Present the options to the client and key stakeholders, and be as transparent as you can about the associated assumptions, risks, and constraints. Build a prototype or run a demonstration of your proposed solution if possible, as this will illustrate your proposal much more effectively than simply explaining it.

Ultimately, the choice of solution will be the sponsor's, but beware if the steering committee cannot agree on a solution. The best solution is one that satisfies all of your stakeholders' needs and success criteria.

✔ Are you confident that the proposed solution is the best one to solve your customer's problem?

✔ Are you certain that the customer, users, and key stakeholders understand what your team is proposing to deliver?

✔ Have you or are you planning to demonstrate or prototype the proposed solution?

Estimate the proposed solution

Devising a thorough, accurate estimate of the proposed solution is one of the most important activities when starting a new project. If you get the estimates significantly wrong, your project is likely to be seen as a failure no matter how good the end product is.

On big projects, the estimation process can be an onerous task, so make use of all of the support available. Research and experiment with different estimation tools, and look at past projects of similar size and complexity for guidance. Involve as many experienced people as possible (even if you have to temporarily borrow them from another project), and make use of different methods and control groups. Make an effort to engage all of the teams that will eventually be part of the project.

Before you start the estimation process, it is critical that you have a really good understanding of what you are estimating. The better you understand the project's scope and requirements and the solution you are proposing, the easier it will be for you to estimate.

Break functions and features down into as much detail as possible and provide both best-case and worst-case estimates for each. Factor in all project phases and activities, and add contingency to every part of your estimate. Also consider to what extent you need to factor in the cost of unexpected events, such as the cost of replacing a valuable team member or finding a new vendor. Play devil's advocate, as not everything will not go smoothly. Remember, Murphy's law: If anything can go wrong, it will.

Of course, it is not just the *scope* of what you are delivering that determines the estimate. Potential *time* constraints and the speed at which you need to deliver may also influence how much the overall project will cost.

- ✔ Are your estimates as robust as they can be at this stage of the project?

- ✔ Have you used several methods and called upon experienced team members to help produce the estimates?

- ✔ Do your estimates include enough contingency, and do they consider scope as well as time requirements?

Produce a high-level schedule

When you have a clear picture of the project's requirements and their relative priority, as well as an estimate for the proposed solution, you can start to put together a high-level schedule. The schedule should outline what will be done when and by whom.

The first step is to identify dependencies between your deliverables and to prioritize them according to business needs and complexity. Find out if there are any milestones you must hit at a certain time. Produce a high-level dependency diagram or product flow diagram to help you visualize the sequence of deliverables.

Arrange your deliverables into phases and iterations with clear milestones, and aim to deliver the core and most critical part of the solution first. Bounce your ideas off the team and stakeholders, and incorporate their feedback into the schedule. Then you can start to break down the initial phases and iterations into more detail.

Identify the resources and the size of the team you need to hit the desired milestones. Play around with different team sizes and levels of efficiency, and get a feel for how these affect the high-level schedule. If your project is under a lot of time pressure, identify and eliminate the most constraining scheduling factor(s) in order to speed up delivery.

Remember to add contingency to your schedule—you may not be able to execute every task in exact sequence. Also, bear in mind that people go on vacation and attend training and that it takes time to bring new team members up to speed.

Scheduling a project is not an exact science, so use your intuition and common sense.

✔ How confident are you that your high-level schedule is as realistic as it can be at this stage of the project?

✔ Does the schedule contain clear phases and milestones?

✔ Does the schedule offer the opportunity to deliver benefits early and gradually?

Highlight risks, issues, dependencies, constraints, and assumptions

Throughout the initiation phase, you will need to pay a lot of attention to the risks, issues, dependencies, constraints, and assumptions that present themselves. Not only do you need to take them into consideration when you design, plan, and estimate the project, but you also need to log them, address them, and highlight them to the sponsor and stakeholders. Doing so will provide everyone with a good understanding of the complexities you are up against and will make your stakeholders appreciate why you need contingency in your estimates and schedule. You may also find that your stakeholders have valuable insights that can help you address some of the risks, issues, or dependencies.

Dependencies, constraints, and assumptions can pertain to just about any element of a project: requirements, materials, technology, resourcing, budget, legislation, and external vendors. Most of your dependencies, constraints, and assumptions are likely to be either risks or issues, so treat them as such, and demonstrate that you have done as much as you can to address or mitigate them. Escalate risks and issues to your steering committee if you cannot resolve them on your own and need senior stakeholders to take ownership. (See Managing Risks and Issues for more information.)

✔ Have you identified the project's risks, issues, constraints, dependencies, and assumptions and made an effort to mitigate and address them?

✔ Have you created risk and issue logs and updated them with all identified items?

✔ Have you communicated the risks and issues to your stakeholders?

Establish a project methodology

One of the key decisions you need to make during the initiation phase is which project methodology you will be using (e.g., waterfall, agile). Many organizations provide guidance on how projects should be run that you can adapt and modify to suit your specific needs.

Keep the application of the methodology simple. Above all, a methodology must be easy and intuitive to use and add benefit to the project. Remember that following a methodology does not guarantee success, although it certainly does help you control your project better.

Make sure everyone on the team buys into the methodology and understands how to apply it. Be prepared to learn from your experiences and adjust your methodology as you move along.

✔ Are you confident that the chosen project methodology is the best suited to the organization, team, and project? If not, how could you tailor it so that it fits better?

Establish project controls

During the initiation phase, not only do you need to establish the project methodology, but you also need to determine how you will control the execution of the project. There is a lot to keep track of once the project kicks off in earnest, so establish the controls up front.

The procedures and checks you need to establish will govern how you will monitor and control progress, costs, scope, and quality. Managing scope, for example, involves identifying, analyzing, approving, and planning any changes that arise (see Managing Changes to Scope). You also need to decide who is responsible for signing off on requirements, user acceptance testing, and external vendor contracts.

For each control you choose to implement, formally agree with the steering committee on what the control is, who will exercise it, and how often they will do so.

Exercise: Setting Project Controls

1. On a separate piece of paper, brainstorm all of the processes, controls, and sign-off points that exist on your project or that you plan to implement. List anything that relates to how you control cost, quality, scope, and progress.

2. For each item, write down who is responsible for exercising the control (e.g., who signs off on a certain document or change).

3. For each item, also write down the frequency of the control (e.g., how often time sheets are signed off).

4. The table below lists some of the project controls that might be relevant to your project. This list is not definitive, so add extra controls as you see fit. The ownership and frequency of each control will depend on your specific needs and requirements.

5. For each entry on the list, provide a score between 1 and 10, indicating to what extent the control exists on your current project.

	Suggested Control	Suggested Ownership	Suggested Frequency	Is it in place? (1–10 score)
Formal sign-offs	Formally sign off business case	Project sponsor	End of initiation and when something major changes	
	Formally sign off project definition document*	Steering committee	End of initiation and when something major changes	
	Formally sign off functional and nonfunctional requirements	Steering committee	End of initiation and when something major changes	
	Formally sign off design document(s)	Steering committee	End of initiation and when something major changes	
	Formally sign off acceptance criteria and test cases	End user/user representatives	End of initiation and when something major changes	
	Formally sign off user acceptance testing	End user/user representatives	End of each user test	
	Formally sign off each phase/stage	Steering committee	End of each phase/stage	
	Formally sign off go-live	Steering committee	When required	
	Sign off actual time booked to project	Project manager	Weekly	
	Sign off external vendor costs (e.g., external consultants, hardware)	Project manager	Weekly	
	Sign off external vendor contracts	Steering committee	When required	
	Sign off change requests (i.e., change to budgets, scope and plan)	Steering committee	Every time a major change happens	
	Review scope and priorities	Project manager	Beginning of new phase/iteration	
	Track progress and schedule	Project manager	Daily/weekly	
	Review resource plan	Project manager	Beginning of new phase/iteration	

Project management controls	Track expenditure / actual cost	Project manager	Monthly/beginning of new iteration	
	Review estimates and budget	Project manager	Monthly/beginning of new iteration	
	Review risks and issues	Project manager	Daily/weekly	
	Conduct project reviews	Project manager	End of phase/iteration	
	Other			
	Other			
	Other			

* Note that the sign-off of the project definition document is an implicit sign-off of the project's approach, including scope, high-level requirements, the proposed solution, preliminary estimates, the high-level plan, roles and responsibilities, and risks and issues.

Prepare for QA activities, and establish a test approach

Quality assurance is intended to ensure that what your team is building and producing matches the requirements, the design specifications, and the end user's expectations. The question is, how will you make sure that every single team member contributes to quality in everything he or she does?

> *Quality assurance is not something you attend to in the last phase of a project. It is something that should be an integral part of everything that is done by anyone on the project at all times.*

To bring quality to the forefront of your team's awareness, brainstorm activities and products that will need to be tested and quality assured, and openly discuss the attitudes the team needs to embrace in order to focus on quality. Make sure everyone gets the message that every single person is responsible for quality. One of the best ways of doing that is to assign clear roles and responsibilities for quality early on. If a team member knows that she is going to be held accountable for a certain test process or quality procedure, she will be much more inclined to live up to that responsibility.

For each test and QA activity you plan to carry out, establish what the objective is, how the activity will be performed, and who will be responsible for preparing and executing it. Also determine whether you need specialists to help execute and manage any of the tests or QA processes or whether the team members will double up as testers, reviewers, and approvers.

Plan for your test and QA activities to take place as frequently as possible during the project (preferably after each small function or product has been built) to catch any potential errors as early as possible. Adopting an iterative delivery approach may help you improve overall quality because deliverables are built and verified step by step, and because there is a frequent feedback loop between the users and developers.

✔ Have you discussed the importance of quality with everyone on the team?

✔ Do you have a document outlining the types of tests and reviews you plan to carry out, how they will be done, and by whom?

Establish a communication plan and reporting

The communication plan sets out what you will do to make sure that project information and status updates are communicated effectively to all parties throughout the project's duration. If you have not already done so, ask your team members and stakeholders how they would like to be kept informed, and group them according to their needs and desires. Distinguish between informal, formal, written, and verbal forms of communication. You will find that some stakeholders want or need frequent informal, verbal updates (e.g., daily catch-ups), whereas others prefer formal, written communication on a much more infrequent basis (e.g., bimonthly project reports). Find out what works for each individual and seek to respect these preferences.

Within the communication plan, make sure you discuss the types, frequency, and contents of your project reports, as well as the audience for the reports. List regular meetings and how often they will be held and who will attend. Note whether the project will have a website, a newsletter, and a document repository and who will be responsible for maintaining them. Mention the tools you will use to communicate with stakeholders.

If you are working with a geographically dispersed team, do not assume that the usual lines and means of communication will work. Extra effort and special tools are necessary to ensure that remote team members become an integrated part of the project.

✔ Have you asked your stakeholders how they would like to be kept informed of project progress, and have they endorsed your reporting template?

✔ Do you have a clear view of the types of information you are responsible for providing and how you can effectively circulate information to all parties?

✔ Does everyone have a clear understanding of the key project meetings that will take place, how frequently they will be held, and who should attend?

Caution

Working with geographically dispersed teams is becoming more and more commonplace within certain industries, mainly to drive down costs, but note that it adds further complexity and risk to your project. Communication will be more challenging on a distributed team, and you may find that the team is less effective than it would be if situated in the same building or the same room.

- Make sure that the steering committee understands the drawbacks of working with a distributed team and that the advantages outweigh the disadvantages.
- Document the risks that distributed work introduces and devise ways to address each of them, for instance by adding more contingency to the plan and by tightening the lines of communication.
- Make sure roles and responsibilities are as clear as they can be and that tasks and their associated acceptance criteria are well documented.
- Use the best communication tools available, and contact remote team members frequently. Do everything you can to make people feel that they are part of the bigger team.

Document the approach (project definition document)

The project project definition document is a tangible outcome of the initiation phase. It is a document that should be created gradually throughout the initiation phase to describe what you are delivering, who you are delivering it to, and how you will deliver it, by when, and for how much.

How much detail you put into the definition document and to what degree you specify your estimate, plans, and methods will depend on your organization's needs and procedures and whether your client is internal or external. If you are dealing with an external client, you may want to write a proposal in addition to the project definition document, as your organization might not want to disclose all of the detailed information around resourcing and estimates.

Your customer and key stakeholders must sign off on this document before you proceed with the rest of the project.

Exercise: Evaluating Your Project Definition Document

1. Look at the last project definition document you produced. On a separate piece of paper, write down all of its headings and subheadings.
2. Look at the list of suggested document sections below and identify to what extent they were satisfactorily covered in your own document. Use the blank columns to record your answers.

Suggested Document Sections	Present in Your Document?	Quality of Section (Score of 1–10)
EXECUTIVE SUMMARY		
Purpose and Benefits		
Project Objectives		
Proposed Solution		
Expected Costs		
Major Risks and Issues		
PROJECT DEFINITION		
Background		
Vision		
Objectives		
Project Scope		
Out of Scope		
Outline Functional Requirements		
Outline Non-Functional Requirements		
Success Criteria (KPIs)		
Project Impact		
BUSINESS CASE*		
Expected Benefits (financial/non-financial)		
Expected Project Costs		
Expected Operating Costs		
Cost-Benefit Analysis		
DELIVERY and PLAN		
Recommended Solution		
Alternative Options Considered		
Delivery Approach		
Road Map and Key Milestones		
Outline Plan		

Suggested Document Sections	Present in Your Document?	Quality of Section (Score of 1–10)
Outline Resource Requirements		
RISKS AND ISSUES		
Project Risk Assessment		
Key Risks		
Key Issues		
Dependencies, Constraints, Assumptions		
ESTIMATED COSTS		
Estimated Project Costs		
Estimated Operating Costs		
GOVERNANCE		
Key Stakeholders		
Steering Committee		
Project Organizational Chart		
Roles and Responsibilities		
CONTROLS		
Main Project Controls		
Cost Controls		
Communication Plan and Reporting		
Quality Plan		
DOCUMENT CONTROL		
Other		
Other		
Other		

*The business case can be included in the project definition document or kept as a separate document.

3. What do the scores show about the quality of your project definition document?

4. Which sections do you need to go back and revisit or pay more attention to the next time you write this kind of document?

5. What additional content would you want include in the definition document? Add the headings for these sections to the blank rows in the table.

MANAGING CHANGES TO SCOPE

It is critical to the success of any project that changes to scope are effectively managed and controlled because they have the potential to significantly impact the parameters and success criteria of your project. These success criteria include specific measures for time, cost, and quality that you, the client, and other key stakeholders agreed on when you initiated the project.

As an example, let us assume that the end users want you to increase scope and include an additional feature in the project. You know that this feature will improve the usability of the end product, but you also know that if you include it, it will have a negative impact on your budget and schedule.

You need to take a step back and recognize this as a change request. Do not automatically add it to the project's task list. You need to log the request, analyze its impact on time, cost, and quality, and get it approved by the steering committee. If you allow the change to creep into the project without formal approval, you may not have enough time or budget to deliver the entire project. The project's steering committee will hold you accountable to the original scope, budget, and schedule unless you have formally agreed to change it.

Test Yourself

- What does a good scope and change management process consist of?
- What is scope creep, and why is it important to control it?

There are many reasons why scope changes. A user may acquire better insight into a problem as the project progresses, or external market conditions or government regulations may drive requests that go beyond the initial scope.

Changes to scope will always happen. The idea behind scope and change management is not to prevent changes but to control them. You need to understand what each change means and what its impact on the project will be. If changes are not controlled, or if they are allowed into the project without proper impact analysis, scope creep will happen, and you may end up not knowing what your project is delivering and how much it will cost.

A prerequisite for successful scope and change management is to have a really good grasp of the project's baseline scope, schedule, and budget. Otherwise, you will not be able to identify what is changing and what impact the change will have.

It is much easier to assess the impact of a change when you know what the existing scope, schedule, and budget are. But again, to properly manage scope, you also need to get the changes approved by the steering committee and effectively schedule and communicate them.

Exercise: How Well Do You Control Scope Changes?

1. Think about past situations and projects that had the highest degree of uncontrolled scope changes. List them.
2. What do you believe the reasons were for the lack of control?
3. On a scale from 1 to 10, how well is scope controlled on your current project?
4. To improve the way you control scope, walk through the seven-step process below. As you read through the steps, keep in mind an example of a scope change from your current project.

Know your baseline

A good change control process starts with a firm baseline. That means that everyone has agreed in writing what is in scope and out of scope and what the budget and time frames are. When you baseline scope, make sure it is documented, signed off, and specified such that it can only be interpreted in one way. If your requirements are too vague or high-level, they will be open to interpretation, and you may have to accept extra features into the scope of the project that you did not anticipate.

The baseline should be made clear within the business case or within the project definition document. In addition, detailed scope should be captured in a requirements traceability matrix and in individual sets of requirements specifications. These documents must be signed off by all relevant stakeholders and should cover functional as well as nonfunctional requirements.

As the project manager, you must fully understand the detailed scope of the project. It is not enough to ensure that scope documents are locked down and signed off. If you do not have a good understanding of what is in and out of scope, you will not be able to pick up on any changes that creep in.

Step 1

- Make sure the project's baseline scope, budget and time frames are captured in the business case or project definition document.
- Lock down the project's detailed scope by getting the stakeholders to sign off on your requirements traceability matrix and requirements specifications.
- Make sure you personally understand what is in and out of scope so that you will be in an ideal position to notice when changes to scope happen.

Have a change budget

To help you successfully manage changes to scope, set aside a budget for scope changes when you estimate the project. If you do not have a change budget, scope changes will eat into the project's contingency, and you may have to go back to the steering committee and sponsor and ask for more money to finish the project. The change budget is different from contingency, which covers a project for risks that may materialize and turn into issues. The change budget explicitly accounts for changes that come up and that get approved. The size of this budget will depend on how sound or uncertain you deem the requirements to be at the time you estimate them.

> ### Step 2
>
> - Explicitly set aside money for scope changes that may come up during the execution of the project. Make sure the change budget is signed off as part of the overall budget.

Proactively identify changes

Changes to scope can come to light in any forum and be verbalized by any team member or stakeholder. Changes are most likely to emerge during user demonstrations, prototyping, requirements workshops, detailed requirements gathering, user acceptance testing, reviews, and risks and issues meetings. The more of these forums you hold and the more you drill down into the requirements, the better placed you are for detecting changes.

When you sense that the scope of your project is being questioned or that it may not match what the users need, do not hesitate to discuss this—proactively explore the situation. Put your detective's hat on and talk the solution through with the team and customer to identify any gaps. It is much better to proactively identify changes and get them out into the open than to hide them away and delay dealing with them.

Beware of changes that creep in as a result of requirements that are not detailed enough. The customer may believe that a certain feature is in scope, while the team believes it is out of scope. When you consult the requirements, they may be too vague to determine who is right. Communicate closely with all team members so that you are able to pick up when scope creep is about to happen. If you cannot resolve these scope issues with the users, escalate to the steering committee for guidance, and revisit the requirements to make them more specific. Drill down into the details, and expand the requirements traceability matrix and the underlying requirements specifications.

Step 3

- Explore, demonstrate, and prototype as much of the functionality as you can, and actively investigate whether it matches the users' needs and requirements.
- Drill down into the requirements and help identify any gaps or inaccuracies. Determine if any of the gaps could cause a change to baseline scope.

Carry out a thorough impact analysis

It is all too easy to conduct a superficial impact analysis and to authorize scope changes prematurely. But remember that it is in the project manager's interest to know exactly what the impact of a change will be. You are the one who has pledged to deliver a certain amount of scope within a certain budget and time scale. If you are to deliver more scope, and maybe even change the proposed solution as a result, you need to know how these changes will affect the existing budget, schedule, and quality.

To carry out a thorough impact analysis, invite anyone from the team whose knowledge you require to help. Map out the proposed change and how you plan to implement it. Consult the requirements traceability matrix and assess whether the change will affect other requirements. If so, which ones? Also look at how you might fit the change into the schedule, and consider the impact of potentially having to reprioritize work to accommodate it.

This impact analysis will show how much more funding or time you need if you are to incorporate the change.

Step 4

- Involve your team in carrying out a thorough impact analysis of all proposed changes.
- Assess the effects on cost, time, and quality if you accept the change.

Get the changes signed off

Always resist the temptation to accept small changes into a project without formally analyzing or approving them. Many small undetected changes can end up derailing your project just as much as one big sudden change can.

Present the findings of the impact analysis to the steering committee or change control board. When you present a thorough analysis of how you plan to implement a change and how it will affect cost, schedule, and quality, your sponsor and stakeholders are well positioned to make an informed decision. If the committee accepts the change but is unable to allocate extra funds or more time, you may have to cut back on other work in order to accommodate it.

Step 5

- Present all proposed changes to the steering committee for approval (or rejection).
- Clearly outline what the impact of accepting the change will be, and tell the committee whether you need further resources such as time, money, people, or materials to implement the change.

Document and log all changes

Be disciplined enough to keep an up-to-date log of all historic changes and how they have affected the baseline. This is a small but important task. Your log becomes a register of all approved changes, what they relate to, what the impact was, and whether any extra funds were allocated to the project as a result. It becomes a very powerful piece of evidence that shows how scope has evolved over time and what the rate of changes has been. At some point, you may have to remind senior executives why your project now costs more and is taking longer to implement than originally estimated. People can have very short memories, so cover your back by keeping a record of approved changes. For the same reason, you should always document key decisions and approved scope changes and circulate them to your key stakeholders for the record.

Step 6

- Keep track of all historic scope changes in a separate log with comments about what was approved (or rejected) and what the acknowledged impact was on cost, time, and quality.
- Document all key scope decisions and circulate these minutes to all relevant parties.

Schedule and communicate changes

If a proposed scope change has been signed off and is going ahead, it must be incorporated into your schedule and other key project documentation and communicated to the rest of the team. Involve the team in the planning process for implementing the change, and explain why this change has been signed off and why it needs to be incorporated. Everyone likes to be kept informed of project decisions and the rationale behind them—proper team communications are essential to understanding and overcoming resistance to change. If changes are not properly communicated, team morale can suffer—the team will feel left out and may not understand why the focus or direction of the project has all of a sudden changed.

Step 7

- Communicate the approved change to the team, clearly explaining why it has been accepted.
- Involve your team in the planning process.
- Schedule the change according to its assigned priority.
- Update your project definition document, requirements traceability matrix, requirements documents, metrics, and other affected documents to reflect the change.

Questions

- Which parts of the change control process do you need to pay more attention to going forward?
- How will doing so help you manage scope and address the kinds of issues you have seen in the past?

TEAM MOTIVATION

Leading and motivating your team members is one of the most important roles you have as a project manager. A team with good motivation will perform better and will make significant contributions to the overall success of the project.

Test Yourself

- What factors affect a person's motivation?
- What can a project manager do to create a highly motivated team?

A team's performance is heavily dependent on motivational factors such as drive, confidence, and attitude. In some cases, highly motivated and driven teams may outperform other teams that are more qualified.

At the most fundamental level, your team members can only be truly motivated if their individual aims and purposes are aligned with those of the organization and project. The better the alignment, the better a platform you have for motivating your team.

People are motivated to do things they relate to and believe in. They want to work on projects that have meaning and purpose and that give them a sense of achievement and satisfaction.

People are truly motivated when they feel that their core personal values are being fulfilled by the work they do.

Although some of the factors that help motivate a team fall outside your control (such as the fundamental structure and business of the organization), you still have an amazing range of tools at hand and significant power to influence the team and improve its motivation and performance.

Questions

- On a scale of 1 to 10, how motivated would you say your current project team is?
- What methods and techniques do you currently use to motivate your team?
- How successful are these methods?
- How motivated are you personally?

There is no universal source of motivation. Different people have different values, and what motivates one might not motivate another. Being thanked personally may motivate some people, while others may want to be given challenges as a thank you. Money motivates some people, but others are more driven by the chance to be creative and innovative or the opportunity to be promoted.

The questions you need to ask are "What motivates each person on my team?" and "What will enable them to do what they do even better?" To answer these, and to tap into your team members' strongest sources of energy, you need to spend time with them and understand who they are and what makes them tick. Remember that there are more people out there who are not like you than are like you, so be careful not to rely on your own criteria and values when motivating others.

Some of the things that motivate your team members may be relatively easy to implement and will have a big impact on performance—for example, giving a certain person more challenging work and playing better to his strengths. Another team member might want your support to promote a certain task or initiative on behalf of the team, while a third person would be much more motivated if she were allowed to work flexible hours. These are all things you can control and can make an effort to do.

Sometimes you will come up against organizational or managerial constraints that you can influence but may not have any direct authority over. Many project managers do not have line management responsibilities for their team members. If you are in this situation and you sense that a team member is unmotivated because his line manager does not provide adequate recognition, or because he is not being adequately remunerated or appreciated by the wider organization, you need to do your best to be an advocate for that person and help resolve the problem. First, talk with the team member and his line manager with the aim of understanding the details of the situation. Then use your negotiation skills to help identify a solution that is beneficial for all parties. You will be amazed at the difference such efforts can make in a person's motivation and performance.

Stand up for your team members, value them, and play to their strengths. Help resolve any nagging issues that might be preventing them from performing at their best, even if the matter is outside of your direct sphere of responsibility.

Take Action

- Spend some extra time next week on a one-on-one basis with each of your team members. Have a general chat about how they feel about the project, the team, and their individual performance. Ask them how they believe the team could improve and what would make them enjoy their job even more.
- Actively listen to what each team member says, and continue these discussions until you fully understand what motivates your team members and what could help them enjoy their work more.
- Make one or two key changes for each person that will have a significant positive impact on his or her motivation and performance.

In addition to spending time with individual team members to understand their values and motivators, there are other things you can do and behaviors you can adopt that are likely to increase motivation across the team.

Exercise: Using Motivational Techniques

Look at the motivational techniques listed below. Score yourself on a scale from 1 to 10 to indicate how often you currently use that particular method to motivate your team.

The more of these techniques you adopt, the better the chance that you will have a positive effect on your team's motivation.

Build strong relationships

There are few motivators more powerful than relationships. When we trust someone and we believe he or she has our best interests at heart, we are willing to go the extra mile and give more effort. Team members will go above and beyond to help a project manager they believe would do the same for them. Value your team members and do what you can to help them thrive. Every interaction you have with them is an opportunity to listen to and appreciate them and to strengthen your working relationship.

✔ On a scale from 1 to 10, how good are you at building strong relationships with your team members?

Be a project champion

Fully embrace the goals, objectives, and plans of the project, and visualize the end state. Really feel it. Keep this vision alive and share it with the team. When you feel inspired and motivated, your team is likely to feel inspired, too. Unite your team around a common goal, and provide focus and direction by sharing the strategy for achieving it. Your team members will feel motivated to follow because they have bought into the vision and want to contribute to achieving it.

✔ On a scale from 1 to 10, how successful are you at inspiring your team and uniting it around a common goal?

Be the best you can, and lead by example

Greatness is contagious. Be the best you can in all that you do, and others will notice your example. They will be inclined to follow because they want some of whatever you have. There are many ways in which you can be great and lead by example. One way is to treat others the way you want to be treated yourself and to treat everyone as an equal. Another is to sincerely embrace values such as integrity, honesty, and positivity. A third way is to be an impeccable manager who works with focus and determination and who is able to stay calm in stressful situations. Whatever you do, do it well; the way you conduct yourself will be the most you can possibly expect from your team.

✔ On a scale from 1 to 10, how good are you at leading by example?

Give constructive feedback, and praise others

People respond well to praise, encouragement, recognition, and being thanked. When you let others know that they are appreciated, they will want to give you their best. Be generous with praise for a job well done, and say thank you when someone helps you or does something for the team. Make team members feel welcome when they call or stop by your desk. Give constructive and objective feedback when something can be improved, and help people reflect on how they can learn from their experiences. Never criticize a team member in public.

✔ On a scale from 1 to 10, how effective are you at giving constructive feedback and praising others?

Act as a mentor rather than a micromanager

Encourage and empower team members to research problems and make decisions on their own. Mentor them and lead them on the way rather than telling them what to do. No one likes to be micromanaged, especially not if he or she is perfectly capable of working autonomously. Instead, strive to adjust your level of direction and support for each person, depending on how capable and committed he or she is. If you give away some of your power as a manager, your team will take on more responsibility and will be motivated to grow even stronger.

✔ On a scale from 1 to 10, how good are you at acting as a mentor rather than a micromanager?

Establish clear performance standards and expectations

Ensure that team members have clear and attainable goals they are working toward and that they know exactly what needs to be accomplished and when it will be considered done. Knowing what is expected is a major performance motivator and is essential for creating a high-performing team.

Make the individual's goals SMART (Specific, Measurable, Attainable, Realistic, and Timely), and ensure that they are consistent with team members' personal aspirations and aligned with organizational objectives. A goal will be truly motivating and engaging only if it is linked to the individual's aims and purposes.

✔ On a scale from 1 to 10, how effective are you at setting clear performance standards and SMART goals for your team members?

Pick your battles, and forgive small mistakes

We all make mistakes; no one is perfect. Depending on the nature of the mistake a team member makes and the intentions behind it, consider letting it go, with just a small comment or no comment at all. If someone has ever let you off after you made a small error, you know how motivating it can be to have another opportunity to justify that person's faith in you. Remember, too, that you could be wrong; perhaps the team member put forth his best effort, but your instructions were lacking.

✔ On a scale from 1 to 10, how good are you at forgiving small mistakes?

Hold people accountable

Be brave and confident enough to hold a team member accountable for bigger mistakes or behavior that is detrimental to the project. Although this may not always be pleasant, it can save you a lot of stress in the future and can help improve performance. Base your feedback on facts, and be as specific about the problem as you can. Give concrete examples of why you are concerned about the team member's performance. The more specific you are, the more likely it will be that the team member will receive your feedback as it is intended.

Again, before talking with the individual, consider your own responsibilities; were the directions and support you offered sufficient? Assume that people mean well and that they are doing the very best they can with what they have. Focus on the way forward and encourage the team member to take steps in that direction.

✔ On a scale from 1 to 10, how effective are you at holding people accountable?

Encourage a culture of communication and contribution

Every person has ideas and opinions they want to share. Set up forums and initiate activities to give your team members chances to share their knowledge and contribute to the project. This will help them connect as a team and will build a culture in which various skill sets, opinions, and capabilities are accepted. Keep the format loose so that team members feel free to share ideas without constraints. Welcome feedback and new initiatives. Show appreciation of good ideas and support them by taking action and implementing them.

✔ On a scale from 1 to 10, how good are you at encouraging a culture of communication and contribution?

Provide good tools and facilities

Do your best to make sure that team members have an optimal working environment and that the tools and information they need are available. Put yourself in their shoes: imagine the tools, facilities, and information you would need if you were doing what they do. Ask the team for feedback. What is working and what is not? What tools and facilities would help them work more effectively?

✔ On a scale from 1 to 10, how effective are you at providing your team with good tools and facilities?

Give team members training and education

Projects often require people to work in domains they do not know much about. Organize training and knowledge-sharing programs for your team. For example, ask the end users or business owners to talk about their jobs and the business. These presentations will increase the team's business knowledge, improve motivation, and contribute to successful delivery of the project. Invest in people, and they will invest in you.

✔ On a scale from 1 to 10, how successful are you at providing training and education for your team?

Take Action

Add up your scores. Which of the following brackets does your total score fall into?

0–49 points: RED. You spend much too little time nurturing your team and setting a good example for others to follow. This could be the one thing that is currently preventing you from becoming a highly valued and truly successful project management leader.

1. Choose three of the motivational methods and behaviors and make a decision to start using them next week.
2. Set aside time in your calendar to plan out exactly how you want to start using these methods and what you want to achieve. Find a slot in your planner now.
3. Take action: Test out the methods you have chosen on the least motivated team members and those who are in most need of a positive change. After trying this for a couple of weeks, look at whether team morale has changed—and how.

50–87 points: AMBER. You know how important it is to provide the right amount of support and challenge to others but have not quite found a truly effective way to serve your team. When you start to tune in to your team members and their motivators, you will find that team motivation soars, and so will your value and success as a project management leader.

1. Identify which of the motivational methods and behaviors would have the biggest positive impact on team motivation.
2. Set aside time in your calendar now to plan out exactly how you want to implement the methods, which team members you primarily want to work with, and when you will start doing so.
3. Take action, and monitor the change in team morale over the next couple of weeks.

88–110 points: GREEN. You spend a lot of time focusing on each individual team member and probably have a highly motivated and highly performing team. After reading through these motivational methods and behaviors, you know exactly where your focus should be if you want your team to produce even better results.

1. Set aside time in your calendar to plan out what you want to achieve with your team and how you will achieve it.
2. Take action, and monitor the impact on the team over the next couple of weeks.

Further Information

There are many ways to find out more about what motivates and drives people. Read up on motivational theories by people such as Abraham Maslow, Frederick Herzberg and Victor Vroom. Also consider using tools such as the SDI® (Strength Deployment Inventory®), DISC® (Dominance, Influence, Steadiness, Compliance), MBTI® (Myers-Briggs Type Indicator®), and Belbin® Team Roles. They are all good starting points for learning more about your team members' preferences. From there, you can run people-development programs to further improve team engagement and motivation.

ADAPTIVE LEADERSHIP

To become a highly valued and truly successful project management leader, you must adapt your leadership style to the people you interact with and to the situation at hand.[2] Every person and situation is different, and your behavior as a project manager needs to change accordingly. Adaptive leadership means adapting your style to suit unique circumstances.

To effectively adapt your style, you first have to establish the needs of the person you are managing, leading, supervising, or mentoring. Second, you have to learn a variety of leadership styles to use flexibly.

A person's individual needs depend on his or her job-related skills and experience as well as their level of motivation, drive, and commitment. Someone who is very experienced and motivated needs to be led and managed differently than someone who is relatively inexperienced and who lacks motivation. The amount of support and direction you offer each of these individuals should vary dramatically.

First consider the individual's skills, situation, and needs, rather than focusing solely on what you want to say. When you focus on the other person and adapt your approach accordingly, you communicate more effectively and are able to better motivate, inspire, and lead that person.

The following four methods illustrate how you can adapt your approach and use a different leadership style in response to how much support and direction an individual team member needs from you.

Instruct: When you *instruct* someone, you give precise direction and tell the individual what you want accomplished and produced. Instruction helps people who are relatively inexperienced and therefore need more direction. Instructing others is also effective when you have to quickly make a high-stakes decision. You should not use this style when people are very competent or when people lack commitment. If they lack commitment they will need more support from you than this style offers.

Nurture: When you *nurture* someone, you offer the individual a lot of support and praise in addition to precise direction. Use this style with relatively inexperienced people who lack motivation and drive. These individuals may have low self-confidence and will need as much of your support as possible. Explain decisions, listen to their concerns, provide perspective, and praise progress. Involve them in decisionmaking and show them how to do things; this will help you restore their confidence and competence.

Encourage: When you *encourage* someone, you offer a lot of support and praise without giving a lot of direction. This type of encouragement helps people who are competent and skillful, but who are also discouraged or lack confidence in their own abilities. You may find that, despite their skills and experience, these individuals are cautious or reluctant to contribute. They need a lot of support and recognition from you to improve their confidence; otherwise, they need hardly any direction.

Self-govern: When you use a *self-governing* style, you give relatively little support and direction to the individual and effectively turn over responsibility for decisionmaking and problem-solving to the individual. Use this style with people who are both competent and committed and who therefore need minimal support and direction. They are capable and willing to work on a project by themselves with little supervision and support.

As the four styles illustrate, you need to assess an individual's competence and level of motivation before you decide which style to use. Members of your team who are more junior or inexperienced will need more direction. Members who are unmotivated or lack confidence will need more support and encouragement. The most competent and committed individuals on your team will need very little direction and very little support and encouragement. In fact, over attending to or micromanaging these individuals could cause them to underperform.

Exercise: Leadership Styles

1. On a separate piece of paper, list all the people you are currently leading. Note that even if you do not have line management responsibilities over people, you are still leading them through a project in some capacity.

2. Write their names in the matrix below, in the space that best corresponds with their level of experience and competence as well as their confidence and motivation. For example, if a team member is neither competent nor motivated, write his name in the bottom left hand part of the matrix.

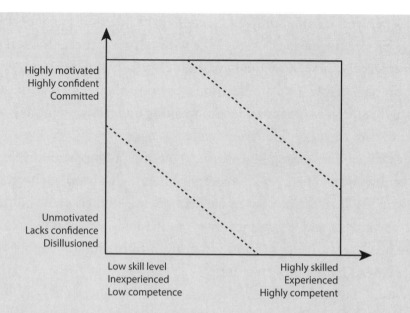

3. Consider the leadership style you use with each person you have placed in the matrix.

   • Do you use a different style with different people, or do you tend to use just one style?

   • Does your chosen style take into account the degree of competence and commitment of the individual you are leading?

4. The matrix below links the four leadership styles to the characteristics of people for whom each style is likely to be most effective.

   The arrows indicate that you want your team members to gradually move into the self-governing section. Not only will this free up your time, but also it means that your team members will be happier in their jobs, because they will be highly motivated and highly skilled.

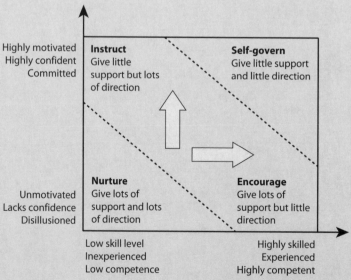

5. Do you think you are using the correct style with each person on your team? If you are not, determine what you can do to become a more adaptive leader.

Did you find that it was difficult to position certain people within the matrix? Did you want to write the same person's name in several different sections?

If so, then you are perfectly right. We must be careful not to judge people and put a static label on them that suggests they have only one level of competence and commitment. We must seek to assess people's level of development with a specific task or goal in mind. This means that the same person could be placed in several sections of the matrix, depending on the situation. In that case, you would need to use different leadership styles with the same person at different times.

Your goal as a project management leader is to gradually increase the confidence and competence of the people you work with. When you get to a stage in which most of your team is self-governing, you will spend less time micromanaging people but will still get quality results.

Caution

Be careful not to rely solely on self-governance when you first form a team and start a project. During the initial phases of a project, your team members are likely to need more direction and support from you—unless you are dealing with a well-established team that has worked on similar projects before and knows exactly what to do.

Hold regular performance review meetings or one-on-one catch-ups with people to discuss the leadership style that is likely to work best for them. Talk about their motivation and competence and how much support and direction they need from you. If you do not talk openly with your team members about their needs, they may misunderstand your intentions. They may not understand or appreciate why, over time, you have gradually started to spend less and less time with them as their confidence and competence increased.

STAKEHOLDER MANAGEMENT

Stakeholders are individuals (or groups) who have a vested interest in your project and who are directly or indirectly affected by it. Project stakeholders include the project sponsor, customers, user groups, suppliers, your line manager, senior executives, team members, shareholders, government bodies, the compliance department, and the public.

For the purpose of this exercise, we will focus on the senior stakeholders, who are managers with authority to allocate resources (people, money, time, materials, and services) and set priorities on behalf of their department or organization. They will often be part of the steering committee and can make or break a strategic change.

In order for you and your project to be successful, you need the support of as many of your stakeholders as possible—especially those who are more senior. You need their buy-in to effectively move the project forward. For example, your sponsor's support is vital; he or she has the power to withhold finances and stop funding if the project starts to deviate from the plan or if the business case is harmed. A good relationship with the end users (or user representatives) is equally important; you are dependent on them to provide accurate requirements specifications and acceptance criteria and to perform user acceptance testing. If the users are not supportive of the project, they will care less about the final product, and quality will definitely suffer.

The exercise below will help you uncover who your stakeholders are, how influential and supportive they each are, and what you can do to optimize the way you interact with them. Ideally, you want to build a strong and trustworthy relationship with all of your main stakeholders.

Step 1: Identify Your Project's Stakeholders

Make a list of all of the stakeholders on your project.

Think of all of the people who are affected by your work, who have influence or power over it, or who have an interest in its successful (or unsuccessful) conclusion. Who are the people with authority to allocate time, money, people, materials, and services to your project? Who are the people who are responsible for signing off the requirements and who will ultimately need to accept the products you are creating?

You now have a list of people, groups, or organizations that are affected by your project. Some will have the power and influence to block it or advance it; some will be very supportive of your work, while others will not. The ideal is for all of your stakeholders to be supportive of you. You cannot easily change how much power other people have over your project, but you can change how supportive they are.

Step 2: Classify Stakeholders by Level of Power/Influence and Support

Add your key stakeholders' names to the grid below, classifying them by their power over your project and by their support of your work.

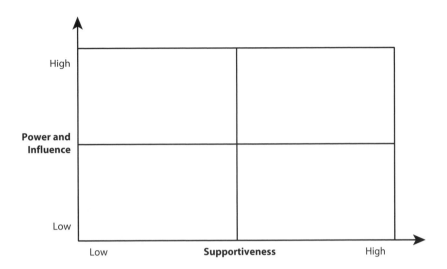

High power/high support

People who have a lot of power and are very supportive of the project and your work are your closest allies. They view the ideas and purposes of the project positively and have the power to influence others. They are happy to spend time with you and to help resolve problems. They genuinely want the project to succeed. Communicate new ideas to this group first, as they can help improve them and promote them to others. This is also the group to go to if you have major risks or issues that the project team cannot handle or resolve on its own. Make sure you nurture relationships with these stakeholders so that they continue to work in your favor.

High power/low support

People who have a lot of power and influence but who are less supportive—or who actively oppose your work—have the power to negatively influence others and could derail your project if you do not win them over. Be as flawless and pragmatic as possible when communicating with this group. Spend time building honest relationships. Listen to their concerns, and make a genuine effort to understand their points of view and the cause of their reservations. Speak to them as equals; do not be daunted by their power or skepticism. There is likely a good reason for their lack of support, and if you manage to get to the root cause and address it, the dynamics of your project could dramatically change for the better.

Sometimes you may come across people who are opposed to the project for political reasons but who otherwise have no issue with you or the way the project is being run. Discuss the situation openly (and tactfully) with these stakeholders. Ask them how they believe you can best navigate through it. If there is nothing you can do to change the situation, discuss it with the project sponsor or executive. A stakeholder who is opposed to the project as a matter of principle is someone you would rather avoid having in a key position or on your steering committee.

Low power/high support

People who have little power but are in favor of the project and your work are often very helpful with the details of the project. They can help you find the right information or put you in touch with the right people. Maintain good relationships with them and ensure they are kept in the loop regarding project progress and issues, but do not spend more time with them than you have to. If you are pressed for time, make sure you spend it with stakeholders who have relatively more power and influence than this group has.

Low power/low support

People who have little power and who are not supportive of your work can be a real nuisance. Keep these people informed and do what is reasonable to gain their support, but do not otherwise spend unnecessary time with them or trouble them with excessive communication. If you focus on winning the support of the high-powered stakeholders, this group will often follow suit.

Questions

Look at the power/support grid you filled in and reflect on it.

- Are your stakeholders generally supportive or not very supportive of your project?
- With which stakeholders do you tend to spend the majority of your time?
- What are you doing on a daily basis to build relationships with and win the support of your stakeholders?

You now have a good understanding of who your stakeholders are and where your time is best spent. To build rapport with and gain the support of these stakeholders, you need to tailor your method and frequency of interaction with each one of them. The best way to find out what your stakeholders are all about and how they prefer to receive information is to spend time with each person and build a relationship based on honesty and trust. Most people are quite open about their views, and asking them about their opinions is the first step in gaining their trust.

Eliciting answers to the following questions can help you get to know each of your stakeholders better and understand their interests and concerns. Note that you should not ask most of these questions directly; you can glean this information from more informal conversations.

> What is his interest in the outcome of the project? Why might he want to see it succeed (or fail)?

> What is worrying her about the current project? Are there any risks she thinks you are not mitigating or issues you are not addressing?

> Is he happy with the frequency and content of project communication and status reports?

> What information in particular is she most interested in, and how would she like to receive it (e.g., face-to-face, email, telephone, in a weekly report)?

> Has he been involved in similar change projects before? If so, what lessons did he learn, and how can you best leverage his knowledge?

> Who influences her opinions generally? Who influences her opinion of you?

> What could influence him to be more supportive of you and your project?

Step 3: Document Stakeholders' Characteristics

Spend time with each of your key stakeholders to understand their motives, thoughts, and communication needs. Try to answer most of the questions listed above.

Record your notes in a table or matrix (as illustrated in Figure 5-3), listing the stakeholders' names in the leftmost column and the information you gather to the right. Consider adding the following fields across the top to better structure the information: Level of Power and Influence, Level of Supportiveness, Interest/Stake in Project, Success Criteria, Concerns, Communication Needs, and Knowledge/Expertise. Also add a field for the relative priority of the stakeholder and any actions you may take to strengthen the relationship.

Stakeholder Analysis Matrix									
Stakeholder Name	Power/ Influence	Suppor- tiveness	Interest/ Stake	Success Criteria	Concerns	Communication Needs	Knowlegde/ Expertise	Priority	Action
Name 1	High	Medium				Formal/Written		1	
Name 2	Medium	Low							
Name 3	High	High				Informal/verbal		1	
Name 4	Low	High							

FIGURE 5-3. Stakeholder Analysis Matrix

Now that you have completed the first three steps of this exercise, you should have a good understanding of who your stakeholders are, how they relate to your project, and what each of them is looking for. The next step is to plan how you will win them over or deepen their support of your project.

Step 4: Win or Strengthen Stakeholder Support

Look through your list of stakeholders and the information you have gathered about each of them. Determine the level of support you want from them and the role you would like each of them to play (if any). That is, decide if you want something different from each stakeholder from what you are getting today.

Questions

- Which stakeholders' support is most important? (These stakeholders may or may not currently be supportive.) Mark them as priority 1 in your stakeholder analysis matrix.
- What do you need to do to maintain or improve your relationship with the stakeholders you have marked as priority 1?
- In what ways can you better use and leverage the goodwill you have from the most supportive stakeholders?
- What can you do to win over the non-supportive stakeholders? What is the root cause of their skepticism, and what can you do to address it?
- Update the stakeholder analysis matrix with the actions you will take.

In summary, the key to stakeholder management is to first and foremost understand each stakeholder's interest in your project and to spend sufficient time gaining and maintaining the support of the stakeholders that matter the most to the success of your project.

The best way to gain and maintain a stakeholder's support is to listen to and respect that person and to appreciate his or her motives and needs. Make sure you always keep the most influential and supportive stakeholders abreast of project progress, risks, and issues, and do not hesitate to ask them for help when needed.

Pay attention to stakeholders who have a lot of power and influence but who are not supportive of the project. Approach them with honesty and openness and listen to their concerns. When they sense that you have integrity and that you are doing your best to accommodate everyone's needs, they will soon start to respect you and support you.

Step 5: Use Principles for Building Trusting, Lasting Relationships

In addition to the individual relationship-building strategies you have devised for each stakeholder, always rely on the general principles discussed in the next section for building trusting and lasting relationships when communicating and interacting with people.

BUILDING TRUSTING AND LASTING STAKEHOLDER RELATIONSHIPS

As we have already established, to become successful, you must be capable of much more than producing a plan and tracking its activities. To set yourself apart, you must have drive, confidence, and attitude, and you must focus on people as much as you focus on tasks. To become a project management leader, you must take the time to fully understand the motives of others and know how to gain support and buy-in from the project's stakeholders.

> *An ability to build trusting and lasting relationships is one of the most critical ingredients to becoming a highly valued and truly successful project management leader.*

Exercise: Building Strong Relationships

1. Think about a person with whom you have an excellent working relationship. Write his or her name on a piece of paper.

2. What makes this relationship good? What do you do to maintain the relationship?

3. Think about a situation in which someone was generally skeptical or even hostile toward you, and you managed to turn the relationship around. How did you do that? What skills, beliefs, and capabilities did you make use of?

4. Read each of the guiding principles for building trusting and lasting relationships below. As you read through them, ask yourself how good you are, on a scale from 1 to 10, at using that particular principle in your daily interactions with your stakeholders.

Note that although this exercise relates to stakeholder management, you can also use these principles to build great relationships with your team members.

Listen to others and seek to understand before being understood

When you invest time in actively listening to and really understanding your stakeholders, the dynamics of your conversations and your relationships change. People become more open and receptive when you actively engage with them and comprehend their situation. Only when you fully understand their position should you speak up about your own topic and agenda.

➤ Forget yourself for a moment.

➤ Listen with your entire body.

➤ Make eye contact.

➤ Make every effort to really understand the position of the stakeholder you are talking with.

The better a listener you are, the more valuable you are to others. When your stakeholders feel that you truly listen and understand them, you will be able to tap into one of their deepest yearnings: the need to feel valued and valuable.

> ✔ On a scale from 1 to 10, how good are you at listening to and fully understanding the other person before you speak?

Have empathy, and encourage win-win solutions

Empathy is the ability to put yourself in someone else's shoes and understand how he feels and what he really means. When you are considerate and empathetic and adopt a cooperative mindset, you will see that you can derive synergies and mutual benefit from every situation. This approach will draw your stakeholders to you and will help you develop effective, creative, and beneficial solutions together.

➤ Forget your own agenda for a moment and fully focus on the person you are talking with.

➤ Avoid being judgmental, inflexible, or thinking in terms of either/or.

➤ Consider situations and responses from your stakeholder's perspective.

➤ Make a commitment to find solutions that will truly benefit all parties.

➤ Strive to always make your stakeholders look good.

> ✔ On a scale from 1 to 10, how good are you at facilitating solutions that benefit all parties?

Set a good example as a project manager

Your stakeholders will respect you for being an effective project manager who keeps tabs on risks, issues, decisions, and actions. Set a good example and demonstrate that you are on top of plans, tasks, and budgets and that you understand how project deliverables are linked to the ultimate business benefits. Your stakeholders will be impressed by your business knowledge and your ability to deliver to their needs.

➤ Create accurate, concise project reports in an easy-to-understand format.

➤ Write and distribute minutes on key decisions.

➤ Hold stakeholders accountable for the activities they take on.

➤ Always come to meetings prepared, and have the necessary information ready at hand.

➤ Ask stakeholders for feedback on what they believe you could do better.

✔ On a scale from 1 to 10, how effective are you at setting a good example as a project manager?

Be honest and open about project progress, and have the courage to ask for help

Have the confidence and courage to talk openly about contentious issues. Say things the way they are and ask for help when needed. Your stakeholders will respect you for being honest and will appreciate being given the chance to help out before the situation gets worse.

➤ Be transparent about project risks and issues.

➤ Strive to always be honest and open.

➤ Never overpromise or feel pressured to say yes to unreasonable demands.

Making promises you cannot keep will put you and your team in a bad position and will end up damaging your relationships. You will score points for being realistic and for having your project's interests at heart.

✔ On a scale from 1 to 10, how open are you about project progress, and how willing are you to ask for help?

Be proactive and take responsibility for your actions

You can earn your stakeholders' respect and admiration by proactively resolving risks and issues. Proactive people face the world with an action-oriented attitude and a firm belief that they have the ability to change a situation for the better. You may not always have control over what impacts your project, but you do have control over how you respond when things go wrong.

➤ Make every effort not to let stressful events overwhelm you.

➤ When problems arise, remain composed and direct your energy into proactive risk identification, decisionmaking, and problem-solving.

➤ Look for durable solutions.

➤ Take full responsibility for the consequences of your actions.

> ✔ On a scale from 1 to 10, how would you rate your can-do attitude and proactiveness?

Maintain a positive attitude, and do not be afraid to show your funny side

Do your best to maintain a positive attitude. The positive energy you radiate will draw others to you and make them feel good about themselves. A positive attitude makes you look good, too; it gives your stakeholders the impression that you are in your comfort zone.

➤ Be cheerful and friendly, and smile.

➤ Show your resourcefulness by using the word *and* instead of *but*.

➤ Say thank you to people to show that you appreciate their efforts.

➤ Think in terms of solutions as opposed to obstacles.

➤ Do not be afraid to be funny or clever.

Most people are drawn to people who can make them laugh. Use your sense of humor as an effective tool to lower barriers and gain people's affection.

> ✔ On a scale from 1 to 10, how would you rate your positive attitude?

> **Questions**
>
> • In what situations do you need to become a better listener? How can you do that?
> • How can you become more proactive and positive?
> • In what situations do you need to get better at asking for help?

Take Action

- Identify two principles from this exercise that would have the biggest positive impact on your stakeholder relationships.
- Identify the situations in which you will begin to implement these two principles, and explain how you will do it.
- Commit to taking action and determine a specific time for when you will start doing so.

TIME MANAGEMENT

Good time management skills are essential for effective project managers. To be the best at what you do, you must be able to focus single mindedly on your most important task and get it done quickly and well. The better you are at managing your time, the more you will achieve and the easier it will be for you to leave the office on time and maintain a healthy work-life balance. Not only does effective time management allow you to perform better at work, but it also helps you withstand stress and fuels your passions outside of work.

Questions

- On a scale from 1 to 10, how well would you say you managed your time today?
- Do you normally achieve what you set out to do during a day, or do you leave the office with the feeling that you got very little done?
- How do you keep track of things you have to do? Do you have a prioritized list, do you keep your tasks on sticky notes, or is your list simply in your head?
- What kinds of assignments are time-management challenges for you? Are there certain types of tasks you never seem to get around to? List them.

Effective time management is all about working smarter, not harder. It is about focusing on the end result and doing the things that contribute the most to that end result.

To be effective, you have to consciously work on the highest-value tasks before moving on to the lower-value tasks. To figure out what these high-value tasks are, ask yourself the following questions:

➤ What do my project, team, and stakeholders need most from me right now?

➤ Who is urgently waiting for information or decisions from me?

➤ Which critical path activities need to be completed?

➤ What blockages need to be removed, and what risks need to be addressed?

➤ Which stakeholders do I need to communicate with and report project information to?

➤ What do I need to do to focus the team on quality and deliverables?

➤ What is the biggest contribution I can make right now?

➤ What will cause the most trouble if I neglect to do it?

The following tips can help you improve the way you manage your time. As you read through them, identify how each of them can help you complete your assignments on a daily basis.

Keep a dynamic task list or workbook

Keep a written or electronic list of tasks and activities you have to do and update it regularly during the day. Add new items that come up at meetings or in conversations to your task list right away. Be sure to revisit this list frequently.

If you are not a fan of task lists, consider setting up a workbook, perhaps in spreadsheet form, that contains different sections (or sheets) for the most important project management activities, such as risks and issues, actions, milestones, and dependencies. Regularly reviewing your workbook will help you easily assess where your time is best spent.

The layout of your list or workbook is not important; the key is to pick a format that gives you a quick overview of all urgent tasks and important recurring project management activities to which you need to attend.

Prioritize your task list, and focus on the most important tasks

Prioritize your task list every evening before you leave the office and decide what you absolutely must do the next day. It is important to update your task list and set your priorities in the evening, as that is when everything is fresh in your mind. This will make it much easier to pick up the thread the next day.

To determine what is most urgent and important, identify the items that will have the biggest positive effect on the project and the well-being of your team. What issues need to be resolved, and what risks need to be dealt with? Who do you need to liaise with? Which project controls need to be checked?

Schedule all your urgent and important tasks in your diary, even those that involve no one but yourself. If an activity appears too big to be done, break it up into smaller activities. Resist the temptation to clear smaller, unimportant issues first. Always start with what is most important.

Minimize interruptions

The more uninterrupted time you get during the day to work on important tasks, the more effective you will be. Make an effort to identify the things that disrupt your work, and find a way around them. Resist the temptation to check and answer emails, answer the phone, or enter long, unimportant conversations when you are in the middle of an important task. Once you have broken your flow, it can be difficult to reestablish it. Let incoming calls from numbers you do not recognize go to voice mail. If a call is important, the caller will leave a message. If your email program is set up to notify you every time a message comes in, consider turning this feature off. Stop working only if something urgent comes up that is more important than your current task. Otherwise, discipline yourself to deal with it later.

Limit multitasking

Many of us multitask and believe we are effective when we do so, but we are often not as productive as we think. On the contrary, multitasking seems to waste time; we cannot effectively focus on more than one thing at a time. To improve the quality of your work and become more efficient, you need to stop multitasking. Plan your day in blocks and set specific times aside for meetings, liaising with people, returning calls, and doing detailed planning and analysis work at your desk. Whenever you find yourself multitasking, stop and sit quietly for a minute.

Stay focused

Once you start a task, discipline yourself to work on it singlemindedly until it is complete. Practice being in the moment, and guide your thoughts back to what you were doing if your mind starts to wander. If you have difficulties staying focused or tend to procrastinate, reward yourself for completing difficult or unpleasant tasks. Make it a habit to complete the most unpleasant tasks early in the day, and you will feel much lighter afterward. You can also improve your focus by creating a commitment external to yourself—for instance, by scheduling a meeting in two days' time where you will be presenting your work and by which point you will have had to complete your actions.

Optimize meetings

Conducting project meetings as effectively as possible saves time, both for you and for the attendees. Let everyone know what the purpose of the meeting is in advance and make sure people understand the outcomes you want to achieve. Listen carefully to all participants, but tactfully interrupt if they go off on a tangent. It is your role to keep the participants focused.

These tips can help:

➤ Have a clear agenda.

➤ Start on time, and come prepared.

➤ Chair the meeting in a polite but firm manner.

➤ Make sure your own contributions are relevant, clear, and timely.

➤ Ask questions that lead to deeper understanding or prevent hasty decisionmaking.

➤ If you identify a significant issue that is not immediately relevant, set up a separate meeting to discuss it rather than sidetracking the current one.

➤ Always summarize and document agreements reached, as well as actions that need to be taken, by whom, and by when.

Spend your time proactively

To become a highly valued and truly successful project management leader, you must spend as much of your time as possible on strategic and proactive activities and as little time as possible on nonproductive or reactive activities.

As Figure 5-4 shows, there are three fundamental ways you can spend your time: Proactive, Firefighting, or Time-wasting.

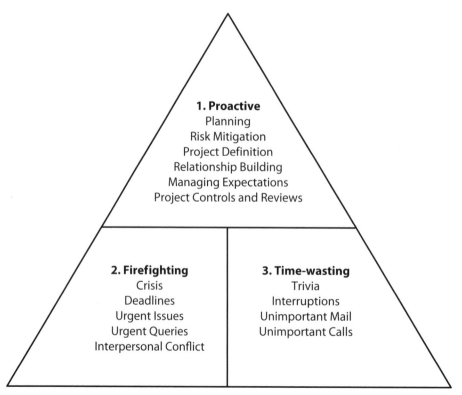

FIGURE 5-4. Ways You can Spend Your Time

Category 1, in the top part of the triangle, represents time you spend on proactive and strategic activities. These activities lead to real results, and this is where most of your time should be spent. Category 1 activities encompass planning, preparation, project definition, project reviews, risk mitigation, relationship building, inspiring and providing focus to others, and improving your professional skills and knowledge.

Category 1 activities are fundamental to becoming a highly valued and truly successful project management leader. By spending your time on activities in this category, you proactively influence the future and gain control over the project. When you are in control, the need to firefight (that is, spend time on category 2 activities) drops significantly.

A lot of people are driven by urgency and get drawn into category 2 activities, which are urgent but not strategic. These are activities that you must absolutely attend to, such as a crisis or a pressing deadline. If you spend all of your time in category 2, you will have very limited time to attend to strategic and proactive activities.

Avoid spending time in category 3. These are the most unimportant and time-wasting activities, such as surfing the internet, chatting about trivia, or attending to unimportant queries. These activities will consume your time but will not contribute to the achievement of your goals or the success of your project.

Exercise: How Do You Spend Your Time?

1. Take a look at how you spend an average day. First, make a list of all your daily activities on a separate piece of paper.
2. List all of your daily activities by category in the triangle below.

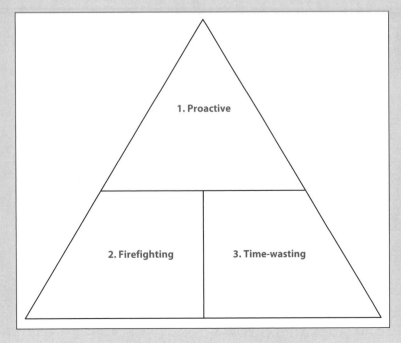

3. How much time do you tend to spend on activities in each of the three categories on an average day?

4. What can you do to minimize the time you spend in the bottom half of the triangle and spend more time on proactive and strategic activities?

5. What actions can you take to optimize the way you spend your time?

Delegate

We have touched upon delegation several times in this workbook. You will recall that delegation allows you to leverage your strengths and facilitate the growth and development of people you lead and manage. Effective delegation is an important complement to time-management skills because it frees you up to focus on the work you do best; in so doing, you add greater value to the project.

Get in the habit of asking yourself what the best use of your time is right now and if someone else could do any of the tasks you would otherwise do. Do not come up with excuses not to delegate. Thinking *and* instead of *but* can help you develop creative win-win solutions that benefit all parties. And keep an open mind; perhaps the person you need to delegate work to is not yet part of the project team.

Exercise: Delegating Tasks

- Look at your to-do lists. On a separate piece of paper, write down all of the tasks you must complete within the next week, including planning, estimating, tracking, conducting meetings, and writing project reports.

- For each of the tasks, determine whether someone else *could* do it if he or she had the skills, time, and desire. Some tasks are simply not fit to be delegated—for instance, those that are highly complex, confidential, sensitive, or personal.

- For each of the items you could delegate, identify what each task requires in terms of time, skill, and commitment. Prioritize these requirements by importance.

- Identify people who could potentially complete the tasks you have identified. Think outside the box. If it is difficult to think of anyone, ask around. Maybe someone on a different project or in a different department can help out temporarily or permanently.

STRESS MANAGEMENT

Negative stress is a feeling of not being in control. It is something you experience when the demand for your time and services exceeds what you feel you have to offer, or when there is a significant difference between what you expect and what actually happens.

Many people believe that stress is a direct result of external events, such as a demanding stakeholder or boss. But emotional stress does not stem directly from external events. It stems from the beliefs you hold about them.

Events themselves do not determine how you feel; what is stressful to one person may not be stressful to another. The meaning you choose to attach to an event is the meaning it takes on. When you interpret an event as negative or bad, you get into a negative or stressed state. You become unable to work effectively; in fact, you stop using the entirety of your brain.

Many project situations can be stressful if you interpret them as such: being asked to plan a large new project; having to quickly make major decisions; presenting at and conducting steering committee meetings; dealing with unexpected issues; facing off with senior executives; dealing with challenging people; having to justify project estimates and time frames; and being responsible for delivering the project on time, within budget, and to the required quality—among others. But just as your beliefs about whether an event is stressful determine your feelings and actions, your response to a potentially stressful event influences the outcome. You may not be able to control an unreasonable stakeholder or boss, but you *are* able to control how you choose to respond to him or her.

Questions

- How stressed are you at the moment, on a scale from 1 to 10?
- What are you stressed about? Write down everything you can think of. If nothing stresses you right now, identify situations that would normally trigger you to feel anxious.
- How do you know when you are stressed? What are your symptoms?

To be a highly valued and truly successful project management leader, you must be as resourceful as possible. You also need to be able to deal with several things at once, while maintaining a broad perspective *and* delving into details when necessary. You need full access to your brain to effectively make decisions, resolve issues, delegate, and motivate. (Evidence suggests that men and women react differently to stress. In general, men narrow their focus, whereas women broaden their focus. Men become unable to concentrate on more than one task at a time, while women do too many things but none of them properly. Regardless of gender, stress is detrimental to intellectual functioning.)

You need to feel good about the work you do and try to embrace the moment, even when doing so is challenging. When you let external events stress you, you feel constrained and tense. Letting work pressure get you down is a major hindrance to being resourceful and performing at your best.

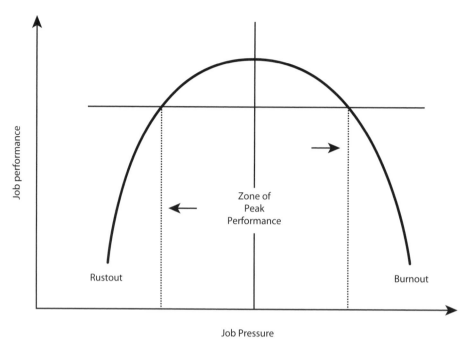

FIGURE 5-5. The Effects of Pressure on Job Performance

As Figure 5-5 shows, you do need some pressure in order to perform, but too much pressure (or stress) leads to declining performance and potentially burnout.[3] If you approach burnout, you may lose your energy, drive, and initiative. You will feel overwhelmed and find it difficult to respond to external demands.

Too little pressure is also not ideal. If you do not feel that there is a need, demand, or desire for your skills and capabilities, you will slowly lose your motivation and feel less inclined to contribute and perform. We could call that *rustout*.

In the exercise below, we look at things you can do to combat negative stress and avoid burnout so that you can remain within your zone of peak performance.

Exercise: Are You Rusting Out, Burning Out, or in the Zone of Peak Performance?

1. Look at Figure 5-5. Where on the graph would you place yourself? Are you operating within your zone of peak performance, are you on the downward slope toward burnout, or are you rusting out?

2. Indicate where you currently operate by putting a cross on the graph. Explain why you put the mark exactly where you did.

3. What would need to happen for you to move into and remain within the zone of peak performance?

The first step in combating negative stress is to realize that you are indeed stressed and to accept that something needs to change. There are many things you can do to reduce stress. Some of them will help you deal with the immediate situation and release physical tension, while others will help you get to the root cause and change the events and beliefs that trigger stress. Below is an overview of tools and techniques you can use in various stressful situations, depending on what you want to achieve.

Breathe deeply and slowly

One of the most powerful things you can do when you are stressed is to breathe deeply and slowly. Sit still for a moment and breathe deeply and calmly from your stomach. Pay attention to your breath as it fills up your lungs completely. Then follow it as it empties your lungs completely. Shut out all other thoughts for a couple of minutes, and just feel your breath in your body.

This technique has many benefits: it restores your body's equilibrium, your heart rate decreases, your lungs expand, and your muscles loosen up. It also calms the brain and releases endorphins into the system. These are natural painkillers that help relax the muscles and nerves.

Try this now and see for yourself how powerful it is. Relax your body and breathe as deeply and slowly as you can. Use this technique any time you feel tense, or use it to unwind after a long day.

Try visualization and relaxation techniques

There are many different types of relaxation techniques. Most of them serve to relax your muscles and to take your mind off the things that stress you. They will make you focus on a place of calm and stillness within, making external events seem less important. You will feel refreshed and calm afterwards.

➤ Experiment and use the relaxation techniques that suit you best.

➤ Try meditation, yoga, guided visualization, or self-hypnosis.

➤ Sit quietly for five minutes every morning and every evening, and focus on being calm and peaceful. Breathe deeply and slowly. Focus on how you want the day to go. Visualize yourself being powerful and in control. Imagine lots of tasks and issues being thrown at you while you calmly prioritize, delegate, and decide where to focus your attention.

Try it now. Sit quietly for a moment and feel your internal source of power. Make it a habit to put yourself in a positive state before you begin your day.

Exercise regularly

Regular exercise is one of the best ways to reduce the physical effects of stress. It improves your health, loosens up your muscles, and helps you slow down and sleep well. When you exercise, the blood flow in your body and to your brain increases, and endorphins are released, which gives you a feeling of happiness and well-being. The most effective kinds of exercise for stress relief are those that work the muscles in your upper body, as that is where stress tends to build up.

If you exercise regularly, you will have a healthier, stronger body, and you will also be psychologically stronger—and better able to handle the long-term effects of stress. When you assume the physiology of someone who is strong and resourceful, it is more difficult to be stressed. Try it now. Stand up tall. Be strong, and feel the power of your being. How does that make you feel?

Focus on your circle of influence

To reduce stress and make you feel more in control, focus your attention on those factors you can truly influence, and accept that some factors are outside of your control.

Your circle of influence as a project manager is vast. You can influence your stakeholders and your team, as well as the products you develop and how you develop them. You have the power to make decisions, delegate, and resolve issues. This is what you should focus on. If you focus on things that concern you but that you cannot control, such as the arrival of a new project sponsor, you will feel powerless and frustrated. Put in place mitigating actions where you can, but if there is nothing you can do about a situation, let it be. Trust that if you do whatever you can, the rest will fall into place.

> *Let go of the things you cannot control. Instead, expand your circle of influence by asking how you can take action to mitigate or address a concern.*

Put things in perspective

When we are stressed, we tend to magnify issues. We get stressed over things that seem big, although in the grand scheme of things, they may not be. To put things in perspective, ask yourself how awful the stressing event is on a scale from 1 to 100, or how much it will matter in a year's time. Compare your situation to other situations that are truly terrible. If you assign your own situation 20 points out of 100, make sure your stress response is in line with the situation's actual level of difficulty and is not exaggerated.

Remember, too, that adversity gives you the opportunity to show your real strengths. You can only really grow and develop when you are being stretched and tested.

Slow down

If you have a tendency to become stressed easily, chances are that you have a "type A" personality. People with type A personalities are typically high achievers who are full of energy and drive. They are competitive, critical, and impatient, and they often try to do more than one thing at a time. They operate at their maximum possible speed and generally feel that time is running out. Type As tend to interrupt and often seek recognition from others.

If this description sounds familiar, make a conscious effort to slow down. Actively make time for other people, listen to them, and try to focus on one thing at a time. You cannot operate at 100 percent capacity on an ongoing basis, so allow yourself to have lazy times. Make time for yourself every day, even if it is just ten minutes. Even the most driven warriors save their energy for when they need it the most.

Exercise: Do You Have a Type A Personality?

1. Take a step back and look at how you generally operate. Would you say that you are often rushed? Do you put high demands on yourself and others?

2. What is the impact of operating in this way? On the plus side, you probably get lots of things done, but what are the negative consequences?

3. In what situations would you get the most benefit from slowing down? How can you start doing that?

Identify unhelpful thinking patterns

Notice when you fall into unhelpful thinking patterns, indicated by thoughts such as "It has to be 100 percent perfect," or "I must/I should/I cannot _____." Instead, focus on your preferences. If you *prefer* things to be a certain way, rather than *need* them to be that way, it will stress you less if they turn out to be different. Things do not have to be perfect; they have to be good enough.

Also, take control of negative thoughts, such as "I am not good enough" or "I am stupid." Look at the situation from a rational perspective by asking whether your viewpoint is reasonable and accurate. Think positively about yourself and your contributions. Imagine yourself as a positive and energetic individual, and give yourself words of encouragement. Remember that there is no such thing as stupidity or failure—only opportunities to grow and learn.

If you continue to have negative thoughts and put yourself down, work with a mentor or coach to help change the way you think and feel about yourself.

Shift your locus of control

People who have an *external* locus of control believe that most of what happens is controlled by fate or by other people and that they can do little to influence situations. They tend to be more susceptible to nervous tension and stress and will often feel powerless to change their own circumstances.

Make an effort to shift your locus of control to an *internal* focus. Remind yourself that events happen as a result of your own decisions and actions. You choose how to react to a situation, and you have the power to change your circumstances.

Realize that you always have a choice. Sometimes the only option may be to change your attitude, but you always have a choice. If you feel trapped, make a list of all possible courses of action. Brainstorm and write ideas down without evaluating them first. When you have listed all possible actions, *then* evaluate each one and select the best one for you.

Prioritize and plan your time

Stress and time management are closely related, as it is easy to feel overwhelmed when you have too much on your plate. Learn to manage your workload so that you do not get stressed by its volume and by upcoming deadlines. Your task list will change many times during the day, and urgent issues will invariably crop up, so make sure you are prepared.

➤ Keep a list of things you *must* do, and prioritize it every evening before you leave the office.

➤ Resolve to always start the day with the most important task; resist the temptation to attend to the small and easy tasks first.

➤ Be proactive and work on important tasks well before they become urgent and stressful.

➤ Before you start something new, always consider whether it is the best use of your time right now and whether you could delegate it to someone else.

Learn to say no

Sometimes we cause ourselves unnecessary stress by saying yes to things when we really do not want to. We might agree to do something small, like performing a small favor, or something major, like taking on an extra project even if we are already running one full time. Remember that there are only so many hours in the day. Accepting additional work limits your ability to focus on the most important aspects of your current project and to produce good results. Even if you *can* somehow fit in a new commitment, you really *should* not, unless it is more important than what you are currently doing.

If you are uncomfortable saying no or are dealing with a pushy boss, just say, "Let me think about it and get back to you." This gives you a chance to review your schedule and think about how you really want to respond.

If you do want to say yes but do not have the time to do what you are being asked to do, think about what you *can* fit into your schedule. Say "I cannot do this, but I *can* do…", and make a lesser commitment. This way, you will still be partially involved, but it will be on your terms.

Follow your passion

Take time out to follow your passion and do what you love in your spare time. This will take your mind off work and energize you. When you are energized and happy outside of work, you are more likely to be energized and happy at work. Laugh, relax, and be good to yourself. Forget your to-do lists and what you "must" and "should" do. Allow yourself to just be and do whatever feels good.

Exercise: Resolving Your Stress Factors

1. Identify the three biggest factors or situations you find stressful at the moment. Write them down.
2. How are your beliefs influencing your perception of these factors or situations as stressful?
3. Imagine that all of these stressors have been resolved. Describe how this makes you feel.
4. What actions can you take and what beliefs can you change to get the outcome you want in each of these three situations?
5. Which of the techniques and guiding practices listed above can you start using on a daily basis to keep your stress level under control?

LESSONS LEARNED

Well done! You have read and taken in a lot of information. Take a deep breath, and acknowledge how far you have come. Congratulate yourself. You are well on your way to becoming a highly valued and truly successful project management leader.

Exercise: Reviewing the Guiding Practices

1. Review the most important aspects of what you have learned from this chapter. Go back through the chapter and look at the notes you have made.

2. Identify the guiding practices, ideas, and techniques that inspired you the most and that would have the most significant effects on your success and efficiency if you were to implement them. Write them down in the space provided below.

3. Revisit your action plan from Step 4 and identify how these guiding practices, ideas, and techniques complement the goals you previously identified. How will they help you unleash your potential and become a highly valued and truly successful project management leader?

4. Commit to taking action by incorporating these guiding practices, ideas, and techniques into the way you currently work. Update your action plan now. Write down what you are committed to doing and by when.

Notes

_____

_____

_____

_____

_____

_____

_____

_____

_____

_____

NOTES

1. Tim Lister and Tom DeMarco, "Risk Management during Requirements," *IEEE Software* 20, no. 5 (September–October 2003): 99–101.

2. Adapting your leadership approach to suit unique situations is a concept popularized by Paul Hersey and Kenneth Blanchard, who have both published extensively on the subject. See Paul Hersey, *The Situational Leader* (Upper Saddle River, NJ: Prentice-Hall, 1986); Kenneth H. Blanchard, Patricia Zigarmi, and Drea Zigarmi, *Leadership and The One Minute Manager: Increasing Effectiveness Through Situational Leadership* (New York: William Morrow, 1999); and Paul Hersey, Kenneth H. Blanchard, Dewey E. Johnson, *Management of Organizational Behavior: Leading Human Resources* (Upper Saddle River, NJ: Prentice-Hall, 1977).

3. A similar stress curve appears in *The Seven Strategies of Master Presenters,* by Brad McRae and David Brooks (New York: Career Press, 2004).

Progress Review: Examine Your Progress and Determine Next Steps

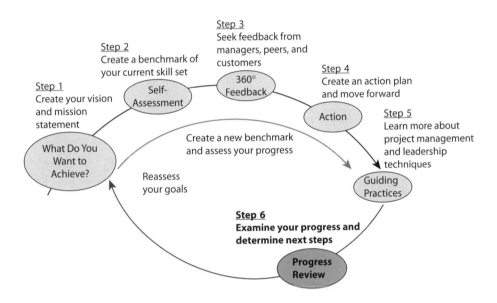

The purpose of Step 6 is to help you review the progress you are making as a result of completing the exercises in this workbook and as a result of your actions in real life. If you are not seeing the results you expected, this is your opportunity to identify why that might be and to examine the factors that are preventing you from moving forward.

If, on the other hand, you are making excellent progress, this step will help you determine exactly how much you have developed and ensure that your next steps match your new level of knowledge and awareness.

Depending on the speed at which you are working, do the first review four to eight weeks after you finalized your action plan (Step 4) and after you began to actively pursue your goals. If you do not review your progress within a reasonable time span, you may lose momentum and move forward more slowly and less effectively than you otherwise would have.

To carry out the review, revisit your vision and mission statement and complete the self-assessment again. When you compare your new scores to the original benchmark, you will be able to assess your progress and identify what your next steps should be for moving even closer toward your goals.

You can carry out this review process several times, until you have established a good routine for setting and achieving goals. When you continually review your progress, adjust your targets, and take action, you will consistently move forward toward your goals.

After completing Step 6 you will know if you are making progress in line with your expectations and you will have determined what you need to do in order to get back—or stay on course.

REVIEW

In the first part of the review, you will consider what has happened to you as a person and project manager, and how much progress you have made, since you started working on the exercises in this book.

Date: _____

Review Your Progress

1. List one or two key successes you have had since you started using this book to work on your professional development.

   _____

   _____

   _____

2. How are these successes contributing to your becoming a highly valued and truly successful project management leader?

   _____

   _____

   _____

3. List one or two efforts that did not go quite as you expected.

   _____

_____

_____

4. What has prevented you from taking action or getting the results you wanted, if anything?

_____

_____

_____

5. What do you need to do going forward to leverage your successes and address the factors that prevented you from making progress?

_____

_____

_____

To continue the review, please go back and revisit your vision and mission statement (Step 1). Then complete the self-assessment (Step 2) again. You should be able to finish it much more quickly the second time around.

When you reexamine the ten spider diagrams, notice the competencies and duties on which you now score yourself differently and where your perception of what is required to do a good job has changed. For example, you may originally have given yourself 7 out of 10 in Inspiring and Motivating the Team, thinking that a score of 10 would be easy to achieve. But as you take action and move closer to your goal, you have found that your idea of what 10 out of 10 looks like is changing. You might now score yourself 6 out of 10 despite your progress. This is perfectly normal and shows that you are developing. Just make a note that your benchmark has changed, and take this as a sign that you are moving in the right direction.

Go back and review your vision and mission statement and do the self-assessment now. Record any revisions with a different colored pen to distinguish them from what you previously wrote.

Questions

1. Has your vision and mission statement changed? If so, how?

_____

_____

_____

2. In reexamining your self-assessment, what key differences did you notice?

_____

_____

_____

3. In what ways do you need to adjust your action plan to take into consideration your recent development and growth?

_____

_____

_____

4. What are the main areas for improvement you will focus on going forward?

_____

_____

_____

5. What specific actions are you committed to taking?

_____

_____

_____

6. By when will you take these actions?

_____

_____

_____

7. How committed you are to carrying out these actions?

   What could get in your way?

   What do you need to do to avoid potential roadblocks?

   What do you need to commit to in order to follow through with these actions?

_____

_____

_____

8. By when will you complete your next review?

_____

_____

_____

CLOSING NOTE

Well done for staying on course and for completing all six steps of this workbook. The fact that you have come this far means that you are undoubtedly on your way to becoming a highly valued and truly successful project management leader. You are dedicated to achieving your goals, and you know what you need to do to fulfill your ambitions.

This workbook has given you a toolkit and a framework you can continue to use on your own or with others. Identify the approaches and topics that had the most significant effect on you, and keep using them. Also, think about which tools and exercises might be of use to other project managers, and share the materials so that your peers can benefit, too.

Reflection

1. Which approaches and topics from this workbook will you continue to use going forward?

2. Which tools and exercises can you share with other project managers?

3. Who in particular will you share this material with, and when will you do so?

4. What is the most important thing you have learned from this workbook?

5. What is your most important talent or gift?

6. How will you continue to nurture this talent?

_____

_____

_____

_____

_____

Keep looking inward, reassess what you really, *really* want to achieve as a project manager, and do not let anything deter you from reaching your goals. Be the best you can in everything that you do, and you will set a great example for others to follow.

Continually set new goals that stretch and challenge you, and keep reviewing your progress as you go along. Enjoy the journey, and remember that there is no such thing as failure—only experiences that help you learn and grow.

Index

Project Team Dynamics:
Enhancing Performance, Improving Results
Lisa DiTullio

Companies that embrace the power of collaboration realize that the best way to solve complex problems is to build cohesive teams made up of members with different skills and expertise. Getting teams to work productively is at the heart of project management. Developing the structure for teams to work dynamically at a high level of efficiency and effectiveness is at the heart of this book.

ISBN 978-1-56726-290-2 ■ Product Code B902 ■ 179 pages

The 77 Deadly Sins of Project Management
Management Concepts

Projects can be negatively impacted by common "sins" that hinder, stall, or throw the project off track. *The 77 Deadly Sins of Project Management* helps you better understand how to execute projects by providing individual anecdotes and case studies of the project management sins described by experts in the field.

ISBN 978-1-56726-246-9 ■ Product Code B777 ■ 357 pages

The Virtual Project Management Office:
Best Practices, Proven Methods
Robert L. Gordon and Wanda Curlee

New technology and global businesses and organizations are making virtual project management offices (VPMOs) more important and more prevalent than ever. Successfully operating a VPMO requires project managers to employ additional skills and address different challenges from those necessary to operate a traditional PMO. For example, the virtual project manager must have effective soft skills to build trust among a dispersed team and to select the best forms of communication. He or she must also ensure compliance with the unique policies, procedures, and laws relevant to maintaining a VPMO.

ISBN 978-1-56726-327-5 ■ Product Code B275 ■ 232 pages

Pragmatic Project Management:
Five Scalable Steps to Success
David Pratt, PMP

This book will help you select the methodologies and tools that will enable you to expend minimum effort to achieve maximum gain on your project. This clearly written guide lays the groundwork with a chapter on project sizing and management scaling and follows with chapters on each of the five essential elements of pragmatic project management. Practical tips and a checklist are included at the end of each chapter. Use the checklists as you plan and execute your project to keep it *on track* and *to scale*.

ISBN 978-1-56726-274-2 ■ Product Code B742 ■ 234 pages